Politically Speaking

Language in Society

GENERAL EDITOR
Peter Trudgill, Professor in the Department of Language and Linguistics, University of Essex

ADVISORY EDITORS
Ralph Fasold, Professor of Linguistics, Georgetown University

William Labov, Professor of Linguistics, University of Pennsylvania

Politically Speaking

The Pragmatic Analysis of Political Language

John Wilson

Basil Blackwell

First published 1990

Basil Blackwell Ltd
108 Cowley Road, Oxford, OX4 lJF, UK

Basil Blackwell, Inc.
3 Cambridge Center
Cambridge, Massachusetts 02142, USA

British Library Cataloguing in Publication Data

A CIP catalogue record for this book is available from the British
Library.

Library of Congress Cataloging in Publication Data

Wilson, John, 1928–
  Politically speaking : the pragmatic analysis of political
language / John Wilson.
      p.   cm.—(Language in society)
  Includes bibliographical references (p.
  ISBN 0–631–16501–0 — ISBN 0–631–16502–9 (pbk.)
  1. Political oratory. 2. Pragmatics. I. Title. II. Series:
Language in society (Oxford, England)
PN4193.P6W55 1990
306.4′4′088329—dc20   90–181
                                                         CIP

Typeset in 9.5 on 11 pt
by Photo·graphics, Honiton, Devon
Printed in Great Britain by Billing & Sons Ltd, Worcester

Contents

Editor's Preface

The language of politics is something we are all exposed to and involved in, and something we all have preconceptions about. In this book, John Wilson subjects the language used by and about politicians to analysis from the perspective of linguistic pragmatics. This means that he looks at political language in its social context of use, and that he is particularly concerned to investigate meanings inherent in political talk over and above what has actually been said or written on any given occasion. He is concerned with what speakers do not say as well as with what they do say, and with the implications and underlying assumptions associated with what is and is not said. In so doing, he shows that preconceptions we might have about political talk being manipulative are not unfounded, but he also demonstrates how listeners too bring unstated assumptions with them in their interpretation of political discourse. The book provides many very interesting insights into the use of language in politics in the Western world and is also an important contribution to pragmatics theory. Sociolinguists like Wilson are uniquely qualified to submit speech used in real-life situations to linguistic and social analyses, and this book, lying as it does at the intersection of linguistic and societal concerns, represents an excellent contribution to the study of language in society.

Peter Trudgill

Acknowledgements

My thanks to Lesley Milroy, Mike McTear, and Philip Carpenter for their comments on early drafts of chapters 1–4. Special thanks is due to Karen Maitland whose work I have drawn heavily upon for chapter 3 (see below). Apologies to Kelly and Lauren who both wanted a children's story in the mould of R. Dahl; just another academic text I'm afraid, but one which I hope, when you are older, you will find interesting enough to read.

Several publishers have been kind enough to allow me to reproduce selected materials from previously published works; my thanks therefore to the following: Macmillan Press, for permission to reproduce a quotation from K. Hudson (1978), *The Jargon of the Professions*; Elsevier Science Publishers, for permission to reproduce materials from K. Maitland and J. Wilson (1987), 'Pronominal Selection and Ideological Conflict', which appeared in *Journal of Pragmatics*, 11, 495–512; Routledge, for permission to reproduce examples from J. T. Dillon (1990), *The Practice of Questioning*; John Benjamins BV, for permission to reproduce diagrams from A. H. Jucker (1986), *News Interviews: A Pragmalinguistic Perspective*; the epigraph at the beginning of chapter 3 is reproduced from *The Complete Yes Minister* by Jonathan Lynn and Anthony Jay with the permission of BBC Enterprises Limited; Extracts from Hansard (1986), *Parliamentary Debates (Oral Answers) House of Commons Official Report* are Parliamentary copyright.

For Linda

Introduction

This book is concerned with the analysis of political talk from the perspective of linguistic pragmatics. Pragmatics, as a sub-discipline of linguistics, is an area of some confusion and controversy. The confusion arises from the difficulties involved in delimiting the boundaries of the area (see Leech, 1983; Levinson, 1983; Verschueren, 1987; Horn, 1988); the controversy, like so many in linguistics, is concentrated on the legitimacy of particular methodological and theoretical approaches to pragmatic questions (see Newmeyer, 1980).

There are those who believe that pragmatics must concentrate only on the role and functioning of meaning as it is displayed within the linguistic system: i.e. on how context becomes encoded (grammaticalized) within the structures of the language (see Gazdar, 1979; Kempson, 1979; Levinson, 1983); others will certainly show an interest in the linguistic system, but will also focus on the formal status of socially or interactionally oriented rules of behaviour (Grice, 1975) as they operate in guiding the communication process. Under at least one interpretation, one which treats 'conversation analysis' (see Levinson, 1983: chapter 6) as pragmatics, only those rules generated through the inductive analysis of participant activities are legitimate empirical pragmatic phenomena.

These distinctions are perceived rather than real, and there is a great deal of overlap within pragmatic work. One need not be constrained to only one particular viewpoint however, and as Horn (1988) notes, it is always possible to offer a mixed account of specific pragmatic phenomena. To a greater or lesser extent, this is the approach adopted in this book. Although the analysis has been heavily influenced by the Anglo-American view of linguistic pragmatics, various different theoretical and methodological ingredients will be added where these are seen as relevant or necessary in exploring particular issues. In many ways this approach is consonant with the definition of *linguistic pragmatics* adopted by Green (1989: 2): 'Linguistic pragmatics . . . is at the intersection of a number of fields within and outside cognitive science: not only linguistics, cognitive psychology, and philosophy, . . . but also sociology . . . and rhetoric.'

The mixed approach (to use Horn's phrase) seems particularly relevant where one is involved in an applied exercise (see Ochs and Schieffelin, 1979; Tannen, 1979; McTear, 1986; Stenton, 1987; Wilson, 1989). My aim is not to resolve the many controversial theoretical issues which abound within pragmatics, but rather to highlight, in the case of political talk, the various insights which may be gained from the application of selected pragmatic concepts. The term selective is apt, in that one could not hope to cover, or apply, in this book, all the myriad techniques and conceptual components of a linguistic pragmatics which encompasses detailed scholarship from within a variety of intersecting disciplines.

Nevertheless, having said that, I will not shy away from theoretical controversy where it impinges on any particular analytic question raised by the application of pragmatic concepts. Consequently, on occasion, as well as elucidating certain aspects of political talk, I may also indulge in contributing to core theoretical debate. This is particularly the case in chapters 4 and 5, where core theoretical issues are explored in conjunction with an applied perspective on political talk (see below). This has been necessary in that pragmatics, as an area, is relatively new, and, consequently, is still in the process of establishing sound and agreed parameters of practice, along with concise definitions of core categories and accepted procedures of analysis. Applying pragmatic theory is not always simply a case of matching data to concept, but may involve the development of speci- fied concepts, or the introduction of new concepts. This is where application feeds back into the development of theory, and in some respects it is hoped that this book contributes not only to our under- standing of how the pragmatics of political language operates, but also to the ongoing development of a pragmatic theory of language itself.

The term 'applied' has been used several times now, and in one sense this book may be seen as an exercise in *applied pragmatics*, defined here as the study of the selection and manipulation of prag- matic elements within specified communicative contexts. In one respect the term 'applied pragmatics' is odd, in that if pragmatics focuses on meaning in context, then applied pragmatics, presumably, focuses on meaning *in context in context*. The conclusion need not be so absurd, however, and a simple example here will help clarify the issues.

Take the case of verbs like regret. Such verbs are known as factive verbs, in that, pragmatically, they are said to presuppose the truth of their complements. For example, if I say, 'John regrets beating his dog,' then we assume that it is the case that John has in fact beaten his dog. The behaviour of presuppositional verbs is quite complicated (see chapter 2; also Levinson, 1983; Green, 1989), but, in general, since they carry an implication of truth, they would not seem particularly useful in the case of lying.

In a study by Epstein (1982) this was in fact the conclusion. Epstein analysed the distribution of factive and non-factive forms in the testimony of the major figures involved in the Watergate trials (*The White House Transcripts*, 1974). In comparing the output of John Ehrlichman, John Dean and Richard Nixon, it was noted that 'both Ehrlichman and Nixon used an overwhelming, and therefore disproportionate, number of non-factives' (Epstein, 1982: 136). As we now know, at the time of the trials, Dean was telling the truth, the claims of others being clearly lies, or close to the edge of truth. Seemingly, in this case, the degree to which one was lying was matched by an avoidance of factive verbs, and, conversely, the degree to which one was telling the truth matched with an increased incidence of factive forms.

This simple example indicates one way in which an applied pragmatics can offer some insight into communicative intentions as they operate within a specific context. It is not suggested that every time a politician (or anyone else) avoids factive verbs they are lying; the process of lying, however, may, it seems, be supported by a direct manipulation of pragmatic aspects of the language system as it is employed in communicative contexts.

Pragmatic Arguments: the Mix

But what, then, do I mean by the term pragmatics? The details of the problems involved in exact definitions and delimitations of the area of pragmatics are available in the work of Leech (1983), Levinson (1983), Verschueren (1987), Horn (1988) and Green (1989), so I will not repeat them here. Rather, let me explain in brief the pragmatic perspective adopted in this book.

First, I want to argue that pragmatics is concerned with the way in which meanings are constructed or calculated within particular contexts of interaction, the simple meaning in context view (Levinson, 1983). Central to this is the fact that we can mean much more than what we say. Such a claim is the core of Grice's theory of conversation, and is endorsed, from a completely different perspective, by Garfinkel and Sacks (1970: 342) when they say 'speakers in the situated particulars of speech mean something different than what they say.' The question is, how are we to explain this process? How does one account for the fact that there is meaning beyond the words produced by any speaker within a particular context?

The answer one provides to this question is in part dependent upon the theoretical perspective one brings to bear, as much as whether the answer is the best one for the job. Linguists, for example, have turned to pragmatics as their theories of semantics have become radically inadequate as accounts not only of how people understand each other, but as accounts of the role of meaning within a language system with interacting levels of structure. Philosophers, for very similar reasons, have converged on pragmatics as a way of dealing with those troublesome sentences which do not easily sit within particular truth-based formalisms. Sociologists, influenced (at least originally) by a phenomenologically motivated view of explanations of social reality, have turned to the study of how meaning is constructed by participants themselves, not by some pre-formalistic view of what meaning should be like.

In order to look at what all this means, and what exactly the differences are between these viewpoints, I want to suggest that we have three types of pragmatically based argument: the L-pragmatic argument, i.e. one which focuses only on how contextual meaning is encoded in the language system; the P-pragmatic argument, an account based on rules or general principles of behaviour, which although generally reflected in the linguistic system may be found beyond this; and the O-pragmatic argument, where meaning is constructed through the orderly negotiation of talk within contexts.

The L-pragmatic argument is a conventionalized one, and assumes that there are certain forms and structures within the linguistic system which act in specific pragmatic ways. A classic case here would be the concept of a *presupposition*. Although presuppositions are somewhat controversial (see Karttunen and Peters, 1979; Oh and Dineen, 1979), they are, in the main, associated with specific elements of language structure (although one can talk of social presuppositions, or psychological presuppositions; Green (1989) also uses the term 'connotative presupposition'; for a general discussion see Bates, 1976). Levinson (1983) highlights a number of these, ranging from definite descriptions to adverbial clauses. The important point is that presuppositions, as inferences, are based on the lexical item or clausal structure chosen, and fall directly, therefore, within the realm of linguistics.

A similar argument has been made for certain types of implicatures, specifically what Gazdar (1979) has called scalar and clausal implicatures. Here we have a kind of L-pragmatic/P-pragmatic mix. The argument is that for certain sets of linguistic elements, for example the quantificational range 'all, some, not many', where a lower bounded element is chosen it implies that negation of all higher bounded elements above it. If I say 'some of the boys are happy,' I am said to implicate (scalar) that 'not all of the boys are happy.' This rule emerges from the fact that, according to the principles of behaviour outlined by Grice (1975), one should not say that which is false, or for which one lacks adequate evidence. Consequently, if I knew that all the boys were happy then I would have said so.

Although Gricean principles are essentially independent of the linguistic system, in this sense they can be motivated in an account of a specific linguistic phenomenon, i.e. quantificational selection and interpretation. For this reason, such examples would still be treated as L-pragmatic types. In general, however, Gricean principles, and other principles of behaviour, may be utilized to account for actions which are not (or not only) purely linguistic; in this case we would have a P-pragmatic account.

An example might be the use of 'It's cold in here' to convey, through indirect means, that the speaker wants the window closed. In order to explain how this utterance means something other than simply a description of relative temperature, we might invoke the concepts of intentionality (Davidson, 1984; Searle, 1983) and rationality, and perhaps elements like beliefs, desires and wants (see Leech, 1983; Bratman, 1984; Wilks, 1986; Wilson, 1989). We might construct an argument from the speaker's desire to be warm, to his/her belief that he/she will be warm if the window is closed, and that the hearer will close the window if requested to do so. Rationally speaking, therefore, if the speaker wishes to be warm he/she should request the closing of the window.

This would not explain why the speaker did not simply say 'close the window' however. In order to explain this, we would have to invoke cultural as well as purely logical or rational principles. Principles of *face* wants and desires, for example, or principles of tact and politeness (see Leech, 1983; Brown and Levinson, 1978). Since all these various strategies and principles may operate independently of the linguistic system, they are not directly linguistic phenomena; although they may be utilized to assist in the explanation of linguistic phenomena (as noted above; see also Sperber and Wilson, 1986).

The O-pragmatic account focuses on the orderly construction of meaning as it is negotiated within a context of interaction. This radical perspective provides no pre-theoretical guidelines; meaning is an ongoing accomplishment. Silverman (1973: 176) notes that within interaction, 'people find out by the replies to their statements what they were taken to be talking about in the first place.' This approach, in one sense, denies the legitimacy of the application of the L-pragmatic and P-pragmatic approaches to actual talk, since both approaches would, of necessity, impose meaning on the structures employed via both linguistic and socially or rationally motivated principles of behaviour. Such pre-formalizations would be rejected by the O-pragmatic's perspective, since meaning is not imposed from the outside, as it were, but negotiated through the interactional construction of talk.

The O-pragmatic approach has had a widespread influence on the pragmatic study of conversation (see Atkinson and Heritage, 1984; papers in Schenkein, 1978), and a number of O-pragmatic analysts have focused on the organization of political talk (see for example, Atkinson, 1984; Heritage and Greatbatch, 1986), an issue which we will look at in more detail in chapter 1. Nevertheless, there is some confusion within this perspective, since it is hard to see how claims about practical reasoning, or negotiation, could be predicated without some prior knowledge of the language, or indeed social and rational principles of behaviour (see Wilson, 1989: chapter 6; also chapter 6 below).

The fact that one can describe the orderly operation of conversation without reference to prior formal rules of language or principles of behaviour does not indicate that they are not in operation at a level beyond the gross manifestation of the talk itself. In phenomenological terms, while one may not need the law of gravity to explain our accepted understanding that stone will fall if I drop it from a height, it does not suggest that such laws do not exist, nor that they cannot be fruitfully explained in a manner beyond the limits of the context of an individual experience (see Gurwitsch, 1978; Husserl, 1962).

The most important fact about the O-pragmatic approach from the perspective of this book is that it draws our attention to the role of sequencing in the construction of pragmatic meaning; the fact that meaning may be constructed, reformulated and changed across turns. But this process, in my view, is best understood where we have some (formal) idea of the tools and structures the participants are drawing upon in this process of development and manipulation.

These three pragmatic positions need not be mutually exclusive, and may enlighten each other within a mixed perspective. This is not to say that every problem must be tackled in a tripartite manner, merely that particular problems within the applied field may be more thoroughly grounded where the analyst is open to the various analytic options available to him/her.

This is the approach adopted in this book. Political talk will be considered from a pragmatic perspective by focusing centrally on meanings which may be derived beyond the context of what has been said. Following, and extending, Lycan (1986) these meanings will be referred to as *implicative relations* (see chapter 1). The aim of the book is to explain, pragmatically, how these relations operate, and in doing this we will draw on a range of arguments from the L- P- and O-pragmatic positions. The validity of this approach resides in the adequacy and insights provided by each analytic account. These accounts are not and cannot be exhaustive, but reflect a selective interest on the part of the author.

In brief then, pragmatics refers here simply to the analysis of meaning which is beyond what has been said, and it is accepted that locating each meaning may involve more than one procedural method of analysis.

The Organization of the Book

Chapter 1 begins by considering, in general, the area of political talk, and looks at a widely held conception that one of the main functions of political talk is to manipulate political thought. This seems a particularly significant case of using language to mean more than is said. It is argued, however, that we must be careful in making claims regarding such manipulation, since it is difficult, if not impossible, within a variable and contextually relative linguistic system, to claim that one has discovered a single and underlying immutable truth. The paradoxical consequences of this position are briefly explored, and the working basis of a pragmatic case is developed from the premise that much political language depends on implications rather than factual claims. Since implications may be cancelled, it becomes difficult to prove, beyond doubt, that any meaning which may be interpreted beyond what is said was intentionally projected.

Chapter 2 takes up the implicational argument and explores it in some detail through the application of two core implicational types, presupposition and conversational implicature, as they apply in a selected debate from the British House of Commons.

Chapter 3 looks at an area clearly pragmatically marked within the linguistic system, that of pronominals. The chapter argues that the

pronominal system of English may be manipulated not only for implicational effect, in terms of the protection of the political self through
the distributional control of projected responsibility (from the 'I' to
the 'we' for example), but also for the building of an ideological
perspective reflecting specific social values and beliefs.

Chapter 4 further takes up the issue of the political distribution of
responsibility and extends it beyond pronominals to the area of self
and other referencing. A core piece of political data is explored from
a variety of broadly pragmatic perspectives, and makes use of the
mixed approach in solving a case of what I will call 'self-reference
under protection'.

Chapter 5 looks at the use of metaphor within political talk. The
area of the pragmatics of metaphor is explored in some detail, and a
theory of *within text* (local) and *across text* (global) metaphorical use
is introduced in producing a pragmatic account of political metaphor.

Chapter 6 offers a broad-ranging account of the pragmatic force
and function of questions and answers within political encounters.
Question types are explored within the contexts of broadcast interviews, parliamentary debates and presidential press conferences.

1

The Truth About Politics and Pragmatics

*I think the inherent right of the government to lie to save itself
. . . is basic.*
Arthur Sylvester, US Assistant Secretary of Defence,
1962, quoted in K. Hudson, *The Jargon of The Professions*

Introduction

The theme of this book is a fairly straightforward one; it is simply
that political discourse may be analysed using various core concepts
from the area of linguistic pragmatics. The aim of the analysis is to
highlight the various insights which may be gained from the application of pragmatic constructs. This is a classic example of the descriptive basis of linguistics, where the aim is to describe not prescribe.
In this sense it is not my intention to reveal some hidden or underlying
truth, or to lay bare the illogicality or unfairness of political rhetoric
(see Chilton, 1985; Norris and Whitehouse, 1988; and, for a general
critique of this position, Richardson, 1989). What is logical or what
is true is relative to your model of truth and logic, or to your standards
of assertability, as Putnam (1971) has put it.

In this sense the approach we adopt in this text is somewhat
different from that frequently found in books on language and politics,
where one of the dominant themes in the analysis of political discourse
throughout the ages has been that political language functions to
influence political thought. In a trivial sense, this is obviously the
case, since politicians present an argument which they want the
electorate to believe. But this is radically different from claiming that
politicians actively create for us a specific cognitive environment which

directs our thinking on various issues. Here we are closer to some assumed concepts of universal truth and honesty which the politicians are ignoring, and which they are using language to subvert and obscure.

In this chapter, I want to explore, briefly, the underlying premise of much political language analysis, both outside and within linguistics. My aim is not to reject such a perspective outright, merely to explore some of its assumptions in the light of a pragmatic view of political talk. Clearly, politicians are making use of the linguistic system for their own ends; nevertheless, my main purpose is not to unmask these ends in any *explicit* ideological sense, but rather to highlight some of the ways in which politicians make use of the available linguistic system in their day-to-day political communication.

Truth, Linguistics and Pragmatics

When, on 15 April 1982, Ronald Reagan was asked by a group of elementary school children for his views on gun control in the United States, he offered an example from British law as part of his response. Under this law 'a criminal with a gun, even if he was arrested for burglary, was tried for first degree murder and hanged if found guilty.' Fascinating though Reagan's example might be, an extensive search by the *New York Times* failed to discover any such law (Green, 1982; cf. Johannesen, 1985). Larry Speakes, the then White House Deputy Press Secretary, defended the President's use of the example, however, by noting that 'It made the point, didn't it?'

It is tempting to offer a wry smile here, if not, indeed, to produce a good hearty guffaw, but why? Perhaps we expect more from senior politicians; as the *Washington Post* noted when discussing the Reagan example given above, 'that's not a good enough standard for public discourse' ('Facts About', 1982). There is a tension between our expectations of political behaviour and what is political reality, and nowhere is this more apparent than in the field of political language.

Since classical times it has been accepted that language plays a role in the creation of political reality. There is an assumption that the aim of the analysis of political talk is to uncover the rhetorical techniques used by politicians to create and manipulate a specific view of the world. As a recent text on the style of Ronald Reagan states: 'recognising the devices of rhetoric and learning how to see through them will . . . help us "clear away the fog so we can face the world we share with all mankind"' (Erickson, 1985: 25, quoting Boorstin, 1962).

This emotive style is typical of writings on political language. What we have here is an extension of basic literary criticism. It's not that such critical considerations are irrelevant, it is often that they are presented as 'correct interpretations', where the standards of assessment are the analyst's own interpretive capabilities. The problem is that there is in action here what Sharrock and Anderson (1981) call a form of 'exceptionalism', that somehow the analyst's own arguments and language are immune from the very same criticisms they have applied to the language of politicians (even radical post-structuralist arguments, of the kind developed by Foucault (1972), would seem to fall foul of this fact; see Harland, 1988).

Further, there is a kind of 'chauvinism' involved here. As Geis (1987) notes, those analysts who claim they have uncovered the truth, or the manipulative assumptions built into the politicians' language, take it for granted that this is something other people cannot do for themselves. Geis (1987: 3) states 'I am sure that some people are sometimes fooled by some instances of alleged *doubletalk*, but this sort of assumption is something which ought to be defended rather than simply assumed.' Such chauvinism, or 'arrogance' in Geis's terms, can be seen in the following quotation from Norris and Whitehouse (1988: 294): 'there is scarcely any prospect of reasoning the electorate (or a sufficiently large part of it) into a real understanding of nuclear issues.'

The underlying premise here is that politicians' language does not merely convey the message, but creates for the listener a controlled cognitive environment from which any interpretation is manipulated (Hudson, 1978; Edleman, 1978, 1988).

This essentially Orwellian thesis finds some support in the linguistic writings of Sapir (1964) and Whorf (1956) who argue that our world view is relatively constrained by the linguistic system we employ in representing the world. In its strongest form, the argument is that our thought is controlled by the language we employ; for example, the Hopi Indians, who have a different tense system from that employed in English, would be said to have a different concept of time from English speakers. It is difficult to maintain such a strong determinist position, however; Eskimos may have more terms for 'snow' than presently available in English, but it is perfectly possible for an English speaker to describe, with already available resources, a range of snow types. The weaker and more realistic version of the Sapir/Whorf view suggests, simply, that the world is not given to us directly by experience alone, but that experiences are, in part, mediated by language. There is undoubtedly some truth in the weak version of this thesis, but the fact that language can influence how we think is a nihilistic one (Strong, 1984). In language use there are no culture-free interpretations; there are simply alternatives, guided by linguistic choices operating at various levels of structure (see Grace, 1987).

One must be careful not to assume that there is somehow a universal truth, at least in linguistic terms; there are alternatives, each representing a relative state or view of the world. To some this is an uncomfortable view, but it is one echoed in that most objective of enterprises, modern science. The progress of science within the twentieth century has brought the realization that what is true is relative to one's standards of assertability. This is not to suggest that one cannot criticize Reagan or other politicians for being, as Sir Robert Armstrong put it (of himself in this case), 'economical with the truth', rather it is simply that if we wish to reject such obfuscations, we must establish sound grounds for our argument.

Truth as Underlying Grammar

One approach which has attempted to provide an underlying structural-linguistic account of political language is to be found in the work of those who might be called broadly 'critical linguists' (Fowler et al., 1979, Kress and Hodge, 1979). Critical linguists are centrally interested in the relationship between language and reality, or perhaps more correctly, the relationship between language and the construction of social meaning: 'there are social meanings in a natural language which are precisely distinguished in its lexical and syntactic structure and which are articulated when we write and speak' (Fowler et al., 1979: 185). Their aim is not merely to describe language, but to consider the role of language in the creation and maintenance of political and social ideologies. They approach their task by making use of standard linguistic theories and concepts.

On the surface, the aim of critical linguistics is to describe how ideological positions are reflected through linguistic choice, and as such this approach has, at this surface level, some relevance to any linguistic theory of political talk. Occasionally, however, one has the feeling that the motivation of critical linguistics goes beyond any descriptive aims and becomes closely aligned with a 'will to truth'. I am using the term 'truth' to suggest that there is a correct reading or understanding of certain linguistic practices, and that if one can only find the correct or structurally sufficient technique this will be uncovered.

Kress and Hodge (1979), for example, seem to advocate a 'will-to-truth' position in their book *Language as Ideology*. They argue that surface language structures (it is not clear whether they mean here sentences or utterances) represent the transformation of an underlying reality, going as far at one point as to claim that the 'grammar of a language is a theory of reality' (quoted in Durkin, 1983). The idea of a transformation is taken from the work of Chomsky (1965), where it was argued that sentences are derived from a basic form (deep structure) by a series of transformational rules.

Chomsky's model, while laying claim to psychological reality, was a formal one operating only, or mainly, at the level of syntax. The work of Kress and Hodge goes far beyond syntax, covering semantics and pragmatics, although this fact is never explicitly considered in any detail. They argue, for example, that when a wife says to her husband, 'Has the garbage been emptied?' it is the result of a two-part transformation of the following type:

(a) Have you emptied the garbage? ==> Has the garbage been emptied by you?

(b) Has the garbage been emptied by you? ==> Has the garbage been emptied?

$$== > \text{means 'has been transformed into'}$$

One consequence of this transformation, according to Kress and Hodge, is the deletion of 'you' in the surface form, with the result that the utterance may be interpreted by the husband as 'sly nagging' (Kress and Hodge, 1979: 16), or by the wife as simply an attempt to avoid any direct request. The logic of this argument is reasonable in pragmatic terms, where one would take account of facts which go beyond simple transformations, but to claim such an interpretation on the part of the husband/wife in terms of a formal syntactic analysis is not only absurd, it is to conflate a series of arguments which operate at different levels of structure (linguistic rules versus social rules for example: see below).

It is not necessary for us to become involved here in a technical reconsideration of Kress and Hodge's linguistic argument. First, because their book is essentially non-technical, as Durkin (1983: 101) notes: 'The deliberately non-technical exposition deprives all but the authors themselves of the opportunity to perceive it as an integrated theoretical system.' And second, because the Chomskyan theory on which the book bases its claims has altered radically since Kress and Hodge published their book in 1979 (Chomsky, 1986; see Botha, 1987 for a review of the various developments and changes in Chomsky's theory of grammar). I would, however, venture a number of non-technical arguments which seem relevant to the debate.

The transformational principle, as employed by Kress and Hodge, raises a significant question which Kress and Hodge fail to answer. If the surface form is a result of a specific transformation (the deletion of 'you', for example), and the hearer can recover the original form (we assume this is why the husband is annoyed in the above example, since the wife is supposedly asking why 'he hasn't emptied the garbage') then how can one manipulate language for a particular ideological purpose since hearers (interpreters) can reinterpret what has been said in its underlying form? As Grace (1987: 121) suggests (arguing from a somewhat different perspective), 'although our language does influence our perception, it does not do so to the extent that we cannot overcome it if there is sufficient motivation for us to do so.'

What I am getting at here is that if we take the base structure to be a form of underlying reality, all competent language-users should have the ability to access this reality (or is it the case that only trained critical linguists have access to the truth? See Geis, 1987: 4). Hence, if I attempt to manipulate an audience by using language to present the world in a particular manner, the audience has the potential to subvert my attempt by simply retransforming what I have said back into its underlying form. The problem is, of course, that we are assuming that any retransformation will not itself be affected by ideology, but this need not be the case.

In a study of political perceptions Pêcheux (1978) presented a group of right-wing and a group of left-wing students with the same economic report, and asked them to produce an analysis of its findings. He noted that each group presented an interpretation of the report which reflected their own ideological bias. Causes and consequences were matched to already accepted views of how economics operates within either a capitalist or a socialist society.

What this indicates is that language mediates our view of the world in both production and interpretation. It is not that there is an underlying reality which we transform to suit our needs; it is rather that there are competing realities which become reflected in the various structures which we employ to talk about the world.

Where such a relativistic view operates, the politician cannot win, accused of insensitivity if he/she refers to 'the poor', and of obfuscation if he/she refers to 'the economically disadvantaged'. The politician is, of course, no innocent, nor unique in linguistic terms. Certainly, it worked to President Nixon's advantage, when, in the summer of 1972, he responded to a question about any possible connections between the White House and those involved in the Watergate break-in by saying that no one 'presently employed' in the White House had participated in the break-in at the Democratic National Committee Headquarters (see Thomas, 1978: iii). But in a very similar way, a young child might say 'no' in response to a question such as 'Did you eat some of the cookies?', meaning, in this case, 'no I ate all of the cookies.' Whatever our moral qualms in each case, they made their point, didn't they?

The question that is interesting from the linguistic point of view is how did they do it, not whether they should have done it or not. In classic terms, we are interested in describing what happened, not in prescribing what should happen. In order to understand what politicans do with language it is important to understand what it is possible to do with language in general.

Such a perspective offers a radically different approach to that normally advocated in the analysis of political talk. It is not that one is arguing here for ideological neutrality (there is no such thing), nor that one is behaving as Van Dijk (1985) has suggested as an 'intellectual paper tiger'; rather, the argument is for a clear discussion of political language in relation to our understanding of the linguistic system itself. The development of a 'socially realistic linguistics' (Seidel, 1985) requires more than an expansion of linguistic concerns into the areas of politics and social action (a view advocated by Lavandera, 1988); it is dependent on an adequate theory of language which may be objectively applied to the analyst's language as much as the language of those analysed.

It is not always enough to simply pin-point particular linguistic styles, as Hudson (1978) does in his book *The Language of Modern Politics*; one must be able to explain the structural basis of such styles, otherwise we become involved in nothing more than English appreciation exercises. Nor is it enough to argue that linguistic categorization delimits and directs perception without fully explaining how this is possible in linguistic as well as political terms.

For example, the political scientist Murray Edleman (1974: 3, cited in Geis, 1987, see also Edleman, 1988: ch. 6) suggests that language shapes beliefs and perceptions to such an extent that politicians use language not merely to explain or describe events, rather the language is 'itself part of events, strongly shaping their meaning'. The linguist Michael Geis criticizes Edleman because Geis knows of 'no theory of meaning, that is linguistic meaning, by which it would make sense to say that events have meaning' (Geis, 1987: 5).

There is some truth in this criticism, but there has been enough work within *sociolinguistics* over the years to indicate that events are in fact defined, to a large extent, by the language employed (see Downes, 1984; Fasold, 1984, Wardhaugh, 1986). Hymes (1977) talks of the concept of a 'speech event', where the organization of talk contributes to a definition of the situation itself (see for example Wilson, 1989). Whether this is 'linguistic meaning' in Geis's sense, or 'event meaning', as Edleman uses the term, will not detain us here. It is enough to note that the concept 'event meaning' operates only as an intuitive rhetorical description without some linguistic theory to validate its underlying assumption(s).

It is the aim of this book to develop an analysis of political talk which is grounded within the framework of a linguistic analysis, specifically a pragmatic analysis, where *pragmatics* refers to the study of meaning in context. It is descriptive, in so far as it explains the way in which available linguistic resources are employed within political encounters. There is no 'will to truth'; politicians manipulate language for their own ends, yes! But the manipulations are frequently no different from those employed in everyday interaction (or by theorists criticizing political language). The stakes and consequences of any manipulation are, of course, much higher in the political game. My aim is not to pass moral judgement, however, but to offer an objective description at the linguistic level; readers may, of course, draw upon such a description to come to their own political conclusions.

Linguistics, Politics and Pragmatics

As I noted above, this book is different from many other texts on political language in that its aim is to provide a linguistic account of actual political talk. In this respect, however, it is similar to the recent work of Geis (1987: vii), who claims in the preface to his book: 'this is by no means the first book on language and politics, but it is I think the first book written by a linguist and the first extensive analysis of actually occurring political language.'

Despite Geis's very reasonable assertions, he does not, in his book, fully deliver on the promise of these initial claims. The term 'actual political language' is restricted, in the main, to political journalism, but as Geis is clearly aware, journalists mediate and transform, in a number of ways, what politicians actually say (see Geis, 1987: 8; also Bell, 1984 on the effects of editing). Consequently, what politicians say and what journalists say they say is not the same thing. We may be being somewhat pedantic here in considering what is political language, but in this book we will constrain ourselves to actual production in the form of what politicians say.

Geis's linguistic analysis, while extremely interesting and worthy, does strike me as odd in a number of places. In a discussion of the Orwellian position for example, that is that political language can influence thought, Geis suggests that many analysts who support such a thesis get the facts wrong because they attend to the political as opposed to the linguistic issues. This claim seems perfectly correct, but I feel that Geis's example case is perhaps badly chosen. Geis takes the example of the word 'pacification' and notes Orwell's claim that the use of such a word to refer to the bombing of innocent villages constitutes language used 'in defence of the indefensible' (Orwell, 1969: 225). Geis argues that if one looks carefully at the actual definition of the word 'pacification' one finds, in the *Shorter Oxford English Dictionary*, a definition which includes 'to bring or reduce to a state of peace; to calm, to quiet'. Further, notes Geis, in the *American Heritage Dictionary of the English Language* (1964 Edition) one finds a definition which includes 'to subdue' (Geis, 1987: 22). From this Geis draws the conclusion that it is legitimate to use the word 'pacification' in a context where force has been employed.

This type of eytmological argument has a degree of linguistic credibility, but it is surely the same kind of argument that might be used by self-styled guardians of the English language when they claim that there is only one correct form of English, with, presumably, a correct definition for each word in the language (see Milroy and Milroy, 1986).

Crystal (1988: 42) sums up mainstream linguistic opinion when he refers to such arguments as being based on an 'etymological fallacy'. As Crystal points out, once we set off on the historical trail there is no agreed point at which we should stop. Take the word 'nice' for example. There are those who argue that its correct meaning must be 'fastidious' because that's what it meant in Shakespeare's time. But as Crystal notes, if we argue that the older meaning is the preferred one, then why stop with Shakespeare; the word 'nice' can be traced back to Old French where it meant 'silly', and further back to Latin where *'nescius'* meant 'ignorant'. Crystal suggests we might go back even further and speculate on an earlier Indo-European form. But the point is made however. Simply referring to dictionary uses and etymological arguments will not deny the force of Orwell's argument, because it has nothing to do with correct or incorrect choices in terms of meaning as defined by lexicographers. The issue is about connotative as well as exact meaning (or perhaps different readings in Derrida's (1978) terms).

If we take a word like 'red' for example, its exact meaning relates to colour in a general and technical sense. But the word may also have psychological connotations, and these may vary depending on the context of use and the individual who is involved in the interpretation process. In some contexts red may have connotations of warmth, in others it may be associated with political beliefs, as in 'he's a red,' meaning 'he's a communist'. When the word 'pacification' is used to refer to the killing of innocent people, we must ask more than what does it actually mean, we must ask why, in paradigmatic terms, was it chosen in this context to refer to these actions.

If we look at related words such as 'passive', 'pacify', 'pacifier', 'pacifist', we can see immediately that the psychological connotations are essentially concerned with peacefulness, not with violence. The fact that one can find a contrived meaning for one of these terms which could include force is irrelevant. Indeed, within the frame of Geis's book this may even be a contradiction. Geis goes on later to argue that in speeches about the Vietnam war, President Johnson alternated reference to American soldiers between 'men' and 'boys'; as in 'I ordered two extra battalions – 2,000 – extra men', as opposed to, 'I want you to know that it is . . . not an easy matter to send our American boys to another country.' What is happening is quite clear; 'men' is the term reserved for martial activities, 'boys' is used when support for policies is required. This is Geis's assessment (see Geis, 1987; chapter 3) but there is no argument here about the correct use of any terms, although I think one could be made, perhaps in relation to the fact that the average age of American soldiers in Vietnam was only 19. No such argument is put by Geis however, because here, as in Geis's own experiments on the so called 'Volatile/Non-Volatile' nature of certain verbs, we are concerned with connotative aspects of meaning.

In many ways we are dealing, in these examples, with subjective and quantitatively delimited aspects of meaning, in the sense that interpretations are not categorical but probabilistic. To most people the contrast between Johnson's use of 'men' and his use of 'boys' will be clear, but this is not guaranteed and there will be individuals who may not agree that there is any strong contrast in the way these terms have been used.

Certainly, politicians use words and sentences in an emotive manner; it is part of their aim to create a feeling of solidarity, to arouse emotions such as fear, hate or joy. But in understanding how this is achieved we must construct our arguments carefully, particularly where we accuse others of failing to recognize the linguistic dimension.

Political Pragmatics

There are other less subjective aspects of meaning, however, which fall squarely within the domain of linguistics, in that such aspects emanate from the interaction of language and context resources. These aspects of meaning are *intentional*, motivated by the speaker's aim of achieving particular goals in a specified context of human interaction. By this I mean that linguistic resources are selected in terms of their interaction with principles of human behaviour in order to achieve specified outcomes. For example, if at the dinner table I say to my partner 'Can you pass the salt?', it will be quite obvious that I am not questioning my partner's ability (although in some contexts this is a possibility) but requesting my partner to perform the action of passing the salt. The meaning of my utterance, then, differs radically from the surface form. But this is not simply a subjectively motivated component of meaning; readers will immediately recognize the conventional form of requesting using a question structure. The details of how this works will be explained later; for the present, the point I wish to make is that there are aspects of meaning which go beyond the surface structure but which are not necessarily connotatively or subjectively loaded.

Since it is quite obvious that political language is designed to achieve specific political goals, to make people believe in certain things, it is a prime example of what we will call 'pragmatic behaviour'; linguistic behaviour, that is, which is sensitive to the context of production. Analysing and considering how this context-sensitivity emerges within political talk is the main function of this book. By focusing on samples of actual political language, the aim is to indicate the way in which a pragmatic analysis reveals, in a structural manner, underlying aspects of meaning.

We have already seen a brief example of how this operates in the introduction. Although the example of factive verbs was chosen in the previous description, this does not suggest that applied pragmatics should (or indeed could) focus only on pragmatic examples defined in terms of the linguistic encoding of context as part of the language system. In this text we will take a much broader and mixed view of legitimate pragmatic phenomena: a necessary step where one wishes to explain the broad sweep of pragmatic possibilities employed within the context of political talk. Consequently, we include analyses of linguistically encoded examples of pragmatic phenomena; examples based on principles of behaviour; examples based on those interactive constraints which operate between the levels of semantics and pragmatics (see Blakemore, 1987) and examples based on psychologically and sociologically constrained aspects of meaning in context (for specific political examples here see Atkinson, 1984; Heritage and Greatbatch, 1986). It will become clear as we proceed that the distinction between these levels of pragmatic concern only operates as a theoretical heuristic, since when one is dealing with actual talk the various levels frequently interact with each other (see, for example, chapters 2 and 3).

In order that we may make some sense of the broad sweep of pragmatic concerns outlined above, I want to attempt to bring order to the range of possibilities by suggesting that the core aim of pragmatics is to account for what Lycan (1986) has called 'implicative relations'. These include what Lycan calls *secondary meanings*; meanings which are not strictly part of a sentence's logical form (semantic meaning). For example, if I say 'It's cold in this room' I may, in some contexts, intend my hearer to interpret what I have said as meaning I would like to have a window closed. There are then what Lycan calls *invited inferences*, which seem to cover a broad range of phenomena. For example, if I say 'I'll give you five pounds if you get a friend to buy this book,' it invites the inference that 'if you don't get a friend to buy the book I won't give you five pounds.' These inferences seem highly dependent on specific aspects of general world and background knowledge. Finally, we have 'presuppositions', an element of inferred information which emerges from the use of specific linguistic forms; we have already come across an example of this in our discussion of the verb 'regret' (see above).

The three types of 'implicative relation' outlined by Lycan cover the main areas presently discussed under the heading of pragmatics. In some ways they are perhaps overly general and somewhat vague; for example in the case of 'secondary meanings', simply saying that it is meaning beyond logical form opens up a wealth of possibilities. What is particularly interesting from our point of view, however, is the idea of an 'implication'.

An 'implication' is an inference type not a fact, and as such, in many cases, it can be cancelled or denied. In the following example (1c) denies that the conventional implication of a request in (1a) was intended, and in (2) the presupposition of truth attached to the verb 'regret' is cancelled by the final clause.

(1a) Can you pass the salt?
(b) Here you are.
(c) I don't want the salt; I only asked if you could pass it.

(2) John doesn't regret beating his dog because he never touched it.

Since many implications are 'defeasible' (the term used to indicate that certain implication types disappear in selected contexts), this makes them particularly useful for directing hearer's interpretations, without, in one sense, from the speaker's point of view, overt responsibility for any inferences which the hearer makes. Further, implicational types are also particularly useful in general social terms for the maintenance of what Goffman (1967) calls 'face', i.e. the way in which we present ourselves and act towards others, and the way in which we expect others to behave towards us (see Brown and Levinson, 1978).

In example (1a) we have a classic case of what would normally be a request. It is articulated in this indirect manner because, as the request is an implication, a secondary meaning, we cannot be accused of imposing upon our hearer, but at the same time we can, by the use of such a form, achieve our own specified goal.

Most important, from the perspective of this book, is the general idea that speakers can employ implicative relations in order to direct a hearer's interpretation. I am not suggesting that this is a form of 'thought manipulation' in any Orwellian or deterministic sense however. It is more of a conjuring trick, where we employ those forms which we predict will lead to the interpretation most conducive to our aims at a point in time.

A sequential example of this may be seen in the work of Atkinson (1984) who has indicated that there are a series of rhetorical devices available to politicians for inviting applause, at party rallies for example. The classic case of this is what Atkinson calls 'the three part list'. Without exploring this concept in any detail, the point is that where certain selected moves are made by the politician, the audience recognizes that applause is being invited and responds accordingly.

This kind of example would not normally be thought of in core pragmatic terms (although see Levinson, 1983); nevertheless I see this type of case as being implicational in kind (an invited inference). I would argue this for the following reasons: first, because applause is not guaranteed and may indeed be cancelled if the speaker continues to talk; second, as Heritage and Greatbatch (1986) note, making applause for an individual may involve 'face' costs. If, for example, an individual applauds too soon he may be highlighted in his isolation. Consequently, the timing of applause is significantly important for any individual in terms of 'face' maintenance. This is similar in a number of ways to the indirect request case in (1).

To take a more traditional example, consider again the earlier quote from Nixon, where he stated that no one 'presently employed' in the White House had participated in the break-in at Democratic National Committee Headquarters; we can see that there is a possible impli-cation here that those previously working in the White House may have been involved in the break-in.

> (3) No one presently employed in the White House partici-pated in the break-in at the Democratic National Commit-tee Headquarters, but a number of past employees were involved.

There is, however, no guarantee that this implication was either intended, or that it is indeed correct, since this implication can be cancelled:

> No one presently employed in the White House participated in the break-in at the Democratic National Committee Head-quarters nor indeed anyone who has ever worked in the White House.

As we now know the implication of the original statement was in fact true, and Nixon's hand might have been forced had reporters questioned further. But as Helen Thomas, who was there when Nixon gave his response, points out, it was not something which the reporters noticed. On the surface the statement seemed to answer the question and deny any link between members of the White House and those involved in the Watergate break-in (see Thomas, 1978: iii). In this sense Nixon achieved his goal, and he achieved it by making use of specific pragmatic aspects of language.

The point is that Nixon did not create any representation of the world which was false. His utterance acted to delimit a set of individ-uals in a specific 'possible world' (Lewis, 1972), or more simply at a particular point in time. Then Nixon noted that this set of individuals had no overlapping membership with the set of individuals designated as being involved in the break-in. However, the set of individuals working 'presently' in the White House is a sub-set of the total set of those who have worked in the White House, and there is in fact an

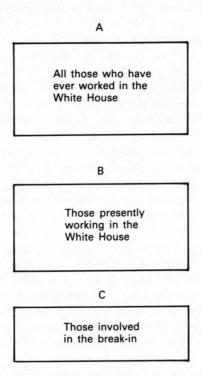

A

All those who have
ever worked in the
White House

B

Those presently
working in the
White House

C

Those involved
in the break-in

Figure 1 The White House and the Watergate break-in: available conceptual sets

overlap of the total set of individuals who have worked in the White House and the set of those individuals involved in the break-in. Diagramatically, we might represent the situation as in figure 1. What the reporters really wanted to know about was the relationship between the total set and the set of individuals involved in the break-in. What they have been provided with is a description of the relationship between set B and set C which have no overlapping members. If we look at the relationship between the total set of those who have worked in the White House, and set C, we can see that there are members of A (those who have worked in the White House in the past) who are also members of set C. This is what the reporters were trying to get at. What Nixon did by forming his response to attend to only those presently working in the White House, was to direct attention to sets B and C which have no overlapping members. The question as to why the reporters could not, or did not, work this out is something we will return to later. For the moment we can see that Nixon made his point, didn't he?

Was Nixon's utterance an example of thought manipulation however? In one sense, yes, in that his utterance led the audience to create a mental model (see Johnson-Laird, 1983; also chapters 2 and 4 below) based on a comparison of set B and set C. But this cannot really be thought control since it is an example of what we all do in directing particular topics of interest in conversation (see Wilson, 1989; chapter 3). Nixon has simply selected a particular picture of the world which suits his purpose on which to focus. As the above analysis (and Thomas's hindsight) shows, however, the reporters were free to select their own focus based on the implication contained in what Nixon said, i.e. that it might have been members of the set of those individuals who had worked in the White House in the past who had been involved in the break-in. The fact that the reporters were not alert to this possibility is something they have to consider.

If this is not thought control in a strong deterministic sense it is certainly a form of manipulation, a process by which specific interpretations are encouraged. It is important to stress encouraged, and not guaranteed, because listeners can locate the principles being manipulated and subvert these. If we want to understand what politicians are up to when they make use of the linguistic system for particular political purposes or functions, and if, in one sense, we wish to redress the balance of power, we must pay attention not only to content but to form as well; and indeed the interaction of these two in specific contexts of production, i.e. we must do pragmatics. In the rest of this book we will do just that, by exploring, through a range of selected cases, what it means to *do pragmatics* within the context of political talk.

2

Talking Politics and Doing Pragmatics

***

Introduction

I argued in chapter 1 that political talk may be analysed from a pragmatic perspective by considering the way in which politicians make use of 'implicative relations'. It was noted that implicative relations frequently lead to inferences and not statements of fact. In this sense implicative relations would seem to present public figures, in particular politicians, with an important communicative tool in their efforts to present the world in any specific ideological manner. For political analysts it would seem to be important also, then, that they are capable of locating and analysing implicative relations and their use in specific political contexts.

In this chapter, I will consider an example of actual political talk and present a pragmatic analysis making use of a number of implicative relational types. The aim is twofold: first, to clarify, by example, how a pragmatic analysis of political contexts might proceed; second, to introduce a number of basic and significant pragmatic concepts which underlie the analyses to be presented in later chapters.

The example I want to explore comes from a question and answer session in the British House of Commons, which took place on Wednesday, 7 May 1986. In particular, I will be focusing on questions, directed to The Secretary of State for Foreign and Commonwealth Affairs (Sir Geoffrey Howe), on US military aid to the Contras in Nicaragua (answered, in the first instance, by Mr Tim Eggar, Undersecretary of State for Foreign and Commonwealth Affairs), and questions on the issue of international terrorism.

Implications

Although the questions I want to focus on seem to attend to two different issues, i.e. military aid versus international terrorism, these issues were linked by a number of questioners who suggested that the United States' support of the Contra rebel group was an example of state-sponsored terrorism. This suggestion was developed, in part, in relation to the US bombing of Libya, which had taken place previously that year, an action justified by the United States in terms of Libyan support for international terrorism.

Several of the speakers who put questions in this parliamentary session suggested that the US actions indicated hypocrisy. The argument was that it was hypocritical for the United States to claim that they carried out the bombing of Libya as a response to that country's involvement in international terrorism, when they themselves (the Americans) supported the Nicaraguan Contras who, in the opinion of some members of the house, were in fact terrorists. This position is summed up in the question put by Mr Dennis Healey:

Mr Healey: Did the Government remind President Reagan at the Tokyo summit that his proposals for military aid to the Contras involved the United States in a most blatant form of state terrorism, because the Contras have engaged in horrifying atrocities, including torture and mutilation, against innocent women and children . . . Does the hon. Gentleman agree that, so long as President Reagan supports such activities he has no right whatsoever to claim to be an opponent of state terrorism. (Hansard, 1986d: p. 136)

In response to this question, and its attendant claims, Mr Tim Eggar, speaking for Her Majesty's Government, made the following statement:

Mr Eggar: I think the right hon. Gentleman is trying to draw a parallel between the United States action in Libya and its action in Nicaragua, which simply does not stand up to any examination. Gaddafi has committed the Libyan Government to organising and directing a world wide campaign of terrorist violence against innocent people outside Libya. In Nicaragua, the Contras and the Nicaraguans have resorted to armed struggle against their own government. *The Contras do not seek to advance their cause by terrorist acts in third countries.* [my italics]

I want to explore, for the moment, Mr Eggar's claim in italics above. My suggestion is that it carries a pragmatic assumption, or implication, which seems at variance with the case I believe Mr Eggar would want to make. The problem is this: to claim that the Contras do not carry out terrorist acts in third countries does not, in itself, deny that they carry out terrorist acts, merely that they do not carry out such acts in third countries. Further, accepting this possibility, and focusing directly on the phrase 'in third countries', which is generally used to mean something like 'in countries other than one's own', then it is perfectly legitimate to interpret that Mr Eggar has said as implying that 'the Contras carry out terrorist acts in *their own country*'.

This would seem odd on any interpretation of Mr Eggar's aim in responding to Mr Healey, since in one sense it gives some credence to those claims made by Mr Healey which Mr Eggar is attempting to deny. Of course, one might argue that the interpretation we have arrived at, or are suggesting, arises because we have taken the sentence out of context. This is not a valid criticism however. First, because the very same option would remain rhetorically available for anyone listening to Mr Eggar's response, and we cannot seriously believe that in the House of Commons, as a forum for confrontational debate, that such an option would be ignored where it is given (intentionally or not). Second, and more importantly, there is nothing within the total context of the response, nor indeed the sequential context of the question and the response, which acts to explicitly block the implications I have identified.

Mr Eggar has claimed that the Contras differ from the Libyans, in that the Libyans carry out terrorist acts world-wide, while the Contras do not. If one were accusing the Contras of carrying out terrorist acts world-wide then Mr Eggar would be correct; there would be no comparison between them and the Libyans. But this is not what Mr Healey claimed; he claimed that the Contras were terrorists, and Mr Eggar has not explicitly denied this.

What evidence is there, however, to support the interpretation I have proposed? In order to present such evidence, we must look again at the concept of a 'presupposition', and introduce another pragmatic concept referred to as a 'conversational implicature'.

In my earlier use of the term 'presupposition' I gave a fairly straightforward account of the concept. It will be necessary now to consider 'presupposition' in a more technical manner. This is not a book on theoretical pragmatics however, consequently the formal nature of the argument will be kept to a minimum (the reader will find an excellent summary of the main issues in the controversial history of presupposition in Levinson, 1983; see also Gazdar, 1979; Kempson, 1979; Oh and Dineen, 1979; Green, 1989).

Presuppositions are inferences which have certain structural qualities. In early studies it was noted that they were elements of meaning which seemed to survive under negation (Strawson, 1950; see Wilson, 1975; Gazdar, 1979; Kempson, 1979). For example, (b) is assumed to be true in both (1) and (2) below:

(1a)   John regrets beating his wife.
 (b)   John has beaten his wife.
(2a)   John doesn't regret beating his wife.
 (b)   John has beaten his wife.

This behaviour under negation distinguishes presuppositions from other elements of meaning such as 'entailments', that is, aspects of meaning logically derived from a sentence relative to its assumed truth value. For example, if (3a) below is true then (3b) and (3c) will also be true. If (3a) is false however, as in (4), then (3c) will not be true, but (3b) may still be true, that is it will survive in the context of negation. (3c) is an entailment while (3b) is a presupposition.

(3a)   John managed to stop in time.
 (b)   John tried to stop in time.
 (c)   John stopped in time.

(4)   John didn't manage to stop in time. (Levinson, 1983: 178)

Put more simply, when we interpret (3a) we assume that (3b) and (3c) are both true, but when we interpret (4) we assume only that (3b) is true (see Harris, 1974 for experimental evidence on the probabilistic nature of this claim). If asked why we made such assumptions, we could readily point out that it is a contradiction to say something like (5), but perfectly acceptable to say something like (6):

(5)   John didn't manage to stop in time and he stopped in time.
(6)   John didn't manage to stop in time but he did try.

Although survival under negation is a basic feature of presuppositions, it is problematic in that in a number of negative contexts presuppositions can themselves be cancelled by the addition of a further clause as in (7):

(7)   John didn't manage to stop in time because he didn't even try.

We have already noted in chapter 1 that this quality of presuppositions is referred to as 'defeasibility'. It was also noted in chapter 1 that presuppositions are tied to specific aspects of surface structure, 'presupposition triggers' as they are sometimes referred to (see Levinson, 1983: 181–4 for a range of examples). Taking these basic (if somewhat controversial) facts into account, let us return to our selected example from Mr Eggar's statement, and compare its negative form with its positive form:

> (8a) The Contras seek to advance their cause by terrorist acts in third countries.
> (b) The Contras do not seek to advance their cause by terrorist acts in third countries.

One implication which seems to survive in both contexts here is that 'the Contras carry out terrorist acts,' which suggests that such an implication is a presupposition. Further evidence for this claim can be provided when we consider that in (8b) one can deny such an implication (an example of defeasibility):

> (9) The Contras do not seek to advance their cause by terrorist acts in third countries because they do not carry out terrorist acts.

As we have already noted, presuppositions have yet another defining quality above and beyond defeasibility; it is claimed that they are 'triggered' by specific linguistic elements (see for example, the case of the verb 'regret' above). Is there any evidence, in this case, that the implication is tied to a specific aspect of surface structure? I think the answer is yes; compare Mr Eggar's statement in both its positive and negative forms with the final adverbial clause removed:

> (10a) The Contras seek to advance their cause by terrorist acts.
> (b) The Contras do not seek to advance their cause by terrorist acts.

It is clear that in this case the implication that 'the Contras carry out terrorist acts' does not survive under negation, in fact it is explicitly denied. Consequently, the argument is that the implication 'the Contras carry out terrorist acts' is a *presupposition* of Mr Eggar's statement. The evidence for this claim is based on the following facts: (a) the implication survives under negation; (b) it is defeasible; and (c) it is tied to a specific aspect of surface structure, in this case the adverbial clause 'in third countries'.

We can see, then, that Mr Eggar's statement carries a presupposition that the Contras carry out terrorist acts, but this would seem to support Mr Healey's claims rather than Mr Eggar's. Why, then, did Mr Eggar make a statement which carried a presupposition at odds, or seemingly at odds, with his aim of countering the claims explicitly made by Mr Healey? We cannot, of course, be sure of his intentions, but since his main aim was to contrast the actions of the Contras with the actions of Libya, and since his main argument here was that Libya carried out terrorist acts beyond its own borders, he seems to have concentrated on making this claim prominent, with the consequence that there was no denial of the Contras as terrorists, simply a claim that they were different from the Libyans who carried out atrocities world-wide.

In one sense, and perhaps within the total context of both Mr Healey's question and Mr Eggar's answer, if Mr Eggar's intention was to deny that the Contras were comparable to the Libyans then his actions are, on one level, *pragmatically* sound. In analysing the pragmatic nature of negation Givon (1979a) suggests that negative statements occur where a corresponding affirmative has either been mentioned or where the content of such a corresponding affirmative is deemed likely, or where the speaker holds the affirmative to be true. Horn (1987; 1988) makes a broadly similar point when he claims that various problems and ambiguities which surround questions about the semantic/pragmatic nature of negation (see Kempson, 1987; Carston, 1987a; 1987b) may be resolved by treating negation as a metalingual concept. Horn argues that in a sentence like (11) a contradiction arises. The contradiction is generated by the fact that the speaker, on one view of negation, is denying that John drank three pints, while at the same time asserting that he drank five pints. Logically, of course, if John drank five pints then it must be true that he drank three pints. This problem is resolved where we assume that (11) is an example of 'metalinguistic negation'. In metalinguistic negation the speaker is denying some aspect of a previous claim, within which it was believed that John drank at least three pints.

(11)   John didn't drink three pints, he drank five.

These arguments about the pragmatic nature of negation would allow us to claim that, within the total context of Mr Eggar's response, the statement, 'the Contras do not seek to advance their cause by terrorist acts in third countries', functions merely to deny a prior claim made by Mr Healey. But what would this claim be? It can't be Mr Healey's claim that 'the Contras are terrorists', since Mr Eggar's statement, 'the Contras, etc.', as we have noted, carries a presupposition that the Contras are terrorists; therefore, it would be a contradiction for Mr Eggar to both deny this and implicate it at the same time.

What he does deny, however, is that the Contras, if they are terrorists, carry out any terrorist acts in third countries. Now, Mr Healey has not claimed that the Contras do carry out terrorist acts in third countries, he has merely said that he believes they are terrorists. However, Mr Healey has also likened the Contras, or rather linked them in his question, with Libya. And Libya does carry out terrorist actions in third countries. Consequently, the only way we can make sense of Mr Eggar's turn as a metalingual form is to see it as denying that the Contras, like the Libyans, carry out terrorist acts in third countries.

Such a claim was never explicitly made in Mr Healey's question; it is, however, implicit in what he says; and indeed it is this that Mr Eggar takes up in the opening remark of his response. In this sense, then, Mr Eggar's statement functions pragmatically to deny an assumed comparison between the Contras and the Libyans. However, if Mr Eggar is going to be selective in his interpretation of what Mr Healey has said, then Mr Healey is free to apply the same approach to Mr Eggar's statement, and despite the metalingual claims attendant on Mr Eggar's statement, he has implicitly left intact a presupposition which is at odds with a more central and core issue, i.e. whether the Contras are or are not terrorists. The problem here is that Mr Eggar has negated any comparison between the Contras and the Libyans at only one level, leaving the presupposition that the Contras are terrorists intact.

Further Implications

This is not the only implication that Mr Eggar has left intact however. I want to suggest that there is yet a further implication in Mr Eggar's statement to the effect that the Contras not only carry out terrorist acts, but they carry out these acts in their own country. Obviously, from a purely political perspective, this is an implication which, in the context of this parliamentary debate, clearly works against any attempt to counter the general tenor of Mr Healey's critical claims (although this is not something which Mr Healey seems to have been aware of).

The implication that the Contras carry out terrorist acts in their own country is based, once again, on the use of the adverbial clause 'in third countries'. The clause, 'in third countries', can be said to mean 'in countries other than one's own', or more simply, 'not in one's own country'. Interpreting the adverbial phrase *in third countries* in this way creates what seems to be a simple bilateral relationship:

third countries   ⟷   not one's own country
one's own country   ⟷   not third countries

There is, I'm afraid, no such simple exclusive relationship in the use of these structures, since it is possible to say the following without contradiction:

(12)   The Contras seek to advance their cause by terrorist acts in their own country and indeed in a number of third countries.

(13)   The Contras seek to advance their cause by terrorist acts in third countries and indeed in their own country.

Clearly, the relationship between 'third country' and 'not one's own country' is more than simply one of semantics, in that the two do not seem inter-substitutable in any sense of synonymy. Are we again, perhaps, talking of a presuppositional relationship? Apparently not, in that the implication which folows from 'in third countries', in this case, is not that which follows from the same form under negation.

(14a) The Contras seek to advance their cause by terrorist acts in third countries.
  (b) in countries other than their own
(15a) The Contras do not seek to advance their cause by terrorist acts in third countries.
  (b) ?in their own country

While the presupposition already discussed, i.e. that the Contras carry out terrorist acts, is available in both (14a) and (15a), I would argue that the implication that 'the Contras carry out terrorist acts in their own country' is only really available in (15a). Indeed (14a) states that 'the Contras do not carry out terrorist acts in their own country'. The question is, then, where does the implication come from in the negative form of the statement, and what kind of implication is it?

If 'third countries' implies 'not one's own country', then, on the surface, the adverbial is behaving in the same way as a word like 'some', which is said to imply 'not all'. Both the adverbial clause and 'some' are similar in that they imply the negation of another form:

(16a)   Some of the boys enjoyed the party.
  (b)   not all of the boys enjoyed the party

  (c)   We play football in a third country.
  (d)   not our own country

They are also similar in that they both provide implications which can be cancelled.

(17a)   Some, if indeed not all, of the teachers were sacked.
  (b)   We will visit a number of third countries and of course our own country.

As we have already noted it is one of the defining features of presuppositions that they are *defeasible*, i.e. that they will disappear in certain contexts. This is not the only defining feature of presuppositions, however, and indeed defeasibility is a characteristic exhibited by several pragmatic phenomena. Consequently, we should not automatically assume that what we have here is another example of presupposition (it was also noted above that the implication we are dealing with does not survive under negation, which we might have expected if it were a presupposition). Let us explore some other possible candidate implication types.

Implications: Scalar and Conversational

In order to try to resolve the question of what kind of implication we are dealing with, I want to consider, in some more detail, the links between the phrase 'in third countries', and the description of a form like 'some', which as we have noted, has a number of features in common with the adverbial 'in third countries'.

The behaviour of a form like 'some' is normally accounted for in terms of what are called 'scalar implicatures', a specific type of implication developed by Gerald Gazdar (see Gazdar, 1979) from the original work of Paul Grice (Grice, 1975).

Grice's work is based on the assumption that when people interact they are guided by a basic principle of co-operation, and that under this principle of co-operation operate a series of maxims which guide conversational behaviour:

The co-operative principle

Make your contribution, such as is required at the stage at which it occurs, by the accepted purpose or direction of the talk exchange in which you are engaged.

The Maxims

a. Quality
   Try to make your contribution one that is true, specifically:

   i do not say that which you believe false;
   ii do not say that for which you lack adequate evidence.

b. Quantity

   i Make your contribution as informative as required for the current purposes of the exchange.
   ii Do not make your contribution more informative than required.

c. Relevance
   Make your contributions relevant.

d. Manner
   i Avoid obscurity.
   ii Avoid ambiguity.
   iii Be brief.
   iv Be orderly.

Where any of these maxims are flouted within interaction, it is assumed that the co-operative principle is still in operation, and that one consequence of this is that the hearer is required to search for meaning beyond the surface structure in order to make sense of what is said. For example:

(18a)   What time did Bill get home?
  (b)   Well the pubs were closed.

On the surface, the response in (18) does not seem to supply information about the time Bill got home, as requested by the question, and in this sense speaker (b) has failed to maintain the maxim of relevance. However, as most readers can work out, the answer supplies much more information than is available from a semantic analysis of the surface structure alone. What speaker (b) indicates is that he does not know exactly what time Bill got home, but what is known is that it was later than X, X being the time at which pubs close. In this example, the hearer flouts the maxim of relevance in order to create what Grice calls a 'conversational implicature', the implication in this case that 'Bill was home later than X'.

Building on Grice's basic model Gazdar (1979) has argued that certain lexical items form scales in terms of the way in which they relate to each other. For example, 'all' entails 'some', and 'some' implicates 'not all'. The relationship between 'some' and 'not all' is one of implication (a scalar implication in Gazdar's terminology) because (like presuppositions) it can be cancelled without contradiction (see above). In terms of a scale such as {A1, A2, A3 . . .} we would say that if one uses {A2} one implicates ˜{A1}, or if one uses {A3} one implicates ˜{A2} and ˜{A1}.

Accepting this basic model for the moment, we might say in the case of countries that we have a simple scale such as the following: {third, one} (where 'one' refers to 'one's own country'). According to scalar principles, 'one' should implicate ˜{third}. This is in fact the case (see above). The problem here, however, is that {third} does not (as would be expected on using normal scalar principles) entail {one}, in fact it explicitly excludes it:

(19a) The Contras seek to advance their cause by terrorist acts in third countries.

(b) The Contras seek to advance their cause by terrorist acts in their own country.

In the case of our simple scale of countries there seems to be a relationship of negative bi-directionality, i.e. that the use of any member of the scale implies the negation of the other in any direction. For example, {third} implies ˜{one}; equally, {one} implies ˜{third}. This is a similar, though a more formal, account of what I referred to above as a bilateral relationship; we are now in a position, however, to explain this relationship. It is suggested that certain forms have a bi-directional scalar relationship, where one implies the negation of the other. These are implicatures, nonetheless, and can therefore be cancelled as in (17) above.

This does not, in itself, tell us why we get the implication from Mr Eggar's statement that 'the Contras carry out terrorist acts in their own country'. The answer is that since {third} implies $^-${one}, $^-${third} implies $^{--}${one}; and by a standard formal rule of double negation we get {one} from $^{--}${one}. Consequently, when one says 'not in third countries' one implies 'in one's own country'. The implication here being a variation of a scalar implicature.

If we accept this argument, however, we must also be able to show that this type of scalar implicature fulfils the necessary requirements for being a conversational implicature in a standard Gricean sense. While the establishment of specific tests for implicature have proved controversial (see Sadock 1978; Lycan, 1986), it would, nevertheless, be worthwhile to consider how our claims stand up to the original tests laid down by Grice.

Four basic tests for implicatures are normally adduced:

1. Defeasibility (that they may be cancelled in certain contexts).
2. Calculability (that they can be worked out: see the explanation of (18) above).
3. Non-detachability (the implicature is attached to the semantic content of what is said, not to the form. In this sense implicatures are different from presuppositions).
4. Non-conventionality (the implicature is not part of the conventional meaning of linguistic expressions).

Let us take each of these in turn, and consider in what sense 'in one's own country' is a conversational implicature which can be derived from the adverbial form 'not in third countries'.

First, *defeasibility*. We have already noted above that 'not in third countries' does provide the inference, 'in one's own country', and that this inference may be cancelled by the addition of a clause giving something like, 'not in third countries, nor in one's own country'. Clearly, this is a case of defeasibility.

Second, *calculability*. In this case we must assume, using scalar principles, that if Mr Eggar had evidence that the Contras carry out terrorist acts in their own country, or that they do not carry out terrorist acts at all, then he would have said so. He did not however; consequently, we may assume that he may not be sure, or lack evidence, that the acts that the Contras are performing are terrorist acts: a not unreasonable claim, since it is sometimes difficult to draw the line between terrorism and democratic struggle (see below).

Third, *non-detachability*. The question, here, is can we generate the same inference ('in one's own country') using a different lexical expression? This seems quite possible as we can see in the following examples:

(20a)   The Contras do not carry out terrorist acts in other states.
  (b)   The Contras do not carry out terrorist acts over the borders of other countries.

In each case the implication that the actions are carried out within one's own country remains intact.

Finally, *non-conventionality*. In this case we would have to claim that 'not in third countries' can have a semantic meaning different from 'in one's own country'. Clearly, this is the case in that, compositionally, one could use the phrase 'not in third countries' to refer to actual multiples of three.

(21)   We will attack every third country to the west.

As I noted above, these tests are a matter of some controversy, and Sadock (1978) has suggested that even if all these tests are taken together, other features may still be required to identify implicatures. However, for our purposes I believe we have fairly strong evidence that the meaning relationship between 'not in third countries' and 'in one's own country' is one of implicature.

The Implications of Using Implications

Returning to why Mr Eggar would make a statement which carries an implicature at odds with the central claim he would wish to defend, it might be argued that there is some advantage in using a phrase which generates a scalar implicature, in that such an implicature may be cancelled (see (18) above). This would offer Mr Eggar some degree of protection in that he cannot be accused, if later evidence should prove against him, that he claimed that the Contras were not terrorists; all he claimed was that unlike the Libyans the Contras did not carry out terrorist acts outside their own borders. Nevertheless, Mr Eggar seems to be in an odd position, unless of course the British Government really believe that terrorism is only to be opposed when terrorist acts are perpetrated upon third countries.

Whether this is in fact the British Government's view is not something which we can prove, on the basis of this evidence, one way or the other. Such a conclusion would, in many ways, be odd in purely political terms, and it may be the case that the Government representatives (and indeed the Opposition) are not fully aware of the implicational consequences of what they have said. Yet a very similar conclusion is further engendered in the very same debate, this time by Sir Geoffrey Howe, who provides a response to an almost identical question to that tackled by Mr Eggar:

Dr Goodman: Has the Foreign Secretary in recent times brought to the attention of Mr Schultz the deep disquiet felt by many people in this country concerning American sponsored terrorism in Nicaragua.

Sir Geoffrey Howe: *that point has already been dealt with by my hon. Friend the Parliamentary Under Secretary of State in answer to a number of questions*, but I make the distinction yet again that there is a total difference between those terrorist organisations that are dedicated to the infliction of indiscriminate damage on innocent people in third countries and the context in which the Nicaraguan subjects are engaged within the frontiers of Nicaragua. (Hansard, 1986d: 141)

The implicational context is less clear in this case, although once again we have the use of the phrase 'third countries'. The problem here is that any presupposition associated with the use of the adverbial 'in third countries' has been tempered by the overall structure of the sentence within which it is embedded (this is an example where one has to be careful not to interpret any presupposition out of context). Presuppositions can be affected by the structural context within which they are located, an issue referred to as the 'projection problem' (see Karttunen, 1973; Karttunen and Peters, 1979). The projection problem focuses on the way in which presuppositions behave in complex sentences. We have already come across a case of this in (7), where the presupposition disappears with the addition of a clause of denial. But there are various other contexts in which presuppositions may disappear; consider the following sentence:

(22a)   Jane took three units in linguistics last year.
  (b)   There is someone called Jane.
  (c)   Jane took two units in linguistics.

It is suggested that (22a) presupposes (22b), and entails (22c). However, when (22a) is negated, only the presupposition survives. This much is clear from what we have already noted about presuppositions above. But when we place (22a) within a modal context, as in (23), then the presupposition disappears:

(23)   It is possible that Jane took three units in linguistics last year.

The projection problem is generated by the fact that within complex sentences certain surface structural elements may allow presuppositions to survive, while other surface structural elements may not. The situation is made even more complex by the fact that within certain contexts some presuppositions may survive while others may not. Karttunen (1974) introduced the concept of a 'filter' to refer to surface structural forms that let some presuppositions through but not others. An example of how filtering works may be seen in the use of certain conditionals:

(24)   If Kelly eats that cake she will regret it.

Here the second clause presupposes 'Kelly will eat the cake', but the whole sentence does not.

Sir Geoffrey Howe, in his response, makes use of a conjunction of two complex syntactic structures. Conjunctions, in general, allow presuppositions to survive, so we might expect that any presuppositions associated with the first complex structure would carry over to the whole. Let us consider the first part of the conjunction:

(25)   . . . those terrorist organizations which inflict indiscriminate damage on innocent people in third countries.

Example (25) clearly specifies a category of terrorist who carries out activities in third countries. The second part of the conjunction states:

(26)   . . . the context in which Nicaraguan subjects are engaged within the frontiers of Nicaragua.

In this case, (26) is vague in terms of what 'the context' is, but in terms of the text it must be one in which the Nicaraguans are involved. Now since the first conjunct has been set up to contrast with the second conjunct, in that Sir Geoffrey refers to a 'total difference' between two elements to be presented, we must look to see what the difference between the conjuncts might be.

The second conjunct is vague as to what the 'context' is, but we know, whatever the context is, it is to be contrasted with another context in which terrorists are carrying out activities in third countries. Again, since, as we have noted, 'third countries' implies 'not one's own', it seems reasonable to assume that Sir Geoffrey is suggesting that the Nicaraguan situation does not involve terrorist activities in third countries. This assumption seems perfectly reasonable, and is supported by the fact that Sir Geoffrey alludes to Mr Eggar's own response to a similar question, suggesting his agreement with Mr Eggar's previous response (see above).

The problem is, however, that Sir Geoffrey Howe has simply talked of a 'Nicaraguan context', which is extremely ambiguous. Nevertheless, the logic of suggesting a contrast between two elements A and B requires a basis for comparison, and the only basis Sir Geoffrey has given is that of terrorists who carry out activities in third countries, which leaves only those who do not carry out terrorist activities at all, or those who only carry out such activities in their own country (the implication of Mr Eggar's statement; a statement which Sir Geoffrey indicates his agreement with) as possible candidates. The second candidate here is a reasonable possibility, since, in Gricean terms, if Sir Geoffrey Howe had evidence for the stronger first-candidate interpretation then he should have provided it.

This kind of argument is based, partly, on what Lycan (1986) referred to as 'invited inferences' (see above). Invited inferences make use of general background knowledge. In this example we are dealing with a claim which contrasts two elements. The dimension of background knowledge involved here is that any contrast must be predicated upon some basis for comparison. Consequently, the hearer must search Sir Geoffrey Howe's statement for the basis of contrast, which in this case is one of whether terrorist acts are, or are not, carried out in third countries.

What we have, then, via a series of pragmatically based arguments is a fascinating (implicative) picture of the British Government's view of Contra activities. The Contras are not international terrorists, because they do not carry out any atrocities in third countries; are they, however, terrorists within the confines of their own border? The Government representatives' responses are unclear on this, but they pragmatically imply (certainly in Mr Eggar's case) that the Contras are carrying out terrorist acts within their own country.

As we noted in chapter 1, implications are not statements of fact and can therefore be cancelled. Therefore, can we really say that the British Government believed that the Contras are terrorists? Perhaps not, but what we can say is that the particular use of language employed by the Government representatives contains a number of implications supportive of the notion that the Contras are terrorists, and that if those questioning the Government on this matter had been more sensitive to the pragmatic context, they could have pushed the representatives to clarify the context implied by what they had said.

Both Sir Geoffrey Howe and Mr Eggar made clear that the Contras did not carry out terrorist acts in third countries and that, therefore, they were not, unlike the Libyans, international terrorists. Sir Geoffrey and Mr Eggar did not make clear, however, the status of the Contras vis-à-vis terrorism within the confines of Nicaragua. The opportunity for making this issue clear was available to both Mr Eggar and Sir Geoffrey Howe; they simply had to drop reference to 'third countries'. Then we would have had, in the case of Mr Eggar, the following unequivocal statement:

(27)   The Contras do not seek to advance their cause by terrorist acts.

If this was what Mr Eggar believed to be the case, there was no need to contrast the Contras with the Libyans, or indeed anyone else associated with terrorism. If the Contras are not terrorists then Reagan's support for this group is not a sponsorship of terrorism. The 'third countries' argument only makes sense if one is contrasting acts in one's own country with acts in other countries, in this case terrorist acts.

With these claims in mind we can also consider again the question of taking Mr Eggar's statement out of context. The context of the question and answer encounter is quite clear: it is concerned with whether or not the Contras are, or are not, terrorists. If they are terrorists then Mr Healey's criticism makes some sense (within the British context); if they are not terrorists then Healey's claims are unfounded. The clearest and simplest rebuttal is that the Contras are not terrorists. There may be many sound political reasons why such a response was not given (the creation of a debate on what is and what is not terrorism for example), nevertheless, the response which was given generates its own problems, problems which are not generated purely out of context, but in conjunction with the context.

National and International Terrorism: the British Context

The story is not over yet, however. Consider, for a moment, the consequences for a British Government which distinguishes between terrorism within the borders of one's own country and international terrorism, where it is implied, in the first case, that it is legitimate for a nation, such as the United States, to lend support for certain activities. This would of course suggest that the IRA, operating within the confines of Northern Ireland, a part of Great Britain, would be, in the main, in a very similar position to the Contras (at least on the basis of Foreign Office responses to questions on terrorism). This position would, of course, be an awkward, if not indeed a dangerous, one for the British Government. It is interesting then to note that within the same question and answer session we have been discussing, Sir Geoffrey Howe took the opportunity, at a later point in the debate (following the examples we have been analysing), to say the following in response to a question about proscribing Sinn Fein (the political wing of the provisional IRA) as a terrorist organization:

> (28)   One important point to be taken into account in this context is that conflicts that arise in Ireland and Northern Ireland take place in the context of a society with a fully representative democratic system. (Hansard, 1986d: 141)

The question on Sinn Fein was out of line with the general debate on international terrorism and the role of the United States; a fact noted by Sir Geoffrey Howe: 'That question raises different considerations.' Nevertheless, in responding to the question Sir Geoffrey made the statement outlined in (28). Within the general debate on international terrorism we might consider what this statement adds.

Consider again the point I raised above, i.e. that if the Contras are different from the Libyans in that they struggle against their own government, and do not carry out terrorist acts in third countries (cf. Mr Eggar and Sir Geoffrey Howe), this implies: (a) that the Contras are terrorists, and (b) that they carry out their actions in their own country. Further, it suggests that other groups who struggle against their own governments, and who do not carry out any actions against third countries, are in a similar position. Such a description, in the main, would fit the IRA. However, Sir Geoffrey's latest comment does draw a possible distinction between the Contras and the IRA, in that the IRA operate within a democratic system, whereas the Contras struggle against a communist regime.

Once again this conclusion is politically interesting. Certainly, it distinguishes the IRA from the Contras, but it suggests that terrorist action is legitimate where the struggle is against one's own government, provided that government is not a democratic one. There are many further conclusions which one might draw from this, but I will leave these to the reader. It is important to emphasize that the claims I am making are based on what the British Government is saying through its own representatives. The logic of the argument is built up through a pragmatic analysis of not only individual responses, but the cumulative relationship between these responses as they attend to the issue of who is and who is not a terrorist, and, therefore, worthy either of support, or ripe for attack.

Since implications can be denied without contradiction, it would be difficult to categorically confirm that my interpretation of the Government's position, via a pragmatic analysis of their responses, was what was intended by the Government representatives. Nevertheless, there is an important point to made: if a democratic system is to be successful it is partly dependent on the quality and nature of the arguments which take place between the various parties and members of the parties within the system. What the analysis in this chapter shows is that there seems to be a certain lack of sensitivity to the interpretation of pragmatic implications. One wonders what the outcome might have been if the representatives of the British Government had been pushed not only on the content of what they said, but on the pragmatic implications of what they have said. It is important to stress that I am not suggesting that there should be only one standard of debate or argument (as suggested by Bitzer and Rueter, 1980), what I am suggesting is that our understanding of political rhetoric may be significantly advanced, both in theory and in practice, by considering how language is used from the pragmatic perspective.

Conclusion

In this chapter I have attempted to show how a pragmatic analysis would operate in the description of political talk. Taking a number of examples from a British parliamentary question and answer session, it was argued that once one goes beyond the surface-level meaning of what is said, a variety of implicational types may be located. Because they are implicational types they can, in many cases, be denied. Nevertheless, at the very least, in the examples we explored, a greater sensitivity to implicational possibilities might have helped clarify the British Government's position on a number of issues of present-day terrorism.

The relevance of this kind of pragmatic analysis is clear. For politicians (like Mr Healey above), for example, a greater awareness of pragmatic concepts would be useful in clarifying responses given to specific parliamentary questions, and of course in constructing such answers. For political analysts the importance of going beyond the surface form of what is said is also significant. In this case, the analyst is provided with arguments which are not simply based on intuitions about ideological beliefs, but facts about language processing and interpretation. And for the public, it is important to be able to evaluate the political product being offered. In all cases some awareness of the pragmatic aspects of political talk would prove invaluable.

3

Political Pronouns and Pragmatic Implications

'May one see the document?' he asked. 'Indeed one may, Humphrey. Better still, one can have it read to one. And one read it aloud to him.'

J. Lynn and A. Jay, *Yes, Minister*

Linguists, among others, frequently describe the pronominal system of English in terms of categorical divisions such as person, number and sex. Recently, however, pragmatic consideration of the way in which the pronouns of English are actually used in context indicates that pronouns are far from categorical, and, indeed, their interpretation is mediated by a range of social and personal factors producing a range of possible uses and interpretations (see Maitland, 1988 for an overview). Most of us are aware, for example, that while 'she' is designated as a sex-specific pronoun (dependent on the sex of the person or animal talked about; Quirk et al., 1985: 342), it may also be used to refer to 'things', for example cars or ships. Equally, and significantly more controversially, it is claimed that where sex is not determined 'he' or 'they' can be used as an unmarked pronominal form.

The problem here is that authors, such as Quirk et al., who support the position of 'he' as an unmarked form, also argue that gender in English is 'natural' (semantic) as opposed to grammatical (formal) (as in a language like French). Cameron (1985) quite correctly asks why, if gender is 'natural' within English, the masculine form is chosen as the unmarked alternative and not the feminine? The reality is, argues Cameron, that 'gender in English is not fixed entirely by sex reference but also reflects a variety of ideologically motivated prescriptive practices and folk-linguistic beliefs' (Cameron, 1985: 26).

What these simple examples suggest is that pronouns may be selected within interaction for reasons beyond those reflected at a purely formal or categorical level; they may function communicatively to reveal various aspects of the speaker's attitudes, social standing, sex, motivation and so on. In this sense one might question Harre's claim that the English pronominal system suffers from a 'social impoverishment' (Harre, 1988: 166). Certainly English does not seem to have an overt system of social ranking and social relations marked within the pronominal system, of the formal kind one would find in Japanese for example. Nevertheless, it may be argued that social relationships and attitudes are marked within the use of the pronominal system, not so much in terms of individual pronominal choice (although a case may also be made here: see above), but rather within the overall distributional use of pronouns by specific groups or individuals.

If this is indeed the case then we would predict that politicians would be particularly sensitive to the use of pronouns in developing and indicating their ideological position on specific issues. This is in fact what happens, and in this chapter we will explore the way in which politicians from various parts of the world select and distribute pronouns for political and personal reasons.

Pronominal Pragmatics

The social and general consequences of pronominal selection are already well accepted. The classic work of Brown and Gilman (1960) is a case in point here. Their work indicates that in certain societies pronominal choice is affected by the perceived roles of the speaker/hearer. In English we have a similar phenomenon. Consider the extract from the well-known comedy series *Yes, Minister* which is given at the head of this chapter. The humour in this extract depends on the exaggerated use of 'one' as a first-person pronoun. Most English speakers are aware that the use of 'one' designates some degree of formality (compare also the use of the 'Royal we', used to extreme effect in Mrs Thatcher's phrase 'we are a grandmother'). Similarly, in a number of British dialects the use of 'yous' as a plural form, instead of the standard English 'you', indicates something about the speaker's social identity or social status.

These examples reflect the sociolinguistic nature of pronominal systems, wherein certain uses reflect dimensions such as formality/informality, status, solidarity, power, class and sex. Sociolinguistic choice is probabilistic, in that what one says about a form like 'yous', for example, is that those speakers who tend to use this form in most contexts (which means they may on some occasions make use of 'you' to designate the plural) are probably speakers of a certain class, and probably from a limited set of geographical regions.

The pragmatic nature of pronominal choice is somewhat different however. If we take the form 'yous' for instance, it means the same as the standard English plural 'you', the choice of one form or the other does not affect the speaker's basic intention of referring to more than one individual. Using one form or the other may affect, however, the hearer's perception of the speaker, but this is not concerned with the meaning, or intended meaning, of the form itself. In pragmatic terms, however, it is possible to use a pronominal form within context with the intention of manipulating the meaning per se. For example, Maitland (1988) suggests that the use of 'we', in Churchill's classic speech following the Dunkirk evacuation in 1940, is an example of what is called 'exclusive we' (see Maitland, 1988). When Churchill says, 'we shall fight on the beaches, we shall fight on the landing grounds', the 'we' here does not include Churchill himself, in that he was by this time an old man and would hardly be enlisted to fight; and further, in the event of an invasion Churchill and other key members of the Government were to be air lifted out of the country. In this case the meaning of the form has been manipulated in context, something which is a pragmatic concern.

What I am suggesting is that where pronominal choice affects, or reflects, certain social facts about the speaker, this is not necessarily a consequence of the meaning of the particular form in context, but rather a matter of paradigmatic choice; i.e. that form X has been chosen as opposed to form Y (a sociolinguistic fact). This is different from selecting a form with a conventional and accepted meaning, X, in order to indicate (implicate) a somewhat different meaning, Y (a pragmatic fact: several examples of this type have been given in chapters 1 and 2).

Clearly, both types of manipulative choice may overlap in actual production, and I do not want to suggest that the distinction I am making between sociolinguistics and pragmatics is an easy one to maintain in all cases. Nevertheless, it is important to try to distinguish between two possible effects on pronominal selection, and indeed in linguistic choice in general, since analysts sometimes confuse specifically pragmatic behaviour with specifically sociolinguistic behaviour, (see, for example, Leech, 1983; Verschueren, 1987).

Myself and Others

(1)   Due to the rising balance of payment deficit . . .
(a)   it has been found necessary to increase interest rates.
(b)   I have found it necessary to increase interest rates.
(c)   we have found it necessary to increase interest rates.

Imagine a government leader (representative) charged with the task of explaining to an audience (the people of the country) that there is to be an increase in interest rates. (1a), (1b), and (1c) are options available to the leader (representative) and each, basically, expresses the same propositional content. Where each differs is in relation to the degree of personal involvement of the speaker. In (1a) we have an agentless passive, the actor is unidentified; in (1b) we have a clear case of personal commitment; but in (1c) the case is less clear: does the 'we' include the speaker, along with some designated others (as in members of the Government), or does the 'we' refer, in a vague and generic sense, to the nation or the state, in which case the actual degree of personal involvement/commitment on the part of the speaker becomes ambiguous?

This example illustrates one of the classic uses of personal pronouns within politics, or indeed within everyday life in general. It is the case that forms like 'we', while designated in grammatical terms as including the speaker plus one or more others, become ambiguous in actual production, between what is known as the speaker-inclusive 'we' and the speaker-exclusive 'we'.

The distinction between exclusive and inclusive 'we' can be illustrated by the following non-political examples. Take case: (a) two doctors are discussing a patient they are about to operate on, and one says to the other: 'shall we get started?' In this context we assume that what is meant is that both doctors, speaker and hearer, should begin the operation. Now let us take case: (b) after the operation one of the doctors goes to see how the patient is recovering and says to the patient: 'how are we feeling today?' In this case, of course, the doctor is not asking anything about himself, but only about the hearer, the patient. The 'we' here excludes the speaker.

Within everyday talk, Goffman (1981) has argued that the use of forms like exclusive 'we' serves to distance the speaker ('animator') from what it is that is being said. In (1b) the speaker specifically indicates that he/she is the instigator of the action; in (1c) the speaker

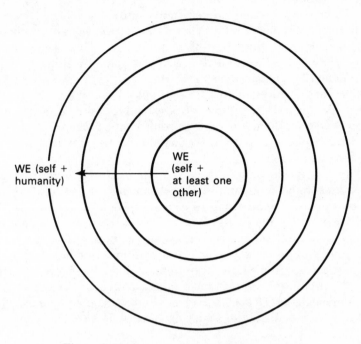

Figure 2 Variation in the distribution of 'we'

may have also played a part in the decision, but the degree of responsibility is less clearly defined.

Urban (1986) talks of this type of distancing in terms of a series of inclusive circles, beginning with the 'we' of speaker/author plus one other and extending out to the 'we' of humanity, as shown in figure 2.

This seems an interesting and reasonable way to model the variation in the distribution of 'we': unfortunately, it isn't clear where my medical example would fit in. When the doctor says 'how are we feeling today', he intends only the hearer to be delimited, not the speaker or any other individual beyond the hearer; it is almost as if, in this context, the pragmatics indicate that the first-person plural is to be taken as the first-person singular. This is not so odd, and can be explained in Gricean terms, in that the well-being of the speaker (doctor) in this situation has limited relevance compared to the well-being of the patient. In which case we might say that a maxim of conversation has been flouted and that a conversational implicature is intended.

The corollary of this situation has been discovered by Christie (1987), who argues that within certain counselling contexts, the counsellor may use 'I' not to refer to himself, but as a means of emphasizing the role, or indicating the role of the client. This is not quite an 'I' into 'we', of course, but the basic principle of a shifting meaning determined by context seems the same.

The consequences of this for a simple distancing model are that the model only sets the range of possible types of others which may be indicated by the use of 'we'. In some contexts the very core of the model, the meaning of 'we' as speaker plus others, may be manipulated for pragmatic effect.

The distribution of I/we (exclusive and inclusive) is clearly marked in political interaction, and this is perhaps not surprising. One of the major aims of a politician is to gain the people's allegiance, to have them believe that the decisions that are being made are the right ones. At the same time no one can guarantee the outcome of any political decision, and since any politician's position is dependent on the support of the people, it is also useful to have the audience believe, in some circumstances, that any actions are perhaps not only, or fully, the responsibility of one individual. First-person pronominal forms can assist the politician in achieving these almost contradictory aims.

I/We: a Political Example

The shifting status of 'we' can be illustrated in the following extracts from the presidential debates which took place between Jimmy Carter and Gerald Ford in 1976. In the extract below, Carter answers a question about his intentions regarding governmental reform, in particular a promise he made to reduce the total number of government agencies:

Well I've been through this before, Mr Gannon, as the Governor of Georgia. When I took over we had a bureaucratic mess like we have in Washington now. And we had 300 agencies, departments, bureaus, commissions, some fully budgeted some not . . . And WE cut those 300 agencies and so forth down substantially. We eliminated 278 of them. We set up a simple structure of government that could be administered fairly . . . It hasn't been undone since I was there . . .

I intend to do the same thing if I am elected President. When I get to Washington, coming in as an outsider, one of the major responsibilities that I will have on my shoulder is the complete reorganisation of the executive branch of government. We now have a greatly expanded White House staff.

When Mr Nixon went into office, for instance, we had 30 million dollars spent on the White House and its staff. That has escalated to 160 millions in the last Republican administration. This needs to be changed. We need to put the responsibilities back on the cabinet members. (Bitzer and Rueter, 1980: 265–6).

In his response Carter follows a pattern of marking out his own position in relation to certain positive and negative issues by generating different I/we choices. In his opening remark he uses 'I' to indicate that the task of reforming a cumbersome bureaucracy is something that he personally has had responsibility for before. He then shifts to 'we', referring to the state of Georgia, and indicates the negative situation he found. This shift is to exclusive 'we', since the mess Carter refers to was not created by him, indeed it was to be resolved by him. In the same sentence he also makes use of another exclusive 'we' which refers, this time, beyond the state of Georgia to the country as a whole: 'like *we* have in Washington'. Next there is a shift to 'we' inclusive, in the phrase 'And we cut' indicating, in the positive sense here, that Carter himself was involved in any major reorganization. In the next paragraph Carter employs a 'block' (for a definition see p. 63 below) of 'I' forms to emphasize his own personal intentions when he becomes President.

When Carter moves on to criticize the present situation in the White House there is yet another shift, this time to 'we' the United States (or we the people), as in the phrase 'we now have a greatly expanded White House staff'. This is a shift back to an exclusive use, since here it is not Carter himself who has the numbers of expanded White House staff, nor indeed would he advocate such an expansion. He is stating that the expanded number of staff is being paid for by the people, by America.

Looking more closely at the initial shift to inclusive 'we', that is, the point at which Carter makes a number of positive claims about his record while he was Governor of Georgia, we (the reader and myself) might ask why at this point he did not shift back to 'I', since then Carter could have claimed sole responsibility for any positive changes in reducing administration costs in Georgia (similar to the move Carter made in describing his future intentions should he be elected President)? There seem to be two possible answers: first, the use of 'I' in this context might not have been positive, in that it could have suggested that Carter was autocratic; second, and more importantly, as I noted above, politicians can never be certain that decisions they have made will always necessarily be seen in a positive

light (or they may be aware that their positive claims could easily be
re-interpreted in a more negative manner; see Ford's response below);
therefore, by the use of 'we' Carter spreads the load of responsibility.
This is a useful ploy in a debate, since it is almost certain that your
opponent will question any positive claims you have made. And indeed
this is exactly what Gerald Ford does:

Ford : I think the record should show, Mr Newman, that the Bureau of
Census – we checked it yesterday – indicates that in the four years Governor
Carter was governor of the state of Georgia, expenditures by the government
went up over 50%. (Bitzer and Rueter, 1980: 266)

It is clear, then, that if Carter had used 'I' to indicate any positive
claims about his achievements in Georgia, this could have been associated, in the minds of the audience, with individual responsibility.
Consequently, when we come to Ford's critical account of the bureaucratic position in Georgia, any negative effect would specifically
rebound on the individual Jimmy Carter, as opposed to the Georgia
state administration as a whole. The use of 'we' with its exclusive/
inclusive ambiguity lessens any possible negative effect in Ford's
counter-attack.

At the point in Carter's response where he did use a 'block' of 'I'
forms, it was to refer to future intentions, which are of course much
more difficult for an opponent to criticize, in that they do not yet
exist.

It should also be said, however, that the ploy of spreading responsibility is only an option, and there will be occasions when one should
perhaps indicate one's individual responsibility for certain actions.
Once Ford has attempted to set the record straight on Carter's claims
this is exactly what he does:

Ford : Now let me talk about what we have done in the White House as
far as federal employees are concerned. The first order that I issued after I
became President was to cut, or eliminate the prospective 40,000 increase in
federal employees . . . And in the term I've been President, some two years,
we have reduced federal employment by 11,000 . . . when I became President
. . . we made a significant reduction in staff . . . So I think our record . . .
shows which is the better plan. (Bitzer and Rueter, 1980: 267)

Of course, if my argument is correct, this now gives Carter the
opportunity to attack Ford's claims, and in this case Ford has taken
the risk of having any such attack interpreted on a personal as well
as (or opposed to) a generic level. Carter does in fact take up this
opportunity, but I think we can move on at this point.

The scope of 'we' in Carter's response ranged over the individual plus others, the state of Georgia, and the United States of America. The shifting scope of 'we' can be broader than this. Urban (1986) discovered, for example, six uses for 'we' in an analysis of the rhetorical choices made by Casper Weinberger (ex United States Secretary of Defence) in an article on nuclear weapons. Urban delimits the following set:

1 The President and I 'we': 'The President and I believe that the answer lies in the Strategic Defense Initiative. We hope that strategic defense will eventually render nuclear missiles obsolete.'
2 The Department of Defense 'we': 'I want to describe the U.S. defense strategies and to summarize the major changes we have made in our thinking at the Department of Defense.'
3 The Reagan Administration 'we': 'The Reagan Administration has made a number of revisions and additions. We have added four pillars of defense policy for the 1990s.'
4 The US Government 'we': 'Even with the SALT II restraints the Soviet Union has built more warheads capable of destroying our missile silos than we had initially predicted.'
5 The United States 'we': 'Should the United States decide that it is necessary to commit its forces to combat, we must commit them in sufficient numbers.'
6 The US and Soviet Union 'we': 'In November President Reagan and Secretary Gorbachev agreed that both governments will examine the possibility of creating risk-reduction centres to lessen the chances of miscalculation or accidental conflicts. We have also conducted a series of policy level discussions on regional issues.'

Urban notes that the majority of 'we' uses are inclusive (68 per cent), and he ties this to the aim of Weinberger's text, which he refers to as a 'rhetoric of fear', in that 'we' excludes the Soviet Union, building a picture of an 'us' threatened by *them* model of the world.

Culture, Topic and Individual

The examples we have looked at so far show the way in which I/we, and in particular 'we', may be manipulated for political effect. This manipulation does not seem to be culturally constrained to Western politicians. The work of Lwaitama (1988), who has analyzed the distribution of first-person singular and hearer-exclusive first-person plurals in the political speeches of two senior Tanzanian politicans; Mr J. K. Nyerere (the former President of Tanzania) and Mr A. H. Mwinyi (the current President of Tanzania), clearly indicates a very similar picture to that described in our discussion of Carter and Weinberger. What is noticeable, however, is that pronominal selection does seem to be variable in terms of both context and individual. It is not that a specific context creates an atmosphere within which the use of 'we' is restricted to either exclusive or inclusive, for example, it is rather that some contexts seem more conducive to particular pronominal choices. Equally, individual politicians themselves reveal, in their selection and use of pronominal forms, particular patterns, which might almost be seen as personal trademarks.

In terms of contextual differences Chafe (1982) has suggested that one is more likely to find first-person references in spoken than in written discourse. Lwaitama notes that for his analysis this seems to be the case. In comparing scripted with unscripted speeches, he found that there were more first-person singular pronominal references in the unscripted speeches. But when one looks at the individual politicians themselves, one finds some interesting and striking differences which are not captured by a simple contextual dichotomy.

When Lwaitama analysed first-person plural pronominal references he discovered that there were distinct differences between Mr Nyerere and Mr Mwinyi. Nyerere used many more exclusive forms in his scripted as opposed to his unscripted speeches; Mwinyi, on the other hand, used far more inclusive forms in his scripted as opposed to his unscripted speeches. Indeed this difference was so strong that Mwinyi used no exclusive forms in his scripted speeches while Nyerere went to the opposite extreme using no inclusive forms in his scripted speeches.

It is not that either politician was unaware of the general distancing principles of exclusive 'we', or indeed the integrative and positive possibilities of inclusive 'we'. Exactly why such extreme differences arose between these politicians is unclear at present. Although Lwaitama tentatively suggests that dialectal differences between Mr Nyerere and Mr Mwinyi's Swahili may have had something to do with the difference, since Mr Nyerere is a second-language speaker of Kiswahili, while it is the first language of Mr Mwinyi.

As we noted, it is difficult to say why one should find such extreme differences, and Lwaitama is aware that he is dealing with a rather limited data base of only 40 paragraphs for each politician (further work is now underway, expanding the data base and the range of politicians). Nevertheless, what this work highlights is the potential interaction effect of both context and individual in the selection and production of pronouns.

If we look at the case of Richard Nixon for example, it is noticeable that in the context of press conferences there is a higher proportion of first-person pronominal choice. In an analysis of a selected sample of responses to reporter's questions over the period 1969–74, (an average of 14,614 words) 'I' was used at a ratio of almost 3:1 (2.8) with 'we'. This pattern is what Chafe (1982) would have predicted, in that presidential press conferences are, of course, unscripted. It is noticeable, however, that the proportion of 'I' to 'we' differs significantly depending on the topic under question.

Separating out what were probably the two major issues for Nixon, Vietnam and Watergate, the ratio in favour of 'I' for each is as follows:

Vietnam . . .   1(1.05):1   (average words: 4,393)
Watergate . . . 5(4.93):1   (average words: 10,218)

Clearly, there is a significant difference here. It would be interesting to speculate on why these differences emerged, knowing now, in retrospect, certain facts about Watergate. We should not assume that the increase in the use of first-person singular pronouns, in response to questioning about Watergate, in any way necessarily indicates an underlying acceptance of responsibility on the part of Nixon; frequently the opposite was the case. What emerges from a consideration of responses to Watergate questions is the effort which seems to have been put into indicating Nixon's own responsibility for actively seeking out the perpetrators of any wrongful acts. A particularly good example of this comes in response to a question which suggested that the administration should make a clean breast of things regarding what they had hoped to 'get done in Watergate' (5 October 1972). Here is part of Nixon's response:

Now when we talk of making a clean breast, let's look at what has happened. The FBI assigned 133 agents to this investigation. It followed out 1,800 leads. It conducted 1,500 interviews.

Incidentally, *I* conducted the Hiss case. *I* know it is a very unpopular subject to raise in some quarters, but *I* conducted it . . . *I* agreed with the amount of effort that was put into it. *I* wanted every lead to be carried out to the end because *I* wanted to be sure no man or woman in any position of responsibility . . . had anything to do with this reprehensible activity. (Johnson, 1978a: 296 [my italics])

Methinks the first-person singular doth protest too much.

I noted earlier that the distributional possibilities of pronominal choice are essentially sociolinguistic. Where pragmatics comes in is when the meaning of a particular pronoun has been changed or developed from its use in context. The data from Nixon's presidential press conferences have been introduced simply to indicate the range of effects on possible selectional choices within the pronominal system; in this case topic and speaker personality.

It need not be the case, however, that all distributional scores are necessarily only sociolinguistic, in that any distributional choice may, in itself, provide evidence for pragmatic assessment. What I mean here is that an individual's choice and distributional range of pronouns may indicate how they treat the meaning of each pronoun. In other words the proportional use of certain pronouns may itself affect the interpretation (meaning) of certain pronouns for certain speakers.

In order to explore this possibility, in the next section I will present the results of a study of a number of selected British politicians, which focused on the way in which a broad range of personal pronominal choices were indicative of how the individual politician viewed the world, and how that politician manipulated the meaning of pronouns in order to present a specific ideological perspective.

Personal Choice and Personal Meaning

This section is based on work carried out with Karen Maitland (see Maitland and Wilson, 1987; also Maitland, 1988). The aim of the original work was to explore the pragmatic manipulation of pronouns within various political contexts by focusing mainly on personal pronoun referencing. We were interested in the selectional choices made by various politicians in referring to themselves and to others. The work goes beyond the discussion of I/we considered above in that it extends the analysis to a broader range of personal pronominal referencing possibilities. The work was based on the system of pronominal distribution shown in table 1, developed from Rees (1983).

In this system 'you' has been allocated to first and third person, as well as to the more conventional second person; 'one' is also given a first- and third-person designation. Support for this position has been implicitly noted in the work of Laberge and Sankoff (1980). It can be argued that you is what is referred to as a 'situational insertion', the conversion of one's own personal experience into experiences which might be, or can be, shared by the addressee; as in (2):

Table 1 Pronominal distribution

	1st person	2nd person	3rd person
Singular	I One² You²	You¹	He/She/It One (indefinite) You³ (indefinite)
Plural	We	You	They Those

(2) But isn't it amazing how when *you* bring down inflation
     to a level far below what they said was possible they take
     it for granted that *anyone* could have done it. [my italics]

Although Mrs. Thatcher is describing her own achievements, she is
speaking to a specific audience, the Central Council of the Conservative Party. Consequently, any overt attempt to explicitly attribute
responsibility to herself as an individual (by adopting the use of 'I'),
as opposed to attributing responsibility to the Government as a whole
(of which, of course, she is the senior member), seems inappropriate.
Nevertheless, the subtle employment of 'anyone' does suggest that
'you' was actually intended to refer to Mrs Thatcher herself.

In this example we can also see the clear pragmatic nature of
pronominal selection at this level. As we noted in chapters 1 and 2,
pragmatics is mainly concerned with implicative relations, and we
noted that implications are not facts but inferences which can, in most
cases, be cancelled. Mrs Thatcher's use of 'you', in this context,
invites the implication that it is she herself she is talking about.
However this cannot be guaranteed, Mrs Thatcher could quite easily
have added on to the end of her statement the following clause:

(3) I am of course referring to the Government's achieve-
     ments, a Government I am proud to be a part of.

Returning to 'you'³, the designation of this form is derived from the
use of what has been called the 'formulation of morals and truisms'.
Quite simply what this means is that occasionally we will employ
'you'³ to reflect upon a kind of conventional wisdom as opposed to
actual experience. Consider the following example from a speech given
by Mr Neil Kinnock, the leader of the Labour Party, in 1984:

(4) Of course money can't buy *you* a loving family, but it can
     buy *you* a separate bedroom for the children. [my italics]

In this example 'you'[3] is employed for indefinite reference, since Mr
Kinnock is speaking about people in general. Any reference to self,
or to addressee, occurs only in so far as they are members of the
wider category mentioned.

It should be noted that 'those' (treated as a nominal demonstrative
head by Halliday and Hasan, 1976) has been added to the Rees
classification, because it was discovered that, for some politicians, it
plays a significant role.

In describing the way in which choices within such a system are
organized we will draw upon a distancing scale for pronouns also
developed by Rees (1983), but extended and modified by Maitland
and Wilson (1987) (see also Maitland 1988). The basic principle
behind the scale is that in considering personal pronouns we begin
from the most fundamental and subjective form, 'I' (and its variants,
'me', 'my' or 'mine') and then progressively move outward, or away,
from this *deictic centre*. This position can be represented for the
individual speaker in terms of the scales shown in example (i).

Example (i)

0	1	2	3	4	5	6	7	8
I	ME	YOU	ONE	YOU	IT	SHE	HE	THEY

          direct   indefinite
          address

(Rees, 1983: 16)

For Rees this scale represents the generic position for all speakers.
Maitland (1988) argues, however, that the scale may vary in terms of
its overall distribution depending on the ideolect of the individual
speaker. Maitland suggests that speakers may shift the relative position
of each pronoun in order to signify some information beyond that of
simply referencing one's self, or any other individual under discussion.
For instance, Maitland notes that certain disturbed individuals who
have great difficulty taking responsibility for their own actions, might
actually have a zero marking for the first-person pronoun, as shown
in example (ii).

Example (ii)

0	1	2	OR	0	1	2
0	YOU	HIM		0	YOU	...

(Maitland, 1988: 82)

To take a more general example, Maitland suggests that it is possible to imagine scales for two individuals A and B of the kind shown in examples (iii) and (iv).

Example (iii) Person A

0	1	2	3	4	5	6	7	8	9	10
I	WE	YOU	ONE	YOU	HE	SHE	THEY	THESE	IT	THOSE

Distancing from self

Example (iv) Person B

0	1	2	3	4	5	6	7	8
I	WE	YOU	YOU	THEY	THOSE	SHE	HE	IT

Distancing from self →

The formation of these scales is dependent on how the speaker perceives particular pronominal uses. For example, if the speaker perceives 'those' as more negative than 'it', with 'those' associated with facelessness, and 'it' being treated as a 'neutral' term, then 'those' will be placed further away from 'I'. On the other hand, if 'it' is perceived as sub-human, with 'those' being perceived simply as not present, then, in this case, it may be placed further away from the 'I'.

What this kind of model offers us, in political terms, is a pronominal window into the thinking and attitude of politicians towards particular political topics and political personalities. For example, if it could be shown for a politician A that 'it' is located at the negative end of the pronominal scale, and this is the term this politician uses to refer to any opposition party, then he or she may perceive the opposition not merely as opponents but perhaps as the enemy. Alternatively, for the same politician to use 'it' to refer to his or her own party would produce a kind of contradiction, or perhaps an underlying antagonism for the present state of the party.

Pronominal Scaling in British Politics

In order to explore such options in the real world we will consider the pronominal scaling of three major figures within British politics; Mrs Margaret Thatcher (the present leader of the Conservative Party and Prime Minister); Mr Neil Kinnock (the present leader of the opposition Labour Party); and Mr Michael Foot (a Labour MP, and ex leader of the Labour Party). A series of nine pre-scripted speeches from the period 1982–84 will be considered, three for each of the selected politicians. We are concentrating on pre-scripted speeches for the following reasons. The first, and main reason, is that in a pre-scripted speech the politician is consciously involved in the organization and selection of each lexical item and each syntactic construction in an effort to achieve the maximum required effect on the audience. We should not be surprised to discover then, that it is in the scripted speech that most attention is given to the selection of pronouns. It is not suggested, of course, that the selection of pronouns in other interactive contexts is any less significant. Indeed, as we have already noted, there is much to be gained from considering the distribution and use of pronouns in various contexts, but one does run the risk of making any comparison and generalization that much more difficult.

A second, and indirect reason, for focusing on pre-scripted speeches relates specifically to the individual politicians we will be considering. Atkinson (1984) points out that Mrs Thatcher, Mr Kinnock and Mr Foot all rely heavily on male script writers; and further, all three tend to adhere very closely to their scripts when delivering their speeches. This makes any comparison that much more significant. It also reduces any differences in sex-based pronominal use (as indicated by Laberge and Sankoff, 1980), since the concentration is focused on script content rather than individual delivery.

In addition to the nine pre-scripted speeches which serve as the basis for the main analysis, two further unscripted speeches of Mr Foot were also examined. The reasons for this will become clear as the analysis proceeds.

In selecting speeches for analysis an effort has been made to make the speeches both representative and comparable (see Appendix, table A.1), the majority being taken from party conferences. The two exceptions to this are speeches D and F (see Appendix, table A.1). Speech D was given specifically for a press conference, and speech F was a party-political radio broadcast. Since all the speeches were designed not only for the party faithful, but also for a larger audience made available through television and radio coverage, these speeches do not present themselves as being significantly diverse from the others.

In the Appendix, table A.2, the overall distribution of pronouns within the text of each speech is outlined. Within this analysis 'they'/ 'them' is included only where the referent was human, or accepted as the personification of an entity. Where 'it' occurred as a dummy subject it was not counted, nor when it was used to refer to inanimate objects or abstract concepts; it was counted, however, where the context indicated that 'he'/'she'/'they' could be substituted for 'it'. For example, we have the option when referring to babies to refer to them using 'it', as in 'it has stopped crying,' or, depending on the sex of the child, as 'he'/'she'; 'he/she has stopped crying.' In more political terms, 'it' is counted when it is used to refer to the Government, since in this case it would have been possible to employ 'they' in such referencing. What this indicates is that the speech writer has a choice of form in such a context; consequently, any actual selection may be seen as carrying, potentially, an ideological loading within the framework of a specific presentation.

If the argument I am making is basically correct, we should not be surprised to find that politicians of different political persuasions would operate with modified scales which they use to represent their distinct ideological position. In order to consider this possibility, we will consider three main areas when looking at the speeches of our selected politicians:

1 *Self-referencing*: the way in which the speaker chooses to portray himself/herself in relation to the topic and addressee(s).
2 *Relations of Contrast*: this refers to the way in which speakers make use of the pronominal system to compare and contrast others on a negative/positive scale. For example, in political debate instead of referring to your opponent by name, you may simply pinpoint them as 'him' or 'her'.
3 *Other Referencing*: this indicates the use of pronouns to refer to individuals and groups outside the roles of speaker and addressee.

The general claim is, then, that each individual may operate with a different scale, or continuum, of pronominal referencing, and that differences will be generated by various aspects of the context, the speakers, the topic, and so on. It is further claimed that such differences are not merely sociolinguistic markers, but pragmatic indicators of shifts in meaning. Although we are interested in the potential pragmatic effects of pronominal scaling, such scales may only be constructed from a more general consideration of pronominal use, and it is here that we shall begin.

Self-Referencing

Indicating self-reference by means other than 'I' or 'we' is said to represent a distancing strategy on the part of the speaker, because the choice of pronoun indicates how close/distant the speaker is to the topic under discussion, or to the participants involved in the discussion. We noted above that this can be represented by a distancing scale of the type developed by Rees (1983), where, as one moved along the scale away from 'I' (and the variants me/my/mine) towards forms like he/it/they, one showed that one was distancing oneself from the issue/individual/subject of the talk.

In analyzing the speeches of our selected British politicians we find that Mrs Thatcher employs the first-person singular pronoun (in the construction of anecdotes, for example) as a means of establishing rapport with her audience (see Lwaitama (1988) who makes a similar argument for the Tanzanian politician Mr Mwinyi):

>   (5)   We have a policy unit and that their job is to think. I understand that this has caused some degree of shock in some quarters. (Speech B)

We also find the use of first-person singular forms (supported by mental-process verbs, for example, 'think', 'want', 'wish') in reflecting intrinsic attitudes, particularly in the communication of *sincerity*:

>   (6)   *I* am prepared to defend to the utmost the things in which *I* believe and *I* wish to hand on to our children as our forefathers handed them on to us. Of course, *I* want to see nuclear disarmament. Indeed, *I* should like to see general disarmament as well. *Wouldn't we all. I* shrink from the horrors of war . . . Should *we* more easily get the Soviet side to the table if *we* had already renounced our nuclear weapons? Of course not. (Speech A; my italics)

Analysis of this text displays how Mrs Thatcher makes use of a *block* (the repetition of the pronominal form three or more times in the same syntactic position in consecutive sentences) of 'I' forms to express her sincerity and personal belief in freedom and dignity. Her attitude to war is presented as perfectly natural and reasonable, an attitude supported by a favourite phrase 'wouldn't we all'. As the text develops there is a noticeable shift from the personal voice, encoded in 'I', to the institutionalized voice encoded in 'we'. This shift is reminiscent of Weinberger's rhetoric, which we noted above. Urban (1986) suggested that Weinberger excluded the Soviet Union from any broad inclusive use of *we*, and Mrs Thatcher seems to be doing the same. Her use of the institutionalized 'we' is ambiguous. Does she mean here only 'we' as Britain? In the context this seems plausible; on the other hand, while Britain may have a nuclear capability it is hardly of the strength necessary to bring the Soviets to the negotiating table. It makes more sense, then, to see the use of 'we' as 'we' the West, or 'we' the Allies. Seen in this way Mrs Thatcher's point is basically the same as Weinberger's, an 'us' against 'them' attitude, where 'we' inclusive is basically everyone but 'them' (the Soviets).

The aim of the shift to the institutionalized voice, therefore, is to separate out the individual from the Government, and possibly the individual government from the Western Alliance (although this is not guaranteed). At a personal level the shift from 'I' to 'we' separates out Mrs Thatcher the peace-loving individual, from the resolute leader who must work with the West as a whole to bring about and maintain peace through negotiation; but negotiation from strength, where one accepts, and does not shrink from, the possibility of war.

As well as employing the pronominal system to distribute responsibility and to distinguish the individual view from the necessary governmental and global view, Mrs Thatcher also makes use of first-person plural pronouns to signal positive associations. By this I mean that Mrs Thatcher reserves particular pronominal forms to reference those groups, countries or individuals who support her general perspective on specific political issues. 'We', for example, is used to reference the Government, Britain, the Central Council of the Conservative Party, President Reagan, NATO and the EEC:

(7)   Mr Chairman, *we* are determined that Britain should not tread that path. *We shall fight* to defend those qualities of tolerance and fairness and courage which have sustained *us* for so long. *We shall fight* for our freedom in time of peace as fiercely as *we have fought* in time of war. (Speech B; my italics)

In this text we see the shifting distribution of 'we'. At the beginning 'we' is restricted to the Government, however by the time we get to, 'we have fought in times of war', there has been a shift to 'we' Britain. For Mrs Thatcher it is almost as if the Government and Britain are one and the same, echoed in the clear parallel between this text and Churchill's classic wartime rhetoric.

This equation between the Government and Britain as a whole is further reflected in Mrs Thatcher's use of the first-person plural possessive pronoun 'our' to refer to organizations, persons or concepts that we might normally expect to be marked by the definite article; for example:

our schools	——	the schools
our forces	——	the forces
our police	——	the police

> (8) What are *we* (the Government) doing because *we all* want genuine disarmament with safety and security for *our people and our way of life*. (Speech A; my italics)

Interestingly, while Mrs Thatcher may employ the first-person plural possessive to refer to the young in the following extract:

> (9) *our* children are fed on a daily diet of violence (Speech A; my italics)

when the occasion arises to discuss juvenile crime, there is no attempt to claim either the children involved (or the parents) as 'ours'. Instead what we find is the use of third-person possessive as a distancing strategy:

> (10) Moreover it strengthens the provisions whereby parents may have to pay *their children's fines*. (Speech A; my italics)

Mrs Thatcher also makes use of 'you'[2], 'you'[3] and 'one' for distancing purposes, sometimes in a very rapid shift within the process of self-referencing (see Rees, 1983):

> (11) Indeed if *one* wants enough resources to do everything *we* wish to do *you* have to be resolute about other matters too. (Speech A; my italics)

It is extremely doubtful, considering that this extract comes from a pre-scripted speech, that what we are witnessing is a production error. What Mrs Thatcher seems to be trying to do is perform a kind of juggling trick. She wants to convey an image of tough resoluteness in the face of problems like high unemployment and issues of poverty, but at the same time she wants to indicate a legitimate concern for those who are disadvantaged. In (11) 'one' indicates the distancing role of authority; however, as we shift to 'we' there is an attempt to present the human face of government, or the Government's position ('we' has strong self-referencing connotations when one wishes to convey a desire to help). But despite any sympathetic concerns, when we shift to 'you', Mrs Thatcher indicates that she has no option available to her other than to be resolute and to stick to her policies.

When we turn to the distribution of pronominal forms in the speeches of Mr Kinnock, it is worth bearing in mind that as a socialist, from a working-class background, Kinnock, not surprisingly, does not employ the pronoun 'one' for either definite or indefinite reference. Kinnock places a greater stress on the use of 'I', and he tends to avoid making use of 'you'[2] as a distancing mechanism.

Interestingly, considering the general findings of this chapter so far, Kinnock makes a limited use of the first-person plural pronoun 'we'. The distribution of 'we' seems to be constrained mainly to reference to the Labour Party; it is also, however, (but less frequently) used for reference to the people of Britain.

(12)   *We* cannot therefore afford to weaken ourselves by divisions even though *our* mood is one of outrage and frustration at the ruthless assertion of the central government dictate. (Speech H; my italics)

Considering the general internal turmoil of the British Labour Party in the 1980s, it is not surprising to find that Mr Kinnock wishes to stress 'we' for Party referencing. Political commentators have frequently questioned Mr Kinnock on the divisive elements within the Labour Party, on the image of what seems to be a neverending internal struggle between the left and right wings of the Party. It is perhaps not surprising, then, to find Mr Kinnock making a positive use of 'we' in his efforts to present a view of the Labour Party as a united force. In 1984 'we the Labour Party' as a concept was particularly central, and it was repeatedly linked to images of strength within the ongoing battle with the Conservative Party. In a speech delivered to the Labour Party Conference in the summer of 1984 the pronoun 'we' is directly linked with the word 'power' 24 times.

The distribution of 'we' is also linked to the use of the first-person possessive 'our'. Unlike Mrs Thatcher, Mr Kinnock uses this form principally for referring to abstract concepts such as ideals, strength, justice and beliefs. These concepts are projected as being possessed by the Labour Party, or as being part of a general socialist doctrine. This is not to suggest that Mr Kinnock, like Mrs Thatcher, does not also use 'our' to talk positively about Britain (our country) or the nation as a whole (our society):

(13)   Action that *recruits* and *mobilises* new people in *our* cause. (Speech I; my italics)

It is the case, however, that Mr Kinnock does not distribute his use of 'our' as liberally (political pun intended) as Mrs Thatcher.

In looking at the speeches of Mr Foot one finds, again not surprisingly, as he is also a socialist and ex leader of the Labour Party, a similar distribution of pronouns to that described for Mr Kinnock. What is interesting about Mr Foot is that he does not seem to make use of the pronominal system in the same political manner as either Mrs Thatcher or Mr Kinnock (or indeed in the same way as several of the other international politicians mentioned earlier in the chapter) and for this reason we will discuss Mr Foot in a separate section.

Relations of Contrast

Within the present British political scene, and initiated by what have become known as the 'Thatcher years', the difference between those elements on the left and right of the political divide within Britain is much greater than it has been for some considerable time. Within this atmosphere of conflict one thing seems abundantly clear; despite the fact that one might consider politics to be based upon the arguments put for different policy solutions to similar problems, much of the present political rhetoric revolves around individuals and their respective competencies and personalities.

It is clear, for example, that Mr Kinnock frequently projects the conflict between the Labour Party and the Conservative Party as being between himself and Mrs Thatcher. We can see this in the way he organizes the presentation of I/she constructions in his speeches.

(14) That is what makes *me* different from Margaret Thatcher.
      I don't have *her* double standards. *I* do not have *her*
      selective and blinkered view of life. (Speech I; my italics)

Government ministers and the Tory Party in general are frequently
referred to as 'hers'.

(15) And in similar slanderous style *her Treasury Ministers*
      blame their failure (Speech H; my italics)

The reason behind this is twofold: first, it can be argued that Kinnock
is attempting to rival Thatcher's personal following as a strong leader,
which would in turn gain him support from those who follow personalities rather than policies, and at the same time provide a central
focus for continuing efforts to unite the Labour Party. Second, and
more controversially, what we have in Mr Kinnock's use of I/she/her
patterns may be a case of chauvinistic politics. It has been noted that
Kinnock has what might be termed a typical male 'working class
mentality' (Harris, 1984). He has enraged members of his own party
by his lack of interest in sexual politics; heavy criticism followed his
use of 'sexist jokes' at a 'Tribune' rally. It might be argued, therefore,
that references such as 'her treasury ministers', reflect not only a
personal attack on Mrs Thatcher, but also on the ministers themselves,
as they allow a woman to dominate them (although one wonders how
this argument stands in light of criticisms that Mr Kinnock allows
himself to be heavily influenced by his wife).

Unlike Mr Kinnock, Mrs Thatcher tries to keep the arguments
between Labour and Conservative to the Party level. This may be
seen in the way she distributes her use of we/they constructions.

(16) And that's exactly what Labour's economics would do.
      They'd destroy the foundation *we* have fought so hard to
      build. (Speech B; my italics)

Other Referencing

In terms of other referencing, the use of pronouns to reference groups
and individuals other than speaker and addressee, Mrs Thatcher
favours 'they' as a distancing strategy. By employing 'they' Mrs
Thatcher aims to distance herself and her Government from other

specified groups. Clearly, 'they' is not always used to convey direct contrast or opposition, but there can be little doubt that it is not simply employed in a neutral manner. As well as allowing Mrs Thatcher to distance herself from certain specified groups, the use of 'they' is also employed to designate vaguely defined groups. The general pragmatic utility of this strategy will be discussed in a moment.

In terms of what we called earlier the 'deictic centre' (see above), 'those' is a deictic marker of furthest distance from the speaker. In the case of Mrs Thatcher, 'those' is for the projection of negative connotations. The general effect of using 'those' to refer to groups is to provide a kind of sinister image. In many cultures that which is abhorrent is marked by namelessness:

> (17)   There are *those who for sinister political reasons wish to undermine* the institutions and values upon which we depend. *Those who call for extra parliamentary action* and the sacking of judges and Chief Constables; *those who viciously attack* the newly appointed Commissioner of Police for the Metropolis before *he* has even taken up *his* appointment – there are some teachers, teachers of all people, who go on strike in pursuit of a pay claim. (Speech A; my italics)

This text is preceded by a 'we' Britain strategy. The result of this is that 'those' are distanced from both speaker and addressee. This, coupled with the use of strong negative forms like 'vicious', 'sinister', 'undermine', increases the sense of menace, allowing Mrs Thatcher to build to a climax where the group are identified (in this instance, the teachers). In this example, the teachers' pay claim does not merely go against Government policy, it is an attempt to undermine the very fabric of society.

Because we are dealing with an example of pragmatic manipulation, however, the above assessment is based on those implications which follow from Mrs Thatcher's text, and as they are implications they can be denied or cancelled. Mrs Thatcher can always claim that she was using forms like 'those' in generic terms, without any intention of specifically identifying any particular group. But, in this example, there does seem to be a link between her criticisms of certain unnamed individuals, or groups, and the teachers.

The implication type employed in this context is an *invited inference*, since the implication is based on general knowledge of a default type which links unidentified elements with identified elements in a text. Textual cohesion is normally maintained through structural processes such as *anaphora* and *cataphora*. Anaphora refers to the way in which elements link backwards within a text, and cataphora indicates the way in which elements may refer forwards. An example of anaphora is given in (18) and an example of cataphora is given in (19):

(18)   John is late, he always is.
(19)   He is always late, John.

In both cases the pronoun is linked in some way with the preceding or following noun. This is a regular process in the construction of texts, and general expectations are set up in processing sentences. Research indicates that when an anaphoric pronoun is encountered, for example, the hearer accesses a set of possible referents and selects the most likely candidate (see Frederiksen, 1981). In an example like (18) this is straightforward, but in the case of (20) the solution is more difficult:

(20)   John passed Bill the ball and then he kicked it.

For the audience listening to Mrs Thatcher there is a problem of pronoun resolution; who exactly is being referred to by 'those'? In processing terms the best link is with the teachers, since this is the only available noun phrase. Further, it has also been noted that the resolution of anaphoric pronouns is influenced by general knowledge. Therefore, since Mrs Thatcher is making her statement at a time of conflict and disagreement with the teachers' unions, it seems reasonable to conclude that the invited assumption is that she is designating teachers' groups under the heading of 'those'.

The pronouns 'they' and 'those' are neutral constructions for both Mr Kinnock and Mr Foot, although as might be predicted, they are used with negative connotations when referring to the Tory Party, and with positive connotations when referring to the trade unions and the British people.

For Mr Kinnock it is not 'those' which is the chosen form for negatively designating groups, but rather 'it'. This form is used to depersonalize government departments as faceless and threatening.

(21)   This was the year when the Government banned trade unions at GCHQ, Cheltenham. Why? In order to demonstrate *its view* that security, patriotism and commitment

to national interest is incompatible with trade unions.
(Speech I; my italics)

This type of use of 'it', taken along with the general lack of the use
of 'our' (see above) in reference to organizations such as the police,
may reflect Mr Kinnock's political position; he is, after all, a politician
in Opposition. As a politician in Opposition he is in conflict not only
with the Government itself, but with all the branches of government.
It cannot be that Mr Kinnock is against the police, the Home Office,
or any other governmental institution per se, they will, after all, be
the very same institutions that he will be working with should the
Labour Party come to power. Rather, what Kinnock is against is these
groups and institutions as manifestations of the present Government's
policy.

Interestingly, this claim about a type of Opposition mentality
towards all aspects of the Government finds its inverted image in the
Government's own position. The aim of the Opposition is to criticize
and question the actions of the Government and all its branches at
every available opportunity; not surprisingly, it is the job of the
party in power to support and defend all branches of government.
Consequently, we find that Mrs Thatcher, as would be predicted from
the above argument, personalizes all the organizations and branches
of government.

(22)   *Any high technology firm* with a suitable invention can get
       a grant from the Department of Industry to cover one-
       third of the cost of *his new products* to the market. And
       that's very good. *He* might not be able to finance it all
       himself. (Speech B; my italics)

Pronominal Scaling and Politics

Earlier in this chapter we noted that pronominal choice could be
related to distancing strategies in terms of a pronominal scale (cf.
Rees, 1983). Such strategies allow the speaker to indicate his/her
relative distance to a subject or individual under discussion. It should
be stressed that the type of scale developed by Rees has no normative
value, since the relative distribution and location of pronouns at
particular points on the scale can vary depending on the individual.
In this way, however, the scale, with its 0 point representing any
selectional choice closest to self, and 9 representing any selectional

choice furthest from self, is a useful device for representing idiosyncratic variation in pronominal selection. In political terms, we would predict, for example, that individuals who construe the world in similar ways, that is, have the same ideology and belief system, would exhibit similar patterns of pronominal choice; and of course, where individual ideologies differ we might predict different patterns of pronominal choice.

Drawing on the analysis of the speeches of Mrs Thatcher and Mr Kinnock given above, it is possible to draw up an individualized pronominal scale for each leader which reflects their own idiosyncratic style in the projection of their political ideologies. For Mrs Thatcher the scale would look something like example (v).

Example (v): Scale of distancing from self for Mrs Thatcher

0	1	2	3	4	5	6	7	8	9
I	WE	YOU	ONE	YOU	SHE	HE	THEY	IT	THOSE
		(direct)		(indefinite)					

On this scale 'it' is employed as a more powerful distancing strategy than 'she'/'he'/'they', as they are scaled by Rees (see above). The increased negative strength of 'it' for Mrs Thatcher is reflected in her refusal to use this form to refer to Government departments, for example. In many contexts using 'it' to refer to institutions would seem innocuous enough. However, the fact that Mrs Thatcher avoids such a use indicates the distancing strength she associates with the pronoun 'it'. As we have already noted in our discussion of Mrs Thatcher's pronominal use, she reserves the form 'those' for referring to those groups which might be considered potentially subversive. For this reason 'those' scores the highest on a scale of distancing for Mrs Thatcher.

The scale of distancing strength for Mr Kinnock is given as example (vi).

Example (vi): Scale of distancing from self for Mr Kinnock

0	1	2	3	4	5	6	7	8
I	WE	YOU	YOU	THEY	THOSE	HE	SHE	IT
		(direct)	(indefinite)					

The first thing to note about the scale for Mr Kinnock is that 'one' is absent. Further, unlike Mrs Thatcher, Mr Kinnock uses 'they' and 'those' in a neutral fashion. However, for Mr Kinnock the scale indicates that 'she'/'he' becomes a significant focus of contrast with 'I'. This reflects the way in which Mr Kinnock views the battle between the Conservative and Labour Parties, i.e. as one between individuals. For Mr Kinnock 'it' carries the greatest distancing potential.

The interesting thing about these scales is the way in which they reflect, for each of the politicians, a particular approach and attitude. This suggests that scaling may be an effective way of objectively assessing the tenor of specific political speeches, and also, over a period of time, assessing the ideological position of individuals with regard to a range of topics.

It is also interesting to note that these scales are not simply reflections of ideolectal differences between the speakers, at least in the sociolinguistic sense. It is not simply that Mrs Thatcher and Mr Kinnock distribute their use of pronouns in a probabilistically distinct way (although this would also be true) it is that they create different meanings from the same pronouns in relation to the context in which the pronouns are used, and in this sense we are dealing with a pragmatic phenomenon.

The Speeches of Michael Foot

In the previous sections some comment was offered on the organization and distribution of pronominal selection in the speeches of Mrs Thatcher and Mr Kinnock. The analysis was mainly comparative and revealed how ideological differences display themselves in pronominal selection. In the case of Mr Foot we might have predicted that selections within the pronominal system would be strongly similar to the choices made by Mr Kinnock. Not only are they both members of the Labour Party, but both have been on occasion associated with the view of the 'left wing' of their party. While there are indeed a number of similarities between Mr Foot and Mr Kinnock, particularly in reference to Mrs Thatcher, it turns out that, in terms of the general use of the possibilities of the pronominal system, Mr Kinnock may have more in common with Mrs Thatcher than with Mr Foot.

In his pre-scripted speeches Mr Foot uses significantly fewer personal pronouns than either Mrs Thatcher or Mr Kinnock. When the scores for pronouns as a percentage of total word output are averaged for each speaker over three speeches (see Appendix, table A.2), we find that Mr Kinnock and Mrs Thatcher use nearly twice as many pronouns as Mr Foot.

Mrs Thatcher	4.85%
Mr Kinnock	5.20%
Mr Foot	2.85%

In pre-scripted speeches Mr Foot rarely makes use of the first-person singular pronoun; indeed in a speech delivered to the nation (December 1983) Mr Foot only employs the first-person singular once:

> (23)   I don't want to bore you.

Mr Foot never seems to use the fervent phrases so loved by many politicians, 'I believe' and 'I hope', particularly prevalent in the delivery of Mrs Thatcher and Mr Kinnock. In the speeches we examined there were no examples of self-referencing using 'you'[2] or 'one'[2], and there was no attempt to make use of either indefinite 'you'[2] or 'one'. Mr Foot uses none of the devices associated with spontaneity such as tags like 'you know', although these are frequently found in the written forms of Mrs Thatcher's speeches; further he seems to employ fewer colloquial phrases; for example, where Mr Kinnock would say 'youngsters', Mr Foot would, instead, employ the phrase 'young people'.

While Mrs Thatcher and Mr Kinnock will both make direct appeals to their audience by making good use of the form 'you', Mr Foot rarely develops his relationship with an audience in this way. In his speech to the nation (noted above) he uses the form only twice, once, as in the case of (23), and the other in (24):

> (24)   What we ask *you* is to come and help us rebuild Britain and help us stop all that.

One might suggest here that, as a concluding statement to an important speech, this is quite clumsy; it is certainly significantly weaker than the punchy rhetorical style of either Mrs Thatcher or Mr Kinnock.

In the same speech Mr Foot also fails to make use of blocks of pronouns. Such blocking techniques, frequently found in the speeches of Mrs Thatcher and Mr Kinnock, serve to stress key points within a speech, to mark issues of contrast, and to give the speech its own individual flavour. Further, for Mr Foot there doesn't seem to be any contrast between 'them' and 'us' (as for Mrs Thatcher), nor between 'I' and 'she' (as for Mr Kinnock). And where Mr Kinnock retains the form 'it' to refer to the faceless nature of government departments, Mr Foot uses the form 'it' to indicate the Labour Party. The possible repercussions of this difference are obvious enough.

The consequences of these findings are (for the speech to the nation at least) that while Mr Foot may put forward clear statements of policy, and offer concrete suggestions, his speeches lack the rhetorical rhythm and forcefulness found in the presentation of Mrs Thatcher and Mr Kinnock.

These findings conflict, however, with the comments of authors such as Harris (1984), who argues that Mr Foot has a reputation as a successful orator, particularly among his fellow politicians in the House of Commons. Harris does accept, though, that Mr Foot may have less appeal to the general public. In an attempt to resolve this conflict between Mr Foot's reputation as an orator and his performance in pre-scripted speeches (as indicated by the above analysis) two unscripted speeches from the same period (J and K) were examined.

In analyzing the unscripted speeches several interesting aspects emerged. For example, the number of pronouns occurring in speeches J and K, (as shown in the Appendix, table A.3) indicates a significant increase in the use of pronouns generally. It is clear that significantly more personal pronouns occur in the unscripted speeches; an average of 7.6 per cent pronouns per total word output, as compared to 2.85 per cent in the pre-scripted speeches.

Those pronouns which Mr Foot makes use of in the unscripted speeches are also used differently from the way in which pronouns are employed in the pre-scripted speeches. It is noticeable that many of the features absent from the pre-scripted speeches are present in speeches J and K. In the unscripted speeches Mr Foot makes considerable use of the first-person singular, in the classic phrases such as 'I believe' and 'I hope'. The indefinite 'you' and 'you'[2] (address) are also used in speeches J and K. However, as in the pre-scripted speeches, there are no occurrences of 'you'[3] for self-referencing. The pronoun 'one' is entirely absent from all speeches. The use of the pronouns 'you'[1] and 'you'[2] and the absence of 'one' in the unscripted speeches matches Mr Kinnock's use of these pronouns in his pre-scripted speeches, and, in turn, is different from Mrs Thatcher's use of these pronouns (as we might have originally predicted).

In speeches J and K, Mr Foot makes considerable use of blocks of pronouns, particularly blocks of 'I' and 'we'. Again, this parallels the block distribution of these pronouns in the speeches of Mr Kinnock.

Further, like Mrs Kinnock, Mr Foot uses the pronoun 'we' to refer only to the people of Britain or the Labour Party. However, unlike Mr Kinnock, the two referents are not always entirely separated and may occur within the same sentence

> (25)   I am deeply ashamed that *we* have permitted that power to rest with such a Government as *we* have in Britain at this time. (Speech K; my italics)

In this example Mr Foot is discussing the failure of the Labour Party to win the election. The first occurrence of 'we' refers to the Labour Party, while the second refers to the British people.

Example (25) also illustrates another device frequently used in speeches J and K, the functional contrast of 'I' and 'we'. This allows Mr Foot to simultaneously present himself as part of the Labour Party and/or people of Britain, while at the same time being seen as detached or outside of the group. This device is used to good effect in his final speech as leader of the Labour Party (October 1983), where he is able to personally accept the 'guilt' of defeat, leaving the Party to move forward undaunted.

In the pre-scripted speeches Mr Foot employs contrastive pronoun patterning using both she/we constructions and they/we constructions. However, when the pronoun 'we' is used in syntactic opposition to either 'she' or 'they', 'we' is frequently used to refer to the British people. Thus, unlike Mr Kinnock or Mrs Thatcher, Mr Foot does not present the political situation within Britain as being between two individual leaders, or between two parties, but rather he presents it as a fight between Thatcher and the Tories against 'The People'. This represents a very traditional socialist ideology:

> (26)   If the reports about the so called Think Tank are correct *they* have chastised *us* with whips, and all *they* have done at recent cabinet meetings is to prepare the scorpions. (Speech J; my italics)

For the run up to the 1983 General Election, the decision was taken that Mr Foot should read from scripts for broadcast speeches. Atkinson (1984) points out that this was a disastrous decision in terms of Mr Foot's non-verbal presentation. Unlike Mrs Thatcher, he did not use the teleprompter and consequently appeared 'hunched', 'glued to the lectern' and 'seldom raised his head'.

It is clear from our analysis of Mr Foot's pronominal distribution that it was an equally disastrous decision in terms of verbal presentation. In his unscripted speeches Mr Foot exhibits all the rhetorical rhythm and forcefulness which has won him the reputation as a good orator. However, in the pre-scripted speeches all these devices are missing and, unfortunately, it was the pre-scripted speeches which the majority of the public saw broadcast at peak viewing time.

It should be emphasized that it is not the pre-scripting of speeches in itself which causes differences in pronominal use, since the devices were in fact present in the pre-scripted speeches of both Mrs Thatcher and Mr Kinnock. It is rather that Mr Foot and/or his script writer, failed to recognize the importance of these devices.

Conclusion

In this chapter we have looked at the way(s) in which aspects of the pronominal system of English can be manipulated for political effect. When one looks at language use, the pronouns of English do not form neat categorical divisions; 'we' can be used to designate a range of individuals moving outwards from the speaker him/herself to the speaker plus hearer and the whole of humanity. Equally, 'I' can be used to refer to the hearer and not the speaker, as well of course as being available for the designation of speaker only. With such manipulative possibilities provided by the pronominal system as it operates in context, it is not surprising to find that politicians make use of pronouns to good effect: to indicate, accept, deny or distance themselves from responsibility for political action; to reveal ideological bias; to encourage solidarity; to designate and identify those who are supporters (with us) as well as those who are enemies (against us); and to present specific idiosyncratic aspects of the individual politician's own personality. All this is revealed through the distribution of specific pronominal types within particular contexts of presentation. The meanings of selected pronouns shift and change depending on the way in which they are textually employed. This is a manipulation of pronominal meaning within context, yet another example of the potential range of pragmatic effects operating within the field of politics.

4

Who Are You Talking About?
Identification and Political
Reference

I think that the American people will support a President, *if they
are told by* the President *why they are there [Vietnam]*.
Richard Nixon: a/the President,
in G.W. Johnson, *The Nixon Presidential Press Conferences*

Introduction

In the last chapter we looked at the way in which the pronominal
system of English may be manipulated for political effect. The so-
called categorical system of person, number and sex is far from
categorical in interactive contexts, where speakers seem capable of
developing and shifting the meaning of specific pronominal forms. It
was noted that selectional choices, such as those which operate
between exclusive and inclusive 'we' for example, offer politicians
ways of directing attention towards or away from their own existential
centre, i.e. themselves.

In this chapter we will explore a broadly similar phenomenon; in
this case however, we will be interested in the way in which selectional
choices made at the level of definite descriptions may manipulate the
hearer's identifications by directing attention away from designated
individuals towards some generic role or conceptual category.

This chapter differs somewhat from the first three in that it is more
theoretical in its argumentation, and bounded by a more limited set
of examples. There are two reasons for this. First, the nature of the
problem to be explained necessitates the use of several competing

explanations of the role of cognitive processing in the interpretation
of definite reference; and second, the phenomenon to be discussed is
so pervasive in not only political interaction but everyday life, that to
extend the set of examples unnecessarily would be to simply labour
the point.

Our main example is taken from a statement made by Norman
Tebbit in the House of Commons on 17 November 1986. Tebbit was
replying to parliamentary criticism of his attack on the BBC's coverage
of the United States' bombing of Libya. In his statement he made
the following claim about those involved in complaining about the
BBC: 'it was not the Chancellor of the Duchy of Lancaster [hereafter
CODL] who made the complaint but the Chairman of the Conservative Party.' What is interesting about this choice and use of definite
description is that Norman Tebbit (hereafter NT) was, at that time,
both the CODL and the Chairman of the Conservative Party. While
the interaction of this dual set of definite descriptions is interesting
in itself, in this chapter I want to focus on the general issue of self-
reference under definite description, and although my arguments
attend to NT's reference to himself as the CODL, they would apply
equally well to his reference to himself as the Chairman of the
Conservative Party.

The type of referring phrase used by NT can be found in a variety
of different contexts. My Dean recently used the phrase 'it is the
function of the Dean to'. The choice of expression used by NT is not
then particularly remarkable. On the other hand, since both speakers
had perfectly acceptable alternatives available to them, that is, it is
my function/responsibility' or 'it was I who complained about the
BBC', we must ask why they chose to refer to themselves in this
particular manner.

Intuitively, one might suggest that the distinction is an indicator
of *role* identification, that speakers who have a variety of roles merely
wish to specify a particular role relevant to the unfolding discourse.
Even if this were the case, it would not explain why it is that such a
choice is not made on every occasion where it is possible, suggesting
some pragmatic grounding in a particular selection. Neither does it
explain how audiences operate in processing such information, since
the effects are significantly different for those audiences who are aware
that the definite description refers to the speaker and those who do
not have such information (it should be noted that parliamentary
debates are broadcast to a radio audience, as well as being available
in a written form in Hansard).

This last claim may seem odd in that it is generally assumed that speakers only use definite descriptions when they can rely on their audience to retrieve the reference (see Clark and Clark, 1977; Sacks and Schegloff, 1977). But this assumption must be assessed against a context where a definite description, even if the reference were retrievable, has been employed when the expected form is more likely to have been a self-referential pronoun. The puzzle of choice is what I attempt to work out below.

In this chapter I want to argue that for both audiences who know that NT = CODL and audiences who do not know NT = CODL difficulties arise, and that the choice of the type of description employed by NT under conditions of self-reference may act as a ploy to deflect, or delimit, what I will call 'existential involvement'.

This last point seems to be supported by Gruber (1987) who claims that politicians operate on two levels of communication. On one level they are communicating with journalists and fellow politicians; on another level they are communicating with (and trying to convince) the public. Using Brown and Levinson's (1978) concept of face, Gruber argues for a 'public positive face' for politicians, and suggests that politicians wish to attack each other while at the same time maintaining their own positive position. For NT then, the choice of referential description may be dependent on maintaining his *positive face* in terms of the competing needs of two potential audience types.

The problem here of course is that the behaviour NT exhibits is not constrained to politicians. Gruber's description does not take account of my Dean's behaviour, nor indeed my own behaviour when I say to my daughter, 'as your father'. In these cases there is only one audience. It is perhaps not so much whether one has competing audiences per se, but rather, as we saw in the last chapter, whether one wishes the core responsibility for what is said, or for some set of actions, to be centred in oneself. For this reason it is not unusual to find specific referential choices associated with the kinds of pronominal shifts we discussed previously. Consider the following response from Nigel Lawson, as the Chancellor of the Exchequer, to Labour back-bench calls for him to place on record a letter sent to the banks: 'In the course of *his* duties as *the Chancellor of the Exchequer my* Right Hon. Friend has confidential exchanges with many bodies and it is not *his* practice to make them public' (Hansard, 1984; quoted in Silk, 1987: 183; my italics). The fact that politicians have differing audiences to deal with undoubtedly has some effect on their discourse, but the basic aim of all communicators is to maintain *face* no matter what or who the audience. When I talk of the difficulties facing audiences who know NT = CODL as opposed to those audiences who do not, it is not that I am separating out political from non-political audiences, but simply audiences of any type depending on whether they have or do not have access to certain kinds of knowledge.

Strategies and Roles

I suggested above that NT's use of a particular type of referring form may reflect an attempt to mitigate existential involvement. Some clarification of this claim is necessary. What I am referring to here is analogous to the options we noted in the choice between 'I' and 'we', or between the use of 'we' as either an inclusive or exclusive form.

Earlier (p. 50), I argued that Jimmy Carter seemed to be distributing his selection of 'I' and 'we' (exclusive and inclusive) relative to the debate context he was involved in, and relative to degrees of personal responsibility, or in more neutral terms, existential involvement. 'I' directly encodes existential involvement, as indeed does inclusive 'we', although this selection would be less existentially salient. Exclusive 'we' may exonerate the speaker from any commitment whatsoever, as in the case of Churchill's rhetoric noted earlier (although exclusive 'we' may include the speaker but exclude some other group or individual: see Urban, 1986). We might represent this on a scale of existential involvement as follows:

$$I > WE(I) > WE(E)$$

This suggests that I indicates a greater existential involvement than WE(Inclusive), which in turn indicates a greater existential involvement that WE(Exclusive).

The argument in this chapter will be that choices of referring forms, in particular definite descriptions, may also carry out a similar function, that is that the use of definite descriptions within certain contexts may reduce the level, and audience processing, of the speaker's existential involvement with certain activities.

Now this may occur for a variety of reasons. Consider the following examples (taken from the Presidential press conferences of Richard Nixon: see Johnson, 1978):

(1) Q: Mr President . . . what problems that *you* have to cope with require *your* most urgent attention?

The President:	. . . the field of foreign policy will require more attention because it is in this field that only the President, in many instances, can make decisions.
(2) *The President*:	As you know the President has authority in that field.
(3) *The President*:	I can only say that by my actions as President I hope to rectify that . . . it will be made clear that the President of the United States, as an elected official . . . represents all the people . . . Putting it another way – as a lawyer – the President is the counsel for all the people.

In the first example the journalist's question personalizes the issue through the use of 'you' and 'your'. In his response, however, Nixon avoids any matching reciprocal pronoun forms, such as 'I', or inclusive 'we'. Inclusive 'we' would have been possible, but perhaps slightly odd as a matching reciprocal in this context. The reason for this is that Nixon was asked specifically about 'his' view of those problems which need most urgent attention. The most obvious pronoun to employ in response here would seem to be 'I'. However, considering what Nixon actually says, the choice of 'I' would have been inappropriate, in that it would perhaps give an impression of arrogance: 'only I can make the decisions'.

Of course, since Nixon is the President, then saying 'only the President can make the decision' would seem to mean the same thing as 'only I can make the decisions', at least in this context. But this is not wholly the case, since, if Nixon is right, then only the holder of the office of President can 'make the decisions'; it is not something solely associated with Richard Nixon.

This will be explained in more detail below, but for the moment we can see how the use of a definite descriptive form in this context gives Nixon the opportunity to indicate that foreign policy is one of the most immediate problems that he (Richard Nixon) has to deal with, but at the same time, if one gives the definite description a broad reading, Nixon's personal existential involvement is only located through his position as President, which delimits any direct claim that it is only Richard Nixon who can make certain decisions.

In the second example Nixon was questioned about his policy on appointments in his Administration. There was an implicit criticism in the question, that *he* (Nixon) was perhaps behaving somewhat differently than previous Presidents. The response, once again, re-routes any direct attention away from a complete existential involve-ment, because Nixon is behaving as the President, and in the field of appointments the President has a specific authority.

In the third example Nixon was responding to criticism of his attitude to the Black community. Once again we can see how the use of the definite description directs attention away from him (Richard Nixon) personally. Whether any of the criticisms were personally true or not, Nixon simply states that the President represents all the people, which is in a sense not an answer at all but a tautology. There is once again the implicit separation of the individual and the role, but it is a separation hard to define or pin down. If I fear or love Richard Nixon, then surely I fear or love the President, where the President is Richard Nixon.

If you feel there is something puzzling here, then I have made my point, and in the rest of this chapter I want to try and unravel this puzzle by exploring not only referential choices as structural options (as I did in chapter 3), but also as cognitive options which have a specific cognitive effect and impact.

Reference and Accessibility

Reference is a major problem for both linguists and philosophers. It is not my aim here, however, to review the vast literature on *referring* (for a general perspective see Devitt and Sterelny, 1987; on more specific issues Castãneda, 1968; 1975; Quine, 1969; Boër and Lycan, 1980; 1986; Cole, 1981; Ariel, 1985; 1988). I would however note, in agreement with Ariel (1988), that there are two basic perspectives on this problem. The first relates to the issue of existential identifi-cation (i.e. existence/uniqueness: see references above, plus Gazdar, 1979; Kempson, 1979; Prince 1981) and the second explores the cognitive issues of accessibility (Yule, 1981; Givon 1979a; 1983; Sanford and Garrod, 1985; Ariel, 1988). These two approaches to the problem of reference overlap, although this is not always made clear in the literature.

There is, however, a problem which the second approach has to face with specific reference to the samples we have discussed so far. One of the aims of the *accessibility account* is to explain how differing referring forms get selected within discouse. The answer, in cognitive terms, relates, inter alia, to such factors as the amount of shared/

mutual knowledge of the participants; the relative distance between an antecedent and an anaphor; and the amount of processing effort required.

One core finding of this work, however, suggests that, in terms of accessibility, definite descriptions are low on the scale of accessibility. This means simply that a definite description will be employed where the speaker, in an assessment of the context of communication, believes that this referring form is the 'best guideline for retrieval' (Ariel, 1988: 59). For example, if I see a man at a party who is standing in the corner, and I want to draw my partner's attention to this individual, then I must take into account such factors as whether this is the first mention of this person, and I must consider whether my partner knows the name of this individual. If we assume that neither I nor my partner know who the man is, and also that he has not been mentioned before, then it is highly probable that I will use a phrase such as 'the man in the corner' to refer to this individual. Once he has been referred to however, he becomes more accessible, and I may then use a pronoun form like 'he':

(4a) Do you see the man standing in the corner?
(b) Yes.
(c) He is wearing a wig.

It would be unusual for me, in the third turn at (4c), to continue to use a definite description, since the object/individual is now more easily accessible.

Now the question I want to raise, with the political examples we have looked at so far, is do they violate accessibility constraints? In each of the Nixon examples pronouns could easily have been employed, since the individual in question was clearly accessible, both in terms of context and shared/mutual knowledge. However, while we noted that it would be odd in the third turn at (4c) to employ a definite description, since the individual was now easily accessible, it does not, in any way, seem odd for Nixon to refer to himself using a definite description, even though a pronoun would be predicted in terms of accessibility theory.

The critic might point out that Nixon is not referring to himself, but to the role or concept of a Presidency, and that therefore this is much less accessible than an individual Presidential identity. But surely we would not want to claim that what Nixon has said does not also apply to himself as a President; nor would we want to say that it was structurally necessary, in any sense, that he employ definite descriptions at specific points in his responses. Consider (5):

> (5) On the other hand it is the responsibility of the President to examine all the options that we have, and if he finds that the course he has to take is not popular he has to explain this to the American people.

Is this example yet another quote from Nixon, or is it a quote from another President, or a journalist, or an expert in politics? We cannot of course say, although all are equally viable possibilities. It is only when the use of a definite description is employed by the same person to whom it refers to does any problem arise. If the quote were from a journalist or a political expert then the normal arguments about accessibility would apply, if, however, the quote is from Richard Nixon we might ask why simple accessible forms like 'my' and 'I' are not employed. It is certainly not for reasons of structure, since if one were to substitute these forms in (5) it remains perfectly acceptable (in both linguistic and cognitive terms). It seems, therefore, that accessibility issues can only be resolved when the initial question of existence/uniqueness is resolved, and that, in this sense, the existence/ uniqueness approach is prior to accessibility studies. In order to consider the puzzle we have targeted, it is with the existence/uniqueness problem that we should begin.

Reference and Intentions

In exploring the existence/uniqueness direction my initial concern is with the distinction made by Donnellan (1966) between the *referential* and the *attributive* use of definite descriptions. This distinction is based on the principle that speakers' intentions play a major role in distinguishing how an expression is being employed in referring (contra Russell and Frege).

Earlier theories of reference were based on a relatively strict language–world relationship. Referring was successful (true) when the reference matched the object designated within the world and unsuccessful (false) otherwise. In terms of real interaction this leads to some unfortunate interpretations. For example, if I say that 'the man wearing a wig knifed my friend,' and it turns out that this individual wasn't wearing a wig, but simply had a bad hairdresser, then, in at least one interpretation of reference, what I have said is false. But if my description is good enough to actually allow the police to pick out the attacker, then in real-world terms the problem of the wig is neither relevant to me nor to the police (although it might be relevant to the attacker and his hairdresser). My intention was to pick out the individual who attacked my friend, and if I pick him out correctly then, in an intentional sense, I have been successful. Alternatively, if I did not see the person who attacked my friend, but simply found a wig at the scene I might say, 'the attacker wore a wig.' In this case I would not be intentionally referring to a specific individual but rather I seem to be referring to *whoever* the attacker was.

This is the essence of Donnellan's view. If a speaker uses an expression *referentially* then he/she intends the hearer to pick out a specific designated individual. On the other hand, if a speaker uses a definite description *attributively* the intention is not to designate a specific individual the speaker has in mind, but rather to state something about whoever or whatever is designated by the description.

Finding Smith's dead body we might draw the conclusion that there has been a murder. We might, in such circumstances, express the view that 'Smith's murderer is insane,' without knowing who the murderer was. In this case one would be using the description attributively. If it turns out that Smith died of natural causes then the description fails as an attributive act. On the other hand, if one were to say at a party that 'the tall woman drinking white wine is a teacher,' and it turns out that she is in fact drinking water, then it is still possible, where you are correctly understood, that you would have successfully designated a specific individual.

This view of reference offers one possible explanation for the behaviour of Norman Tebbit in our original example; at least at a descriptive level. One might argue that when NT refers to himself as the CODL his intention is to use the referring expression *attributively*. The explicit aim is not to specify a particular individual, but *whoever* happens to be designated as fitting such a description. This may seem odd in common-sense terms, particularly for those who know that NT is the CODL. But let us concede, for the moment, that if NT can get his audience (whoever they may be: attributive) to think about the individual who is the topic of talk in attributive terms, then any existential involvement claims will not be embodied in any single identified person, but rather in generic terms relative to whoever or whatever may be the case. The advantage here for any person being attacked for performing certain actions is that hearers are being directed away from focusing on that person as a specific individual.

Taking this claim as a starting point, and assuming that it is plausible (as far as it goes), how can we explain such an interpretation; and further, how does such a claim take account of the interpretive options available to those audiences who know NT is the CODL as opposed to those audiences who do not? For those who are not aware of the identity equivalence (in the real world), they clearly cannot equate any beliefs or attributes of NT with those of whoever is the CODL, since the assumption is that the identity for them is unknown. In the case of those who are aware of any identity equivalence the problem of explaining any interpretive behaviour is more complicated. Surely, they can simply substitute NT for the CODL. For example: NT is speaking, NT is the CODL, therefore the CODL is speaking. I don't want to consider whether such a substitution operates in all environments which might be constructed for the sake of philosophical debate (as in opaque contexts, contexts of self-reference under loss of memory, or contexts where perceptual trickery operates: see Castãneda, 1968; Quine, 1969; Boër and Lycan, 1986); I take it as given that in the real world of discourse, if I know NT = CODL, then it is plausible for me, in constructing models of the actions of NT or the CODL, to treat these (where necessary) as intersubstituable.

If this is true then what is to be gained from using the expression CODL as opposed to some other self-referring expression? Perhaps it is the case that the ambiguity inherent in Donnellan's distinction allows NT to *hedge* (Lakoff, 1972) on any identity claims. Consider the following:

(6) *A*: Can you fix this for me?
    B: I'm busy.
    A: I was only asking if you could fix it.

Most normal speakers of English will recognize that A's first turn has the conventional form of what is known as an indirect speech act (Searle, 1975). Such acts are indirect in that they perform their main function in a non-literal manner. For example, if I say 'it is cold in here' what I may actually mean is 'please close the window.' My direct statement can be reinterpreted as a request for action (see Labov and Fanchel, 1977; Leech, 1983). The problem with the concept of indirect acts is that it is unclear whether the literal interpretation is negated, or whether, indeed, there is only one act being performed (see Labov and Fanchel, 1977). In example (6) the turn may be intended as both a question and a request.

The main point to note, however, is that there is a potential advantage for speakers in using indirect speech acts, in that you can always claim of any two interpretations (a) and (b) (question and request for example) that only one was intended, the one which suits your purpose. In the case of NT's use of the CODL as a referring phrase under conditions of identity equivalence, similar options seem available. NT can claim either that he was referring to himself as a unique identity, or that he was simply referring to a role which he just happened to hold at this point in time (indeed this claim would fit with Donnellan's suggestion that attributive uses may not refer at all: see Searle, 1979a for a counter view).

There are a number of difficulties here, however. First, the use of the referring description has different effects on different audiences, suggesting that whether some expression is interpreted as referring or attributive is not completely constrained by speaker intentions alone. The hearer's knowledge of the world in which the expression is used plays a part. Secondly, despite the social role theory, if NT = CODL and I know this to be true, I know this to be true whether it is explicitly expressed or not. In this case, then, we need some further pragmatic explanation to account for any role interpretation where it emerges via some expressions and not others. Third, why should hearers, as rational agents, believe that the degree or extent of responsibility for actions is any way mitigated by the use of certain referentially equivalent descriptive phrases? I don't believe that they necessarily do, but in order to make my position clear, I must first attend to the problems of differing audience effects and the issue of the pragmatics behind specific choices and expressions.

I intend to do this by exploring several candidate solutions to the identity problem we have identified. The reason for this, as noted in the Introduction, is that pragmatics, as a new area, offers a variety of seemingly competing theories. By exploring a number of these theories, my aim is, (a) to acquaint the reader with relevant pragmatic information useful not only in this chapter but throughout the rest of the book; (b) to consider the overlap of these theories; (c) to see how each theory, in its own way, contributes in part to an overall solution to our problem.

Speaker Models and Hearer Models

In discussing the issue of differing audience effects it will be argued that the distinction between the interpretation given by hearers who know NT = CODL and those who do not, can be represented using Johnson-Laird's (1983) theory of mental models. The general principle underlying the theory is fairly straightforward; Johnson-Laird argues that speakers and hearers construct mental models of the world which they use as a basis for reasoning about what others say about the world. For example, suppose you are told of the various members of an academic conference that:

> All the linguists are footballers.

It can be argued that you organize this information in terms of a mental model which matches linguists with the concept of being a footballer; but since some members of the conference may be footballers but not linguists, you include other slots which contain this possibility, as in example (i);

Example (i)

linguist	=	footballer
linguist	=	footballer
linguist	=	footballer
		(footballer)
		(footballer)

This is a very basic example of what a mental model would look like. Johnson-Laird has shown how such models can be made much more complex and how they can serve as the basis for reasoning about certain relationships based on information within the model. For example, if we are further told of the conference that all the gin-drinkers are footballers, then on the basis of the model we have constructed we might make certain adjustments, as shown in example (ii).

Example (ii)

linguist	=	footballer	=	gin-drinker
linguist	=	footballer	=	gin-drinker
linguist	=	footballer	=	gin-drinker
		(footballer)		
		(footballer)		

This model suggests that all linguists are footballers and therefore gin-drinkers, but that there are footballers who are neither gin-drinkers nor linguists. This is not quite right however, certainly not in terms of the two statements we have been given: (a) all the linguists are footballers; and (b) all the gin-drinkers are footballers. The correct model would look something like example (iii).

Example (iii)

linguist	=	footballer	=	gin-drinker
linguist	=	footballer	=	gin-drinker
linguist	=	footballer		
		footballer	=	gin-drinker
		(footballer)		
		(footballer)		

This model shows that all linguists are footballers (statement (a)) and that all gin-drinkers are footballers (statement (b)), but not the incorrect assumption that all gin-drinkers are also linguists, or indeed that all footballers are either gin-drinkers or linguists.

The point in introducing the concept of a mental model is that it reveals a basic weakness within Donnellan's theory of reference, and potentially a weakness in the use of this theory to account for Norman Tebbit's behaviour. This weakness is outlined in a paper by Johnson-Laird and Garnham (1980), in which they argue that the referential/attributive distinction fails to take account of the potential difference between a speaker's model and a hearer's model. One of the basic principles of attributive reference is that when there is no entity for the description to refer to (as in the case where the phrase 'the murderer of Smith' is used in a situation where Smith died of natural causes) then the speaker fails to say anything.

As Johnson-Laird and Garnham argue, however, this need not be the case. Take the example of Smith (now alive and well) who believes that his sister's husband has been to see two films (a) and (b). Smith believes that his sister's husband (John) believes that his wife does not know about film (b). However, it is another one of Smith's beliefs that his sister does in fact know about film (b). In such a context Smith might say to his sister:

(7)   How do you think John enjoyed the film that he doesn't know that you know that he saw last night? (Johnson-Laird and Garnham, 1980: 373)

Now, unknown to Smith, the husband (John) has found out that his wife (Smith's sister) does know about film (b). Now since Donnellan claims that an attributive expression fails to say anything when it is used where there is no entity to fulfil the attributive slot, Smith has failed to say anything in (7) since there is no film that John doesn't know that this wife knows that he saw last night. The point of all this is that, as Johnson-Laird and Garnham point out, Donellan's view here is too strict and it seems incorrect to claim that nothing has been said in (7). Johnson-Laird and Garnham argue that Smith's sister is quite capable of reconstructing what Smith believes to be the case and of responding in relation to such a reconstruction.

The main point that is being made is that speaker models and hearer models must be considered individually. Further, with relation to definite descriptions, it is uniqueness in a model, rather than in reality, which guides interpretation.

Within this view speakers, where they are aware that hearers may have access to only certain types of knowledge, can intend that only selected aspects of that knowledge become relevant to interpretation. For example, in the case of NT, many of those who do not know that NT = CODL cannot access an identity expression in the construction of a mental model of what NT has said. In a hypothetical extension of the facts, a hearer in this position will know CODL = ?R(BBC), where the expression on the right hand side of the = sign simply indicates that CODL has been accused of being responsible for critizing the BBC. What such hearers do not know, however, is that NT = CODL = ?R(BBC). One consequence of this is that any discussion of those who have criticized the BBC's behaviour will, for the hearer who does not know NT = CODL, be tied only to the slot for CODL as an attributive form, i.e., whoever he may be.

We have two potential hearer models on which what NT says can be interpreted:

(8a) CODL = ?R(BBC)
  (b) NT = CODL = ?R(BBC)

Where the BBC has been criticized, certain implications may follow from each model. On hearing NT's utterance let us assume, for case (8a), that the hearer knows that someone has criticized the BBC. The hearer is made aware that the CODL is accused of being responsible for this action, which suggests (but does not guarantee) that it is the CODL who has criticized the BBC. The hearer in this case does not know specifically who the CODL is, but whoever he is he has been accused of critizing the BBC. Such a view will only hold, however, for as long as the hearer cannot interpret the CODL referentially (at least intuitively, although see below). Whether in fact politicians can maintain a continuous use of seemingly attributive forms for self-reference is highly debatable. Various clues within the discourse, and within the range of general pragmatic expectations, would soon lead the hearer to a referential interpretation of the attributive form. On the surface then there seems to be little point in using definite descriptions of one's self with the intention that they are to be interpreted attributively, when it is the case that the pragmatics of certain contexts serve to supply the relevant knowledge for supplanting the attributive interpretation with a referential one.

This is of course the explicit case for those hearers who already know that $NT = CODL$ (8b above). In this case the speaker's intention that the definite description be interpreted attributively, as opposed to referentially, seems even more futile. On the other hand, in this case, we get a clue to another possible solution and explanation of what is going on.

As NT is the speaker, it would be our normal expectation that when he talks of himself he will use a suitable form (see Sacks and Schegloff, 1977). So if he is responsible for some action he might be expected to use one of the personal pronouns: I did X; it is my job to do Y; and so on; or even where shared responsibility or solidarity is the aim: we must do X; it is our job (see chapter 3; also Boër and Lycan, 1980 on the general expectations of self-reference).

As NT speaks the hearer may have as a model some general association such as $NT = ?R(BBC)$. When NT refers to himself via his role as the CODL, where the hearer knows that he is the holder of this role, then the general associative frame of the model becomes, firstly, $CODL = ?R(BBC)$, then $CODL = NT$, which seems to lead the hearer to $NT = ?R(BBC)$; or perhaps in a more expanded form $NT = CODL = ?R(BBC)$. But in processing time it is not clear what the hearer gains from this extra effort, or from maintaining extra information within the frame of the model, since in the context of this discourse $NT = CODL$ and $CODL = NT$ say the same thing.

One point which emerges from this is that when a speaker refers to himself/herself using a definite description which could (potentially) be interpreted attributively, then for the hearer who knows that the description can refer specifically to the speaker, some extra and superfluous processing may take place. This very fact, however, may offer us another and alternative solution to our problem. It may be the case, for example, that hearers may see Tebbit as flouting Gricean maxims of behaviour and that his intention, therefore, is to have his audience process a conversational implicature of some type. In order to consider what this might be we will look to the most recent development within the general Gricean framework, i.e., at what has become known as 'Relevance Theory'.

The Relevance of Referring

According to the theory of *Relevance* developed by Sperber and Wilson (1986; see also Wilson and Sperber, 1986) from the original work of Grice (see chapter 2), everyday communication (in particular what Sperber and Wilson refer to as *ostensive communication*) is achieved, in part, by the processing of a set of *contextual assumptions* which can be arrived at from an interpretation of the surface discourse within a specific context. *Relevance* within communication is achieved by maintaining a balance between processing effort and information implied or indicated. For example, consider (9):

(9a) *He*:   Can Susan drive a Buick?
  (b) *She*: She can drive any car.

                          (Wilson and Sperber, 1986: 250)

As we saw earlier when we discussed *conversational implicatures*, the answer given in (9) is not a direct response to the question, and may therefore be used to imply other information beyond the simple surface content. It is this general principle which Sperber and Wilson exploit. They argue that communication involves a speaker presenting some form of stimulus in a specific contextual environment, and that the hearer takes this stimulus within its context and accesses and processes information from this interaction in an attempt to make sense of what the speaker has done: i.e. to discover the 'relevance' of what has been presented. In the case of (9) the answer has been presented and what needs to be discovered is its relevance. In attempting to process the answer, the hearer might construct a context containing certain assumptions, which then serve as input into a deductive device which generates contextual implications. A possible context for (9) would be something like (a) and (b), with a contextual implication such as (c).

  (a) A Buick is a car.
  (b) Susan can drive any car.
  (c) Therefore Susan can drive a Buick.

The question for the hearer is, then, since *She* could simply have said 'yes', which would have given the same result, i.e. that Susan can drive a Buick, why has *She* responded in such a way that the hearer has to work (in processing terms) that much harder. Accepting the original Gricean assumption that speakers wish to make what they say as relevant as possible, the hearer might ask whether in fact the indirect response given was not in fact more relevant than a simple straightforward positive answer. Sperber and Wilson construct a context where such an interpretation is in fact possible. If we imagine that (9) has arisen in a context where *She* knows that Susan has asked *He* to lend her his Buick, and *He* is wondering whether Susan will look after the car properly, then the *contextual implications* (given in (10)), which follow from the indirect response (9), will encourage the hearer to lend the car with the confidence that Susan is a good driver and will look after the car.

> (10a) If Susan can drive any car she is probably a good driver.
>   (b) If Susan can drive any car she is probably interested in cars.
>   (c) If Susan can drive any car she may be able to fix engines.
>
>   (a) Susan is probably a good driver.
>   (b) Susan is probably interested in cars.
>   (c) Susan may be able to fix an engine.
>   (from Wilson and Sperber, 1986: 251)

If the hearer does indeed process such extra contextual implications then any worries about lending Susan the car may be limited.

It will be clear, of course, that there are many implications which might be derived from any utterance. There is a control operating in the theory of relevance, however, which constrains implications in terms of the relevance they contain in proportion to the processing effort required. Wilson and Sperber (1986) suggest that there is a trade-off between maximizing the number of contextual implications and minimizing the processing effort involved in interpretation.

If we take a basically similar approach to our NT example, we may suggest that his statement might initially be processed by an audience who know NT = CODL as:

> (1a) The CODL designates the individual responsible for criticizing the BBC.

    (b)   Whoever is the CODL is responsible for criticizing the BBC.

    (c)   NT is the CODL.

    (d)   Therefore NT is responsible for criticizing the BBC.

If we compare this with the way in which this same audience would have processed the use of a personal pronoun such as 'I', given as (12), then it would be possible to argue that the use of a definite description generates a greater processing effort.

    (12)   I was responsible for criticizing the BBC.

    (a)   The person speaking is NT.

    (b)   NT is responsible for criticizing the BBC.

Now it could be said that I have left out a possible contextual assumption in (12), something like, 'the speaker has used a pronoun type to reference him/herself'. If we were to include this then we should also add to (11), a further assumption such as: 'the speaker has used a definite description because he/she assumes either this is a first mention, or that the specific identity is unknown.' If we did include such an assumption in (11) (and this seems reasonable), this would do two things: first, it would maintain our claim that extra processing is required in the case of the definite description; second, and more importantly, it would create, at the same time, a contradiction and a context for the resolution of the contradiction.

The contradiction, obviously enough, is that the speaker is both not sure who the CODL is, and yet is the CODL. It may be argued, however, that this contradiction is in iteself a context for a possible resolution of relevance. It could be argued that since it is the definite description that NT has made primarily manifest, it is this which is more significant than the personal identification which it is also possible to process, or which could have been made primarily manifest through the use of a personal pronoun. But why would that be relevant? A suggested answer is that through the use of a definite description NT is stressing a role rather than an individual, and if we place this within a legitimate and broader, political context as indicated by the following:

    (a)   The BBC is a public corporation and is therefore accountable to the public.

    (b)   The Government (and indeed the public) have a right to expect certain standards under the BBC's charter.

(c) It is acceptable for anyone (particularly members of the Government) to criticize the BBC if they fail to behave in accordance with their charter.

We might claim, in one sense, that NT was simply doing his job. The argument, in relevance terms, is that the use of a definite description generates a balanced output between the number of contextual implications and the processing effort, to give a solution that suggests a reasoned choice in the selection of a definite description.

Such a solution, via the theory of relevance, would be consistent with one's intuitions regarding examples like 'it is the function of the Dean'. In this case also, one has the feeling that the point being made is that it is not the actions of a specific individual identity that is at issue but the actions associated with a role, actions which any individual (whoever he or she may be) would equally be constrained in performing. This would also fit with my suggestion that certain definite descriptions may be used to offset responsibility claims: nevertheless the solution via such a set of contextual implications as those noted above has a certain ad hoc feel about it.

The basic problem with the approach offered by Sperber and Wilson is that it doesn't seem to take account of the fact that hearers are free to bring to bear idiosyncratic information about any topic, or to display particular individually based motivational constraints (see Gazdar and Good, 1982; Wilks, 1982; 1986). For example, consider the following alternative conclusion to (10):

(13a) Can Susan drive a Buick?
  (b) She can drive any car.
  (c) A Buick isn't just any car.

In this case the hearer may work out the relevance intended by the speaker in using an indirect response, but he may reject the implications derived from (10) substituting instead something like (14):

(14a) She believes all cars are the same.
  (b) A Buick is something special.
  (c) She does not believe a Buick is something special.
  (d) If Susan treats all cars as the same she will not treat a Buick as something special.

With these implications any fears the speaker has about lending the car will be far from allayed.

The point is not that Sperber and Wilson's approach is necessarily wrong, indeed it is claimed that their theory takes account of the fact that one cannot predict exactly what the implications will be for each speaker (Blakemore, 1987), in which case, I suppose the implications in (14) might just as easily have been arrived at by the same speaker trying to achieve relevance. The problem here, of course, is that where the intention was to make sure that *He* would feel happy about lending the car then the answer given has clearly failed.

Of course one cannot guarantee how an utterance will be interpreted, but the fact remains that the theory does not seem to offer a clear account of how idiosyncratic motivations effect relevance processing. This is significantly important for NT, since if he is attempting to make a specific pragmatic point (beyond the surface meaning of what is said) it becomes quite clear that he cannot guarantee that any audience which recognizes that his choice of referring expression requires extra processing effort, and may therefore carry certain implications, will necessarily arrive at the implication most relevant for him, i.e. that he was only doing his job. An audience could just as easily arrive at the conclusion that NT is trying to worm his way out of taking responsibility for the consequences of his action.

Perhaps we expect too much of relevance theory in this respect. There is, however, a more worrying aspect. In looking at the processing of NT's use of a definite description within a specific audience/knowledge context, that is where it is known that NT = CODL, we predict that this fact will become part of the processing context (see (11) above). If we compare this with the processing which takes place within an audience/knowledge context where NT = CODL is not known then of course this cannot become part of the processing context:

(15a) The CODL is responsible for criticizing the BBC.
  (b) Whoever is the CODL is responsible for criticizing the BBC.

Clearly, if it was NT's aim to get his audience to redirect their thinking away from himself as an individual, then the context in (15) is a more useful one. But why should an audience who know NT = CODL process his utterance as if they did not know NT = CODL? This would seem absurd! But this is the wrong question however. The question should be why should an audience who know NT = CODL access this information where a definite description has been chosen?

The relevance answer is particularly strong here, and would seem to be that such information is made mutually manifest by NT's utterance; or more simply, the fact that NT is speaking, and that he has used a definite description which refers to himself, would seem to suggest that he wishes the hearer to focus on such a fact. In other words relevance theory would seem to strongly push us towards the use of the knowledge that NT = CODL in this particular context.

I think this is perfectly reasonable, but within the spirit of this chapter I want to suggest an alternative possibility. I want to argue that it is possible that NT's aim was to get both the audience who knew that NT = CODL and the audience who did not know NT = CODL to behave in the same way, that is he wanted both to behave as if they did not know that NT = CODL.

This seems somewhat odd, and so I have a difficult task ahead of me to present a convincing case. The first thing to note, however, is that since relevance theory seems to provide a solution dependent on the processing of NT = CODL where this is available, it would not seem suitable to explain the option I have suggested above.

Beliefs, Environments and Reference

In order to explain the possible processing senario I have just outlined I want to consider what Wilks (1986) has referred to as a 'constructive theory of beliefs'. Wilks argues that beliefs are processed and understood in terms of specific belief environments. These environments are organizational belief spaces which speaker/hearers employ in achieving understanding. What is particularly important about Wilks's perspective is that the model seems to allow for selective processing, by which I mean that one can select specific environments in which to run arguments; with the obvious consequence that each different environment may create different outcomes from basically the same input material. An example from Wilks (1986: 276) will clarify this:

(16) *User*:   Frank is coming tomorrow, I think.
    System: Perhaps I should leave. (I)
    User: Why?
    System: Coming from you that is a warning.
    User: Does Frank dislike you?
    System: I don't know (II) but you think he does and that is what is important now.

The problem in this example results, argues Wilks, from the fact that beliefs of different types are being run in different environments. The basic issue is that one needs to distinguish between the user's beliefs about Frank's beliefs, the system's beliefs about Frank's beliefs, and Frank's actual beliefs. At points (I) and (II) the system is 'running knowledge about individuals in different environments'. Wilks uses the notational approach shown in example (16b) to represent belief relations.

Example (16b)

$$\begin{array}{c} [\ \text{Frank}\ ] \\ \text{System} \end{array}$$

(Wilks, 1986: 277)

This is used to represent the *system's* beliefs about Frank. This kind of structure can be nested as in example (16c).

Example (16c)

$$\begin{array}{c} \left[\begin{array}{c} [\ \text{User}\ ] \\ \text{Frank} \end{array} \right] \\ \text{System} \end{array}$$

(Wilks, 1986: 277)

This represents the system's beliefs about Frank's beliefs about the user. A further distinction is drawn between *A's* beliefs about *B*, and *A's* beliefs about *B's* beliefs. A line is drawn within diagrammatic representations to indicate this distinction, as shown in example (16d).

Example (16d)

$$\begin{array}{c} \left[\begin{array}{c} \text{Smith} \\ \quad \text{Smith is an alcoholic} \\ \hline \quad \text{Smith is an alcoholic} \\ \quad \text{Smith likes Jones} \end{array} \right] \\ \text{System} \end{array}$$

(Wilks, 1986: 280)

Such a distinction is made because it is possible to believe that Smith is an alcoholic without believing that Smith himself believes this.

Now applying this theory to the situation of NT, and considering his utterance as an independent unit, we can construct sample belief environments relative to whether the hearer knows or does not know that NT = CODL. If the hearer knows that NT = CODL then beliefs about the CODL at this point in time will be the same beliefs about NT; consequently, despite the fact that some extra processing effort may be required, this does not seem relevant to the belief environment itself (see examples (17a) and (b)).

Example (17a)   H know NT = CODL

$$
\left[
\begin{array}{l}
\text{NT} \\
\quad \text{NT} = \text{CODL} \\
\quad ?\text{R(BBC)} \\
\hline
\quad \text{NT} = \text{CODL} \\
\quad ?\text{R(BBC)} \\
\quad \text{Criticize(BBC)}
\end{array}
\right]
$$
Hearer

Example (17b)   H not know NT = CODL

$$
\left[
\begin{array}{l}
\text{CODL} \\
\\
\quad\quad @ \\
\\
\hline
\quad \text{CODL} = ?\text{R(BBC)} \\
\quad \text{Criticize(BBC)}
\end{array}
\right]
$$
Hearer

It is clear from representation (17b) that any implications or inferences which might be drawn will not be attached to any specific individual. The symbol @ indicates here that since the identity of the CODL is not known, it is difficult for the hearer to have any beliefs about the beliefs of this unknown individual (although this is perhaps not impossible, but certainly highly implausible). In representation (17a) we would be capable of drawing conclusions (which can be extended in terms of the number and types of beliefs we run) which are clearly linked to the identity of NT. But, of course, we already knew this. What I want to suggest, however, is much more controversial. I want to argue that some of the hearers who know NT = CODL may actually run beliefs in environment (17b) as opposed to environment (17a), which would mean, of course, that even though they know NT = CODL, in this scenario they do not attach conclusions to any specific identity.

Beliefs, Environments and Perserverance

The problem with my suggestion, that speakers who know NT = CODL may nevertheless run beliefs in an environment where he is not specifically identified, is that it seems to be counter to common sense. On the other hand, it would not be possible for speaker/hearers to bring to bear every item of possible relevance to each and every utterance. This is the whole point of Sperber and Wilson's theory of *relevance*. Speaker/hearers must somehow work out the relative importance of certain elements of information (although it is not very clear how this is achieved). As we saw earlier, one factor which plays a part in this process is the speaker's own motivations at a particular point in time. Consequently, for a hearer less interested in proving that individual responsibility for attacking the BBC lies with NT, there may be less motivation to run beliefs about the CODL (as NT) as opposed to attributively (as whoever he may be) (see Gibbs, 1987: 582 on some relevant experimental evidence related to selective reference location).

Evidence for this suggestion can be found in one view of the way in which beliefs are organized. Social psychologists have noted in experiments where subjects' beliefs have been manipulated, that such subjects find it difficult to re-adjust their belief system when the 'contrived and inauthentic nature' of the information they have been given is revealed (see Ross and Anderson, 1982; Harman, 1986). It has been suggested that many beliefs, once established, are maintained by a kind of 'habit theory' (Harman, 1986: 37), and that such beliefs may even be neurologically salient (see Goldman, 1978; cf. Harman, 1986).

Taking up a point made earlier, that the speaker would be expected when talking of himself/herself to make it clear that that is what they are doing (see Boër and Lycan, 1980; 1986), and treating this expectation as a general belief which we would accept unless motivated to reject, then for those hearers who know NT = CODL, but who are not motivated to pay any particular attention to such a fact, the habit of believing that where a speaker talks of himself/herself, he/she will make this clear, may lead them to run beliefs within an environment similar to that constructed by hearers who do not know NT = CODL. Put simply, since NT has not used any explicitly available self-referential form he is not referring to himself. This is a kind of default (if startling) argument whereby unless the hearer is motivated otherwise, all speaker-generic references to self will be treated as attributive rather than referential.

This would account for Nixon's use of definite referring forms where simple pronominals were available. His choice leads the hearer away from a specific identification, and creates an attributive view of the President, whoever he may be. Clearly, in terms of existential involvement, the use of definite descriptions in certain discourse environments has a specific advantage, in that one can exploit the ambiguity of involvement for specific political needs (as was the case with specific pronominal selection; see chapter 3).

The problem here of course, is that such an argument seems to contradict the classic Gricean view, that when speakers flout maxims of behaviour they imply information above and beyond the surface interpretation of the utterance itself. But this is of course a speaker intention; if the hearer, for his or her own purposes, can make sense of the speaker's utterance using the surface form alone, and there is no self-motivating reason to process the utterance any further (hearer intention) then he/she is free to do so. Example cases of conversational implicature within the literature are frequently extreme in that no further sense can be made of the ongoing discourse without recourse to some implicated information. In the case of the NT utterance, hearers who are aware that NT = CODL can still make sense of what is said without explicitly accessing the fact that NT = CODL; they are free to ignore such facts. We should not assume that simply because our theory suggests that further information can be gleaned by processing implicatures that it is compulsory for hearers to do so. I can find nothing wrong with the following interchange:

(18) A: NT was just trying to worm his way out of the situation.
      B: No he was just indicating that he was doing his job.
      C: What do you mean?
      A: Well NT is the CODL.
      C: Of course, that's right, but its not really relevant: someone has to deal with the BBC.

In (18) speaker A has processed the information that NT = CODL and come to a particular conclusion about this; B has processed the same information and come to a different conclusion; C didn't process the information at all although he/she had access to such information, but for C the information isn't relevant anyway since he/she sees a general logic to the argument relative to whoever the CODL is.

Taking account of such facts, my argument does not contradict Grice's position but rather complements it. As Johnson-Laird and Garnham (1980) suggested, information is processed relative to both speaker and hearer models of the world. To suggest of any utterance that it carries an implicature indicates only a potentiality for interpretation (as with indirect speech acts several levels of interpretation may be possible). Speakers may intend an implicature to be calculated or they may not; hearers may calculate an implicature or they may not. Speakers/hearers perform interpretation in terms of their own interests and motivations; these may coincide for discourse processing, but in many cases this is not a sine qua non. Consequently, we should not think of relevance as an optimal informational state agreed by participants (in many cases participants, intentions may only vaguely overlap). This is the ideal, but in real-time discourse there are too many intervening variables to guarantee complete co-ordination of speaker/hearer interests and interpretations.

If my argument is correct it increases the validity of choosing a referring form which, while self-referential, could be treated as attributive, particularly in those circumstances where one wishes to deflect personal responsibility. Since you cannot deter the motivated hearer from tagging you with blame, you can at least attempt to offset this fact by leading the general audience to either a non-identification-based conclusion, or an identity-based conclusion with the added, and mitigating, implicature that you are only doing your job.

This view further suggests that one must be careful in extrapolating from theories of relevance to the processing of relevance in the real world. As Johnson-Laird and Garnham point out, it is possible for the speaker and hearer to operate with different views of the world (which may be adjusted, if necessary, in processing input). Consequently, relevance is itself relative to the contents of speaker/hearer models of the world, and the speaker/hearer's motivation in processing and accessing certain information within such models. This is not, in itself, a criticism of *relevance theory*, particularly where such a theory aims only to delimit underlying or basic cognitive principles. Such principles may remain constant even though the outcomes in terms of the processing of the same information context by different individuals may be different. The point is rather that in searching for pragmatic intentions in actual contexts one must be careful in assuming that these are easily captured by unitary implicature types.

Conclusion

The argument has been that, in some circumstances, when a speaker uses certain kinds of definite description to self-refer, he/she may be attempting to deter the hearer from attaching beliefs or associations, connected with whoever or whatever is delimited by the definite description, to the speaker him/herself.

How this is actually achieved is difficult to specify in exact terms. But we have argued here that where the hearer is not motivated to seek a referentially specific indentity, he/she may simply treat the description as generic as opposed to attributive and run beliefs about the referring description in these terms, with the consequence, of course, that any conclusions or inferences which follow from the belief environment are not bound to any designated individual. Even where the hearer does not run beliefs in a referential mode, the extra processing effort may lead to a mitigating implicature (but this is not guaranteed).

5

Power to the People: Political Metaphors

Now the trumpet summons us again – not as a call to bear arms,
though arms we need – not as a call to battle, though embattled
we are – but a call to bear the burden of a long twilight struggle.
J. F. Kennedy, 1962, in G. W. Johnson, *The Kennedy*
Presidential Press Conferences

Introduction

Metaphors and metaphorical language have a central role to play in
political communication. In general, metaphors can assist in the
explanation of complex political arguments by reducing such arguments to a metaphorical form. They may be employed for connotative
or emotional purposes in arousing emotions and reinforcing particular
perspectives, and they can be used to elicit absurd images which can
then be employed for the purposes of ridiculing one's opponent. (1),
(2) and (3) represent examples of just these points:

(1) inflation runs aways with your most cherished plans – not
to mention your savings. (Mrs Thatcher: Cardiff, 1987)
(2) And constantly I seek to look beyond the doors of the
White House, beyond the officialdom of the national
capital, into the hopes and fears of men and women in
their own home. (Franklin D. Roosevelt: 14 April, 1938)
(3) Custard pie conservatives and slapstick social democrats
hurling social abuse (Neil Kennock, 1987)

The complex economic issues of inflation may be more easily

understood when they are personified through what Lakoff and Johnson (1980: 25) call 'ontological metaphors'. In (1) inflation acts like someone or something which runs away with (steals) your money, and destroys your plans. In (2) Roosevelt makes an emotional plea on a singularly personal level (what Jasinski (1988: 19) calls a 'privatistic turn'), rejecting the distance of power and status and indicating a concern with the basic and personal concerns of individuals. And, finally, in (3) we have the image of political party members behaving as participants in some classic comedy routine.

It is not suggested that these examples in any way represent a definitive set of the possible uses of metaphor within political communication; they are merely illustrative of some of the major functions which metaphors can fulfil. The question is, however, how do metaphors achieve their function in general and where this can be explained, how can such an explanation allow us any insight into the specific orientation of metaphors within political communication? In order to deal with these questions this chapter will, firstly, consider the status of metaphors as pragmatic phenomena. After considering how metaphors may be explained utilizing specific components of pragmatic theory, various examples of metaphors employed within political communication will be analysed in an effort to gain some general understanding of how they operate within political talk, and how various politicians draw upon metaphors as a communicative resource.

Metaphors and Pragmatics

Metaphors represent core examples of language use where any intended meaning is normally assumed to be located beyond the surface structure of the sentence/utterance. In this sense metaphors seem prime candidates for pragmatic analysis. Certainly this is John Searle's view. Searle (1979b) argues that in using metaphors speakers say S is P but mean (metaphorically) that S is R. This is an example of what Cooper (1986) calls the 'standard view' of metaphor, wherein the literal form of an utterance or sentence, which has been employed metaphorically, is assumed in some way to be 'perverse' or 'defective'. For Searle this is the first step in interpreting an utterance or sentence as being metaphorical: 'Where an utterance is defective if taken literally, look for an utterance meaning that differs from sentence meaning' (Searle, 1979b: 114). Once a speaker recognizes any perversity then, argues Searle, they must 'Go back to the S term and see which of the many candidates for the values of R are likely or even possible properties of R' (Searle 1979b: 115).

In terms of the approach we have been developing in this book, Searle's interpretation suggests that metaphors represent, potentially, another example of what we have been calling (following Lycan, 1986) an 'implicational type'. However, in the case of metaphor, it has often proved difficult to describe in a precise sense how any implications are accessed and interpreted. Searle's approach suggests that the process involves the hearer in first noting that the meaning of what the speaker has said, if taken literally, is defective in some way, a view supported, in the main, by the theory of conversation developed by Grice (1975).

There are a number of problems here according to Cooper (1986). First, there is an assumption that we may easily distinguish that which is literal from that which is not; and second, even where such a distinction is made, to treat a non-literal (metaphorical) example of language as defective is to suggest that metaphors are perverse uses of language.

In this chapter I want to suggest that these problems are perceived rather than real. It will be argued that metaphors are clearly pragmatic phenomena, and that they behave, and may be accounted for, in basically the same manner as other pragmatic phenomena. The aim is to produce an explicit account of the pragmatic nature of metaphor which may be utilized in the analysis of political examples of metaphorical language. It is not the purpose of the chapter to present a full and detailed account of the historical and general theoretical background of metaphor. Such an account is beyond the bounds of this chapter, and the book as whole; for the reader interested in metaphors in general the following texts are recommended as a useful starting point: Ricoeur, 1978; Ortony, 1979; Cooper, 1986. Some time will be given, however, to the consideration of a number of basic theories which impinge on the development of metaphor as a pragmatic construct.

The Problem with Metaphor

The most basic question of all is, what is metaphor? This can be both a substantive and a taxonomic question. The taxonomic question focuses on the demarcation of metaphor in relation to other related 'figures of speech' (or tropes), such as synecdoche, metonymy, irony, litotes and so on; the substantive question focuses on the issue of how these types of non-literal speech are distinguished from literal speech.

In this chapter we will accept a broad Aristotelian view of metaphor, and concentrate our energies on the substantive issue.

In using the terms literal and non-literal it is assumed that whenever a metaphor is employed the words/sentence will be interpreted non-literally. There is some debate on this point, particularly in relation to what have been called *dead metaphors*. If I say 'Joe has kicked the bucket', meaning that he has died, it can be argued that what I have said is literal, in that the phrase 'kick the bucket' has now come to mean simply that someone has died. There is no need in this case to construct a literal meaning, look for perversity, and then search for a more logical and reasonable alternative. If this is the case, when I say 'Joe has kicked the bucket' then I mean *literally* that Joe has died.

One problem here, of course, is that we create another demarcation problem, this time between those metaphors which are 'live', and which therefore act to convey meaning beyond the literal content, and those which are 'dead', and therefore, in one sense, not metaphors at all, but rather simply sentences/utterances which are to be interpreted literally. Lakoff and Johnson (1980) suggest that there is a continuum which operates between those metaphors which are 'live' and those which are 'dead'. However, while this is theoretically plausible there are no hard and fast rules for deciding at which point on the scale any particular metaphor lies. Further, Lakoff and Johnson suggest that since our conceptual view of the world is mediated by the kinds of metaphors we employ to structure our experience, then metaphors, as found for example in the language of argument (to defend/attack a position; demolish/shoot down an argument), are not 'poetic, fanciful, or rhetorical' but literal (Lakoff and Johnson, 1980: 5).

Once again, however, such an interpretation will be based on the way in which the term literal is employed. But we must be careful in any assessment of Lakoff and Johnson's claims, since for them metaphor is 'not merely in the words we use' (1980: 3). When Lakoff and Johnson talk of metaphor they refer to a cognitive object, a 'metaphorical concept'. If, as Lakoff and Johnson suggest, we really do represent arguments in terms of some conceptual form like 'argument is war', then in one sense this may indeed be literal: in this case I do not think of argument as being like war, but actually as war. Does this mean, then, that literal does not, as one might think of it in common-sense terms, mean the relationship between the words and the world, but rather a relationship between the words and a motivating conceptual system which is metaphorically encoded or represented?

In one sense the answer is yes, and this representation is, in many ways, a reflection of the way in which a particular culture has decided to reflect or think about the world. For example, in Western culture the metaphor 'time is money' is used as a source for talking about 'time' as a valuable commodity, and for indicating that, like money, time can be saved, wasted, invested put aside, restricted and so on. But on the other hand, Lakoff and Johnson also talk of what they call 'metaphorical projection', which involves 'understanding one kind of thing in terms of another'. Non-metaphorical projection involves the understanding of only one kind of thing. If this is so, then a metaphorical concept must be one which is derived by comparing one thing with another, which suggests that it is not literal. On the other hand, as we have noted, the metaphorical concept has a certain kind of cognitive reality, which suggests that in one sense it may be literal. This would mean, as noted by Cooper (1986), that certain forms may come to be seen as both metaphorical and literal.

Deciding that which is literal and that which is non-literal is a complicating factor in the analysis of metaphor. Nevertheless, whatever the decision here, there are certain other basic facts on which almost all analysts are agreed. From Aristotle to the present day, theories of metaphor have indicated that metaphorical language is relational; one element is used to elicit, or generate, some understanding of another element (or elements).

Early substitution theories described this relational behaviour by arguing that metaphors are understood in terms of available literal paraphrases. Despite the fact that in many cases no literal paraphrase seems available (as in 'Juliet is the Sun' for example), but the question is, why would a speaker employ a metaphor if a clear and literal form was available? Indeed, psychological research on metaphor suggests that metaphors may in part be employed to allow us to talk about experiences which cannot be literally described'; what is sometimes referred to as the 'inexpressibility thesis' (Paivio, 1979: 152).

The 'comparison theory' of metaphor is, in many ways, a more complex version of the substitution principle, with in this case the sentence to be substituted being a literal simile. In the case of something like 'that man is a pig', this would mean, 'that man is like a pig'. Searle (1979b) has criticized this perspective from a number of angles. It fails, according to Searle, to tell us exactly how we compute an intended metaphorical meaning from a substituted simile (which is itself in many ways figurative); it simply tells us that two things can be compared in terms of similarity. This is vacuous, argues Searle, in that any two things can be shown to be similar to each other in some way.

Searle's alternative thesis, as we have seen above, is to argue that metaphors work on the basis of recognizing that the meaning of what has been said is in some way defective, and that therefore the speaker is directing the hearer to reconsider the sentence/utterance in terms of available knowledge of those things being talked about. For example, Searle notes that if one is told that 'Sam's car is a pig,' then any interpretation of this will be different from interpreting simply 'Sam is a pig'. One has to use knowledge not only of what pigs are like, but what they are like in comparison with specific aspects of the target sentence.

In the end of course, Searle is, in essence, still arguing that one element is compared with another in order to gain access to relevant and salient aspects of meaning as intended by the speaker. Searle does, however, explain one way in which this process might take place, with a first step being a recognition that the literal meaning is somehow perverse within the specific context of production.

In a similar sense Grice (1975) makes the same point when he talks of 'implicatures' arising where there has been a gross violation of expected conversational norms (see chapter 2). So if one says 'you're the cream in my coffee,' the violation of Grice's maxim of truthfulness may lead the hearer to an interpretation which compares some person with aspects of the role (or perhaps the substance) of cream in coffee.

Cooper (1986) criticizes this 'standard view' of metaphor, as represented by Searle and Grice, because, despite the fact that both Searle and Grice attempt to get at what the speaker meant by saying X, they do so by implying that metaphor is in some sense a perverse use of language. Cooper, along with Davidson (1984), wants to argue that metaphors are not perverse, nor do they represent some form of meaning beyond the sentence, they are rather 'true or false in a normal, literal way'.

The problem for Cooper is that Grice and Searle's versions of how metaphors operate seem to represent gross violations of what he calls the 'transparency principle', which indicates, basically, that speakers should mean what they say, even if, according to Gricean principles, they also mean something beyond what is said. According to the Gricean view of metaphor however, any understanding is dependent on the flouting of the maxim of truthfulness, which for Cooper suggests that the speaker does not therefore mean what he/she has said, and has consequently breached the 'transparency principle'. One problem with this 'transparency principle', of course, is that if the speaker must always mean what he/she says it becomes impossible to say anything meaningless, unless we treat meaninglessness as a general semantic phenomenon where what is said is marked simply as false.

Nevertheless, the example Cooper gives is instructive here. According to Gricean maxims speakers may say that which is true, yet still intend to convey further meaning beyond that which has been truthfully presented. For example, in response to a statement by a motorist that he has run out of petrol, I might say, 'there is a garage around the corner.' I believe what I have said is true, but further, if I am to abide by the general tenets of the co-operative principle, I could also be shown to have implicated the further information that I believe the garage to be open and that it has petrol. This further information is implicated from what I have said if the hearer assumes that I am abiding by Gricean principles of co-operation.

This is different, argues Cooper, from the case of metaphor. If we look at a statement such as 'you are the cream in my coffee,' any implications which follow, follow because the maxims of conversation have been flouted in some manner. Cooper sees these two cases as radically different. In the garage example, I mean what I say, but also, in terms of the general principles of conversation, I imply some further information beyond the simple meaning of the words I have employed. In the metaphor example, however, Cooper argues that any implications which are derived are derived because one assumes that the speaker does not mean what he/she has said; any implications follow from the assumption that the speaker does not adhere to the meaning of the sentence he/she has employed, but to some implied meaning to be calculated using Gricean principles. In order to explain metaphors, argues Cooper, Grice has to assume that there is something wrong with the meaning of what has been said, and metaphors are treated, therefore, as perverse uses of language, something Cooper wants to reject.

For Davidson (1984), whose views Cooper is basically in agreement with, the issue of perversity, or meaning beyond surface structure, does not basically arise, simply because Davidson argues that metaphors mean literally what it is they say. This is the radical 'metaphor without meaning' view (see Cooper, 1986). This radical perspective refutes the claim that metaphors have a special kind of meaning or cognitive content; they mean simply what they say. Davidson does not deny that by employing a metaphor the speaker can intend all kinds of meaning to be taken up; he simply denies that these emerge from the meanings of the words in themselves. Davidson is in agreement with Searle and Grice on this level, in that he accepts that metaphor belongs exclusively to the domain of use, he does not accept, however, that the fact that extra meaning may be gleaned from the use of certain words means that these words do not also mean something in a quite normal way.

Now how different is all this from the claims of Grice and Searle?

According to Cooper the problem with Grice and Searle is that they assume that in metaphor the sentence does not mean what it says but means instead something else, some form of metaphorical meaning. The issue it seems to me hangs on the use of the term 'meaning', and in turn the perhaps regrettable use of terms like 'defective' and 'perverse'.

Let us look more closely at Cooper's distinction between the implicatures derived from the garage example, and those derived from the example of metaphor. Cooper suggests that in the first case the speaker means what he/she says, but also implies something else; however, in the second case the speaker does not mean what he/she says, but intends to imply something else. What makes us assume that the speaker who uses metaphor does not mean what they say? Where does this notion of defectiveness come from?

Basically, the problem seems to be that the speaker produces a sentence which is false (although this need not always be the case; see below), a sentence which represents a specific state of the world in which the conditions outlined by the sentence do not hold. This is assumed to be 'defective' because, unlike cases where the speaker is simply mistaken, the speaker is well aware of the failure of the sentence to represent a truthful picture of the world. And it is different from lying because the speaker knows that the hearer is well aware that the speaker knows that what he/she has said is false, and that the speaker knows the hearer knows this to be true (for a more precise view of the act of lying see Verschueren, 1985). All I am saying here is that you cannot successfully perform an act of lying when the hearer believes that you want to make it clear that what you have said is intentionally false. But what is the defect? There can only be a defect if there is a norm or expectation of behaviour, or production, which has failed. In Grice and Searle's sense this failure is one wherein there is an expectation of truthfulness, that one would not intentionally say that which is false, specifically where the aim is to have that intention recognized, unless one wished to say something beyond the meanings of the words themselves.

This seems reasonable, but it doesn't necessarily invalidate the meaning of the sentence per se. It seems to me that with the example 'you're the cream in my coffee,' as in the case of the garage example, the speaker (as claimed by Davidson, 1984) means what he/she says, and that the meaning of what is said is simply false. As in the garage example, where the hearer had to assume some further information beyond what was said in order to accommodate a belief that the speaker was at least abiding by the co-operative principle, so in the metaphor example the hearer has to make the very same assumptions. The fact that in the garage example what was said was true, while in the metaphor example what was said was false, is not the point, since in neither case is successful communication possible without further information above and beyond the words themselves. The garage example and the metaphor example are equally defective at the level of communication unless the speaker can glean some relevant information. In both cases it is possible to say that the speakers meant what they said but that they also meant more.

The issue is one of where any defect arises. If metaphor were a perverse use of language simply because no relevant message could be gleaned on the basis of the meanings of the words alone, then almost all examples of conversational implicatures would fall into the same class. The meanings of the words are an input into a context, along with other elements like shared knowledge and Gricean principles themselves, and it is out of the interaction of these elements that some sense is gleaned. Any defect in terms of what the speaker says only arises from this interaction, and not from the meanings of the words alone. I think this is what Searle really means when he uses the term 'perverse' or 'defective'.

This argument allows me to bring together a number of disparate accounts of metaphor. First, it maintains the idea that there is some underlying principle/principles operating within communication, and that the meaning of what is said is assessed in relation to how far the meaning of what has been said allows the speaker to adhere to this underlying principle or principles. This is exemplified in much recent work within pragmatics, for example Atlas and Levinson, 1980; Sperber and Wilson, 1986; Blakemore, 1987; Horn, 1987; Kempson, 1987; Levinson, 1987. Although there are several core differences in the theoretical approach of a number of these cited authors, they all seem to agree that, in a variety of uses of language, there is meaning beyond the surface form of what is said, and that this meaning is accessed through some variation or extension of Grice's model of conversational interaction.

The point, particularly with reference to metaphor, is clearly articulated in the work of Sperber and Wilson (1986) (see also chapter 4) who have developed an overarching principle of communication (developed, as noted, from the general starting point provided by Grice), the principle of relevance. The principle of relevance states that what speakers say must be assessed within context in terms of the information provided, relative to the amount of processing required to get at that information. One should attempt to provide a balance between the information gained and the amount of effort put in. If a hearer recognizes that a more complex statement has been made where a simpler one would have conveyed the same information, then in order for the principle of relevance to hold the hearer must assume that there is some extra pay-off in terms of information which justifies this extra processing effort. An example of how this works was given in chapter 4. But a metaphorical example will be useful here:

(2)   This room is a pigsty. (adapted from Sperber and Wilson, 1986: 236)

On receiving (2) the hearer will access general knowledge that indicates that pigsties are stereotypically filthy places, which suggests that what the speaker intends to convey is that the room is filthy, and untidy. But since the speaker could just as easily have employed a literal phrase to convey the same information, in order to abide by the principle of relevance there must be further information available in (2). In this case perhaps that the room is *excessively* filthy and untidy.

In example (2) the metaphor is a fairly standard one, and the information conveyed is, in Sperber and Wilson's terms, 'strongly implicated'. More complex metaphors, however, may generate many assumptions where it is unclear which of these the speaker may have intended. (3), according to Sperber and Wilson, will generate a wider range of potential implications, with no strong implicature necessarily coming to mind. This set of weaker implications is linked to 'Robert's persistence, obstinacy, insensitivity and refusal to be deflected'.

(3)   Robert is a bulldozer. (from Sperber and Wilson 1986: 236)

The interesting point here is that the less standard, or more live, the metaphor, the more work the hearer has to do in sorting out the range of implicatures. Sperber and Wilson note that this may be best revealed within literature, where the hearer gains in some aesthetic manner from the effort they put in. The stronger and more original the metaphor the greater the variety of possible interpretations.

It is not clear, however, how this notion of a range of 'weak implicatures' differs from the general claim by Schon (1979) that metaphors (original or otherwise) are 'generative'. The term *generative* is adopted by Schon to indicate the way in which metaphors are used to allow us to look at things in different ways. Schon notes the example of researchers working on the improvement of a new type of paintbrush who tackle the problem by thinking of the paintbrush as a *pump*. Using this metaphor the researcher can consider the paintbrush from a completely different perspective, and he can generate ideas on the basis of the metaphor itself. This is also similar to Lakoff and Johnson's position, where they argue that a core conceptual metaphor, such as 'argument is war', may generate a variety of metaphorical perspectives on arguments.

The question is, what is the relationship, if any, between the set of implicatures 'weakly' produced by a metaphor, and the set of perspectives generated by a metaphor? If I say that an argument is war, then I may implicate all kinds of things; I may also generate various perspectives on arguments, and both these implicatures and perspectives may overlap. Further, since we are talking about a set of possible implicatures, is there any mechanism for ordering this set, as one finds with scalar and clausal implicatures for example?

This second question is important in considering the intentions of the speaker, since where a range of 'weakly' generated implicatures are possible we must ask whether the speaker is quite content with a range of interpretations, or whether he would prefer one interpretation from the possible set. Where such a preference exists, it is difficult to see how it might be achieved in metaphor, other than, of course, by choosing a more restricted type of metaphor along the live/dead continuum.

We will not consider the first question about implicatures versus perspectives any further here, since the label we attach to any metaphorically created meanings is not the main issue for us, rather the main issue is how we get at any metaphorically created meanings. Sperber and Wilson's view explains the principles which direct the hearer beyond the surface meaning, and in this sense it is at least a useful starting point. Further, as Levinson (1987) notes, 'among the range of alternative explanations of implicatures presently on offer, Sperber and Wilson's theory emphasizes the particularised' aspect of implicature theory as opposed to the 'generalised' (where much of Levinson's own work might be located). The point here is that metaphors are very much contextually generated, and as such, to respond to an earlier question noted above, it is difficult to see how the issue of multiple interpretational choices could be resolved by focusing on surface structure choices alone.

If we accept the argument put by Sperber and Wilson, then the more *live* the metaphor the more work the hearer will have to do, and consequently, from this extra effort, some other relevant information will be gained beyond simply the meaning of what has been said. Of course, exactly what this will be may vary for each hearer, since, as we saw in chapter 4, each hearer will bring their own idiosyncratic perspectives to bear on what has been said. This suggests, as in our discussion of definite descriptions, one cannot guarantee exactly how certain metaphors will be interpreted.

The consequences of this for political communication suggest that some care in selecting metaphors may be necessary in terms of the particular aim one wants to achieve, not merely in terms of the quality of the metaphor chosen, but in terms of the control one has over any potential interpretation.

To sum up: metaphors are pragmatic phenomena in that there is information conveyed above and beyond the surface form of what has been said; this is accessed because in assessing the meaning of what has been said as input into a theory of communication (such as Grice's model; or in a more advanced form the model developed by Sperber and Wilson) one must assume (and calculate) further meaning in order to make sense (relevance) of the interaction.

Knowing this, however, does not tell us how specific interpretations are accessed at the more *live* end of the metaphorical scale. On the other hand, it does suggest a possible constraint as one moves to the opposite end of the scale, in this case where the more standard or dead metaphors would be located. One interesting question, then, from the political perspective, is how do politicians employ metaphors in terms of the relative scale of metaphoricalness, with the attendant variation in possible limits of interpretation between the open-endedness of live metaphors and the closed set of possibilities generated by dead metaphors?

Metaphors and Politics

In discussing the pragmatic nature of metaphor, I suggested that the distinction between *live* and *dead* metaphors might be described in relation to the relative number of potential (strong and weak) implicatures generated by the choice of metaphor. The problem is, of course, how do we actually calculate these, since any interpretation may vary with each individual speaker. Let us begin our exploration of the pragmatics of political metaphor with a much less ambitious aim, and simply consider, first, how political metaphors may be described as pragmatic constructs.

Consider the following statement made by Ronald Reagan:

(4)   The Lady standing in the harbour has never betrayed us
once.

One of the first things to note about this statement is that without
further contextual information we cannot even decide if this is metaphorical or not, since under one interpretation this statement might
describe an explicit state of affairs in the real world (an example of
the particularized nature of metaphor). Something which we will
return to later is the fact that many metaphors not only cannot be
understood independently of the context in which they occur, but also,
many others gain their sense in relation to the ongoing development of
the discourse sequence.

For the moment let us note that Reagan has made his statement as
part of a speech delivered in the area of New York Harbour, against
the backdrop of New York City, and in particular the prominent
figure of the Statue of Liberty. Interestingly, in the light of the
argument between, on the one side, Cooper and Davidson, and on
the other, Searle and Grice, this statement could be seen as expressing
a semantic truth, but yet still be pragmatically defective. Decompos-
itionally speaking (see Katz, 1987), since the statue is not a lady in
any human sense, the issue of betrayal does not arise, and therefore
what Reagan has said is necessarily true. While this is the case it
would be like claiming that someone who says 'that bachelor is an
unmarried man' has also spoken the truth. Logically this would be
so; however, were such a statement to be made in real-time interaction
it would be interpreted as particularly odd, since it conveys no real
information. It is for this reason that we must look beyond the
meanings of the words themselves in order, in Sperber and Wilson's
terms, to achieve some relevance.

Let us take Reagan's statement in two parts. The first part refers
to 'the Lady standing in the harbour'. What implicatures can we
generate from this? If we look at the statement, using the general
deductive procedures suggested by Sperber and Wilson, we might
suggest that the following assumptions are conveyed (or in more
technical terms, serve as premises):

1   The phrase 'the Lady' refers to the Statue of Liberty.
2   The term 'lady' is normally used to refer to animate objects; the
Statue is not an animate object.
3   The President wishes me to think about the Statue as being like
a real person.
4   The Statue of Liberty is a symbol of American values of freedom
and liberty.

At this point we might argue that the metaphorical projection is one whereby the Statue is imbued with an animate persona; and the Statue itself is noted as having symbolic meaning for the American people.

While this makes some sense, we might recall Donnellan's (1966; see also chapter 4) distinction between *attributive* and *referential* uses of definite descriptions. In one sense, it doesn't matter if the statue does not have an animate persona, if Reagan's aim was to draw our attention to, refer to, the Statue of Liberty, since, according to Donnellan's description of *referential* uses, they are successful if they allow the hearer to pick out the object. In this case it is possible for some hearers to simply interpret Reagan as talking about the Statue without drawing any further implications at this point. This means simply that there is no need to access assumptions about 'ladies', as compared with 'Statues' and so on, one simply accesses 'the Statue of Liberty' since this is the object that Reagan is referring to. Clearly, there are implications here for the amount of processing effort involved, since, where one adopts the referential view, 'the Statue of Liberty' is accessed directly, without the need for any intermediate processing, a point we will return to in a moment.

Taking a look at the second part of the statement, 'has never betrayed us once', what meaning we get here is dependent on how we interpret the first part. We have two possibilities at present. One indicates that we are thinking about the statue in terms of an animate and female persona, the other simply indicates that we are thinking about the Statue of Liberty as a specific object. In both cases, where 'the Statue of Liberty' is accesssed, it is likely that, using general encyclopaedic knowledge, we will also access, as part of our understanding of the statue, that it is symbolic of American values of liberty and justice, values which 'true' Americans could be said to exemplify.

In this sense, what Reagan is claiming is that America and Americans have not betrayed their values of freedom, liberty and justice. Now the same conclusion can be reached whether one takes a purely referential approach, or an approach which has as first step an analysis of the use of the term 'lady' in relation to inanimate objects like statues. The problem is that in this second approach there are more premises required, and presumably, this would require more processing effort, without any clear pay-off in terms of extra informational content.

The problem is whether the first part of what Reagan has said should be treated as a 'dead metaphor', in which case it would act purely referentially, and no further processing would be required, other than accessing 'the Statue of Liberty' along with any general knowledge one had of the symbolic role of the Statue. The difficulty here is, who is going to decide whether the first part of the statement is 'dead' in metaphorical terms?

We could, of course, note the fact that people frequently refer to statues, boats, cars, individuals in portrait paintings, etc., in animate terms, often imbuing them with human characteristics. Nevertheless, the example from Reagan indicates some of the difficulties in interpreting how information is being processed in terms of metaphorical relevance.

Sperber and Wilson's theory is based on the premise that relevance is achieved by deductively assessing the informational balance between processing cost and information gained. The theory would resolve our dilemma here, presumably, by arguing there is least effort in processing the first part of the statement as a 'dead metaphor', or something like a dead metaphor, since the hearer achieves basically the same level of understanding as that which would have been achieved by attempting to work through some step of comparison involving animate and inanimate objects. This seems correct, but would it be true to say that all hearers took the same route and reached exactly the same conclusion; or is it possible that some may have taken the first part of the statement literally and worked from there, not simply to American values, but the values of particular types of individual Americans, where the hearer believes himself/herself to be one for example; or where the hearer identifies Ronald Reagan as an exemplar of the type of American who would never betray the people, or indeed the values for which they stand? This is of course speculation (although see below), but in political terms this extended interpretation may be more worthwhile from Reagan's perspective, although I am not suggesting this is what Reagan intended (see however, Norris and Whitehouse, 1988).

Even if what I have suggested were correct, Sperber and Wilson would of course claim that the noted extra work was giving some more informational pay-off. But this means that the theory is correct whichever route we take. This may be a reflection of the power of the theory. On the other hand, there is no guarantee that anyone who takes the longer processing route will also necessarily come up with any further information. What I mean by this is that since Reagan has employed a metaphor in the first place, different hearers may process different amounts of information with the same conclusion, and each will justify the effort put into processing in terms of the relevance achieved; where the relevance in this case is in terms of exactly the same conclusion for each speaker. The result of this is that since we have no way of comparing the actual amount of processing needed to achieve a particular conclusion, two speakers who have employed different amounts of processing time to achieve the same conclusion could both be shown to be adhering to the principle of relevance since they both gained from the extra effort put in. The fact that one of the speakers could have taken a shorter processing route to the conclusion is not the point, since we cannot assume that speakers will always compute the exact and mathematically optimal relevant choice.

As we have already noted, however, Sperber and Wilson admit that one cannot guarantee how any message will be specifically interpreted on an individual level, their main point is that the interpretational process is bound by the principle of relevance and an effort to achieve a balance between processing effort and informational content. On the other hand, relevance was introduced as a principle which helped guide and control the number of premises one would employ in processing information, since in theory one could employ any premises one wanted, but clearly this would not be acceptable where the main aim was to balance processing cost with informational output.

It seems that if I process information about ladies, animate objects, inanimate objects, symbolic relationships, etc., in Reagan's statement, then this will be acceptable if I can be shown to have gained more information from this route than if I had simply accessed 'the Statue of Liberty' as a referential object. On the other hand what is the status of this extra processing where I do not achieve any informational gain?

Within limits one might not expect Sperber and Wilson's theory to take account of particular idiosyncratic quirks in the selection of individual processing routes. Nevertheless, there seems to be something missing here and perhaps, at times, we are too ready to adopt individual variation as a way of solving our problems. While we cannot, of course, guarantee how a message will be processed in terms of achieving the same outcome, there may be other constraints operating alongside that of relevance which might help us understand the possible weighting of individual choices.

Sperber and Wilson are open to the possibility of other than deductive constraints operating in the processing of information, and they have speculated on such a possibility. While their model of relevance processing is *deductive*, they suggest that 'We would expect . . . the deductive device to be complemented with some non deductive or not directly deductive procedures for checking validity whenever the deductive machinery is insufficient' (Sperber and Wilson, 1986: 102).

The introduction of another non-deductive device is offered in order to explain conclusions which may not have been derived directly from deductive rules. We cannot, at this point, enter into a direct debate about the deductive nature of the model of relevance (or whether it is deductive at all: see Popper, 1963; 1978; Levinson, 1983; 1987), but in order to explain any constraint on the operation of the two possible routes we have discussed as legitimate ways of interpreting the Reagan metaphor, we need to look more closely at the assumptions which serve as input to the deduction of any implicature(s).

We are not interested in where these assumptions come from (they may be from general knowledge, mutual knowledge, knowledge of the linguistic system and so on) but rather their status in terms of any assigned truth value. In a deductive system an argument is valid where the truth of the conclusion is guaranteed by the truth of the premises. In real-world interaction, assumptions (or 'factual assumptions' as Sperber and Wilson refer to them: 1986: 75) are frequently not guaranteed as either true or false, but rather they are held to be true by speakers/hearers with varying degrees of strength. This means simply that you believe some assumptions that you hold to be more or less likely to be true. Consequently, the premises employed, in most cases, in the derivation of particular conclusions (implicatures) are not categorical but probabilistic.

This is not to say that individuals compute exact values for any premise, a point noted by Sperber and Wilson (1986: 76–9). Sperber and Wilson suggest (following Carnap, 1950) that these assumptions are assessed *comparatively*, which means simply that they are treated like gradable forms as being more or less of a type; for example, some puzzles are easier than others; some mountains higher than others and so on.

The reference to Carnap's work seems a bit dated, especially for a theory which focuses so centrally on cognitive processes. There is a range of experimental and computational work now available which considers how reasoning operates under conditions of uncertainty; that is conditions where the outcomes cannot be guaranteed (see for example, Kahnemann et al., 1982; Cohen, 1985). Since most premises which enter into the deductive computations of implicatures are essentially probabilistic (which as I have noted is not to say that individuals compute specific numerical values), it would be worthwhile to consider what evidence there is on how the processing of decisions under uncertainty operates. How are assumptions selected and entered as premises in the first place for example? This alternative approach seems particularly apt in the case of metaphors, which as we noted above may generate a range of interpretations without any clear guide as to which is the correct one, or whether, indeed, there is any correct interpretation intended.

Calculating Interpretations

Recent work by Kuipers et al. (1988) on the making of critical medical decisions in contexts of uncertainty confirms Sperber and Wilson's argument that individuals do not compute, for any assumption, an exact numerical value, as predicted by mathematical probability models for example. What individuals do is to abstract simplified information from a set of alternatives available to them, leaving the introduction of relevant and more detailed information until later. Basically, what this means is that decisions are reached fairly quickly with limited input, even where more information germane to any decision is available. Decisions are based on a process of refinement where abstract general statements are incrementally refined in the light of more detailed information.

In the study by Kuipers et al., it was noted that doctors dealing with a difficult medical problem broke the problem up into locally manageable units. This seems sensible enough, but information from different units impinged on each other, and access to non-local information relevant to solving a particular unit issue was not always assessed. However, with the limited processing facilities of the human brain this may be the best way to approach problems, because one cannot hold in memory all the necessary components which might be relevant to a specific problem at a single point in time.

What is particularly interesting about what Kuipers et al. found was that while the planning involved in solving a decision problem was logically ordered, it also frequently involved what Hayes-Roth and Hayes-Roth (1979) refer to as 'opportunistic planning': 'Their model predicts that the different steps of the planning process will not be strictly ordered: their sequence will be determined partly by the structure of the problem and partly by which information happens to be available or which inferences happen to be activated at which times' (Kuipers et al., 1988: 196). Within this perspective assumptions employed in decision-making were symbolic representations which were marked as *landmarks* in terms of their 'likelihood'.

The findings of Kuipers et al. suggest that making a complex decision, such as deciding exactly what Reagan meant by his metaphor, would begin at a general level with whether what was said was metaphorical or not. In terms of 'landmark' decisions one would predict a literal interpretation of the first part of the statement as a dead metaphor in that the referential interpretation of Reagan's use of a phrase like 'the Lady', in the context of his speech and surroundings carries a high value (or is likely), and is more likely than the search for any female animate object, for comparison purposes or otherwise.

We have introduced a new problem here, however, and that is one of how we explain the selection of 'landmark' assumptions which feed into the initial processing. In the case of Reagan's example one might note that, for most people, the use of phrases like 'the Lady' are a commonplace when referring to inanimate objects. The assumption that a referential interpretation is correct as a 'landmark' premise in assessing the rest of what Reagan has said is supported by its *processing history* (Sperber and Wilson, 1986: 77). Processing history refers to the fact that the more a particular representation is processed (in this case the use of phrases like 'the Lady' to refer to inanimate objects) the more likely it is to become 'habituated', and in our terms the more likely it is to be treated as a 'landmark' value in any processing.

This suggests that we do not have two routes to the conclusion that Reagan is indicating that America/Americans have been true to their values of justice and liberty, but only one. However, on that route *opportunistic* possibilities exist for looking more closely at any of the premises, or for re-evaluating the conclusion, or for introducing new premises. For example, we might, having accepted that Reagan is drawing our attention to 'the Statue of Liberty' consider within its own locally managed domain what reasons there may have been for using the term 'lady' to pick out the Statue; or we might focus on the use of the term 'once' as the final element in the statement and what it adds to the overall meaning of the claim; or, even more idiosyncratically, if one had access to information on the history of Reagan's rhetoric (as in, for example, Norris and Whitehouse, 1988) the statement might be interpreted as confirming Reagan's mythic construction of America as an 'ideal'; 'In the specific instance of Reagan's text language is used in a ritualistic celebration of the game of being American' (Norris and Whitehouse, 1988: 314).

These levels of refinement in interpretation are available for processing, and each may in turn provide extra pay-off in informational terms, although this is not guaranteed. The only thing that is guaranteed is the basic interpretation of Reagan's statement, which has been generated as most likely in this context.

This account of what is happening is not necessarily an alternative to relevance theory, but rather an extension of the same basic point.

However, we have been able, to some extent, to clarify the various alternative choices in the interpretation of Reagan's metaphor by suggesting that there is only one basic or general interpretation, but that this presents itself for refinement in the light of further information, and for extension where 'opportunistic' planning choices are made at an individual level.

The idea that there is only one basic interpretation is similar to Sperber and Wilson's claim that some metaphors may generate a 'strong', or a series of strong, implicatures. As implicatures, however, they are the end result, or output, of the deductive system. Their guarantee of strength does not follow from the rules of the deductive device per se, but rather from having input assumptions with high values, which allow valid and guaranteed outcomes to be computed. These high-valued assumptions are 'landmarks'.

Earlier we noted that the idea of varying numbers of 'weak' and 'strong' implicatures generated by metaphors might serve as a basis for distinguishing metaphors on a continuum between *live* and *dead*. An alternative way of viewing this is to suggest that the more *live* the metaphor the more difficult it is to access a 'landmark' assumption. And without one, one will have a series of alternative assumptions, or different premises, which will in turn produce a range of *weak* implicatures. The question of how politicans make use of different types of metaphors may then be better understood once we know how 'landmark' assumptions are accessed in the processing of statements in general, and metaphors in particular.

We have already noted one way in which 'landmark' assumptions may be selected, that is in relation to the process of habituation; where the more frequently something is processed the stronger or higher value it receives as an assumption. Habituation is clearly not the only process which assists individuals in selecting specific inputs for interpretation. Levinson (1987) notes that components of conversational structure (for example pre-forms, like pre-requests) guide the process of reasoning to interpretation. In the next section we will consider how metaphorical interpretation may also be confirmed in relation to the overall structure of the discourse within which metaphors are embedded.

Discourse Structure and Metaphorical Processing

Levinson (1983; 1987) has argued that the empirical study of conversation, as exemplified in *conversation analysis* (see Schenkein, 1978; Atkinson and Heritage, 1984; for a counter view see Wilson, 1989), has revealed a variety of structural patterns which may be utilized in assessing and supporting a number of the theoretical claims of pragmatics. Levinson has argued, for example, that there is a *maxim of minimization*, whereby the speaker is enjoined to: 'produce the minimal linguistic clues sufficient to achieve his ends' (Levinson, 1987: 169). He has further suggested that such a maxim might account for a number of linguistic phenomena, such as ellipsis, PRO elements, gaps and so on.

We have seen throughout this book that much of pragmatics deals with the fact that speakers frequently mean much more than what they say, the problem is how to account for any derived information which we believe the speaker has intended to convey. Levinson suggests that the minimization strategy is not only revealed in the surface structure of forms, but also in the sequential structure of conversation itself. In the case of *requests* for example, it has been noted that these structures frequently contain a pre-move of some form as in (4):

(4) *A*:   Are you taking your car to the party?

Given the right circumstances this could be understood as a pre-request move, whereby a positive response might lead to (5):

(5) *A*:   Are you taking your car to the party?
    B: Yes.
    A: Any chance of a lift (ride)?
    B: Yes certainly.
    A: Thanks.

On the other hand, it is also possible that B could recognize the first turn as a minimal move in the request sequence, and pre-empt any further need for subsequent move types:

(6) *A*:   Are you taking your car to the party?
    B: Yes, I could give you a lift if you want.
    A: Yes thanks.

The point here is that the sequential structure of requests begins with a minimization strategy, which may be all that is required, but where it is not, further moves may be employed which clarify what had been originally conveyed with minimal resources.

In using metaphors we have seen that any potential interpretation can be closed down where a 'landmark' assumption can be located, but that with more open-ended forms several possible alternative assumptions may be equally plausible. Since politicians are frequently involved in the process of conveying information through speeches, where there is little chance of interactive clarification of their aims, how can they attempt to clarify, through further moves, the nature of the metaphorical choices they have made?

The question is, of course, why should they want to? The obvious answer here is that they need to make sure that they are getting their message across, and since some messages may be more important than others, they may need to be re-emphasized, or repeated in various ways, to increase the possibility that the people are receiving and understanding the message in the way intended.

This repetition is not necessarily a word for word principle but rather the repetition of core ideas or cognitive forms, as exemplified through various metaphorical choices. We have already seen an example of this in the work of Lakoff and Johnson. They argued that a core conceptual metaphor, like 'argument is war' could serve as the basis for understanding argument environments:

(7)   He attacked my position, but I defended each point in my argument carefully, before he tried to shoot down the underlying premise on which my argument was based.

Here it is the themes generated by the core metaphor of 'argument is war', i.e. attack, defend, shoot down, which I am referring to as repetitions. Repetition, in this sense, indicates that the metaphors come from the same core conceptual resource. Or alternatively, since a core conceptual resource must itself have a history, where any set of metaphors create a core conceptual resource through their frequent use. This second case would be an example of habituation in the creation of core conceptual metaphors.

The idea of repetition can operate at two structural levels; the first is the local and internal sequential level of the text itself. This refers to the selective and repeated use of metaphors from a core resource within the frame of a single discourse (a speech for example). The second level operates across individual examples of text and acts to indicate a rhetorical development of a specific position; in the case of politics, a specific ideological position. Both structural levels are of interest to pragmatics in that they both serve to reinforce and develop 'landmark' positions for the interpretation of messages in general, and metaphorically encoded messages in particular. Both these structural levels are not necessarily exclusive, since a local interpretation can be

confirmed by a global rhetorical assessment, and in turn local repetition can serve as the initial step in the formation of global forms.

This may be explained by returning to our example from Reagan.
While it is difficult to say much about Reagan's intentions from a
single metaphor, the local interpretation we offered above has received
support from a recent and more global rhetorical analysis of Reagan's
speeches (specifically in this case in the area of nuclear deterrence: see
Norris and Whitehouse, 1988). One of the main messages consistently
appearing in Reagan's rhetoric is that of America as a heroic and just
nation struggling within a historical frame to maintain peace and
justice in the face of aggression. Norris and Whitehouse (1988; see
also Montgomery, 1985) suggest that this view of America is a mythic
construction, and they wonder how people can believe such 'posturing
nonsense'.

As we saw in chapter 1, there is a danger in assuming that your
own world view is the only correct one. Our main aim is simply to
see that the sequential recurrence of specific statements tends to
support the view that Reagan's metaphorical message was about the
nature of American values; once we know this is the case, then we
can look to a different level of political argument to decide how we
view this individual interpretation of reality.

When we look at the global frame of Reagan's discourse examples
abound to support our original interpretation of the Statue of Liberty
metaphor (examples adapted from Norris and Whitehouse, 1988):

(8a)   How can we not believe in the goodness and greatness of
America. (1984)

(b)   We cannot and must not turn back, we will finish our job.
How could we do less; we are Americans. (1984)

(c)   My fellow citizens this nation is poised for greatness . . .
a second American Revolution . . . a revolution of spirit
that taps the soul of America. (1985)

(d)   History is asking us once again to be a force of good in
the world. (1986)

(e)   with no limits to our reaches, no boundaries to what we
can do, no end point to our hopes (1987)

These examples (some of them metaphorical) are selected across a
period of time, and within the broader frame of discourse (in the way
the term might be employed by Foucault or Derrida); they can be
seen as confirming a specific message, which as an instance, or move,
in an individual text is a minimization of the overall intention. By

this I mean simply that each example is a minimization of the whole, where the force of an individual interpretation is ratified by repeated confirmations through a cumulative set of other individual interpretations.

We are not claiming, of course, that the single instance of metaphor we analysed cannot be understood independently of the global aspects of Reagan's discourse. However, while it is unlikely that any individual (other than those studying Reagan's rhetoric) would have access to all relevant examples from Reagan's various texts, it is equally unlikely that anyone who takes any interest in what Reagan has to say will have only one example or instance to draw upon. Consequently, most people will have global evidence to support their assessment of individual instances of metaphor in Reagan's pronouncements.

The same fact may be shown also in the local production of texts, and in this case we are closer to the original claims of Levinson. It is noticeable in a number of texts that various politicians utilize metaphors which are of a similar cognitive type. Here we are back to Lakoff and Johnson's point that core metaphors may generate a specific view of aspects of the world which are then supported or confirmed by the way we talk about the world. We are not only talking about such confirmation in a general or global sense this time, but within the local frame of an individual text production and text production across time, although it must be admitted that it is hard to see how the local and individual can be easily divorced from the global, indeed it is more likely that they are interactive and mutually supportive. However, for the sake of exemplification we will assume this is so in the following examples.

In a very recent political example we can see how the local frame of metaphorical construction operates. In his inaugural address of 1989, George Bush repeats, in this case both word for word and, more broadly, conceptually, a seasonal rebirth metaphor to represent his new Presidential era. The metaphor 'a new breeze is blowing' occurs several times, and is matched with metaphor types such as:

(9a)   a world refreshed with freedom
  (b)   ideas blown away like leaves
  (c)   new ground to be broken

Other similar metaphors of change are also employed, 'going through a new door'; 'the page turns'; 'hoping the mist will lift'. The interaction of repetition at these various levels drives home to the audience that this is the beginning of something new. This fact was significant for

Bush, in that as a former Vice-President to President Reagan, there was a suspicion among political pundits that Bush would simply carry on where Reagan left off, having nothing really new to offer. Bush took the opportunity of the inaugural address to imply through metaphorical selection that this would not be the case.

Similar examples of metaphorical use can be found within the British context. A number of British politicians, Neil Kinnock, for example, frequently employ metaphors in sets of two or three, which are either clustered together or which are spread throughout a particular speech. One of Kinnock's favourite metaphors for describing what the Conservative party are doing to the country is that of Conservative policy as disease or physical debilitation:

(10a)   Britain can't grow on that diet of decline.
   (b)   The places that have been paralysed by closure.
   (c)   There is no . . . vaccine to inoculate the country against the spread of shut down.

These metaphors follow each other rapidly in this speech, developing a picture of Britain as a sick nation without any hope of a cure. The individual metaphors are cumulative in their aim. In the first, there is a basic landmark assumption relating 'diet' with reduction, and through implication with the need for sustenance. In the second there is a strong relationship between the physical aspect of paralysis and the general idea of the failure of movement, or inactivity. In the third case the onset of disease is uncontrollable with no cure available, at least within the present system of things. Each metaphor in turn lends weight to the next in the creation of an image of sickness, weakness, futility and hopelessness. This type of repetition is an example of sequential habituation, where each representation lends confirmation at different levels to the initial assumption.

Clearly, of course, the strength of any assumptions gleaned from this process will be affected by the strength of some assumptions already available to the individual. An avid supporter of the Conservatives will be less inclined to believe any of Kinnock's claims, since they will have what they believe are alternative assumptions which counter such claims; these counter-assumptions will carry higher comparative values, and will, consequently, be more readily accepted and believed.

These local examples from Kinnock are supported by examples from his global rhetorical behaviour across a range of texts, revealing, once again, the interactive nature of the global and local structures.

(11a)   When she is challenged by the facts of the fracture in our country.

  (b)   Unemployment is a contagious disease. It doesn't stop at the borders of economic regions. It infects the whole economic body.

  (c)   If limbs are severely damaged the whole body is disabled. If regions are left to rot the whole country is weakened.

  (d)   Ailments in a country gradually stain the whole country.

  (e)   If the battered parts of Britain don't get noisy they will just get neglected; silent pain evokes no response.

  (f)   They'll get a dose of decline.

The cumulative effect of these images is to create a potential 'landmark' assumption that Britian is sick and the cause is Toryism; the cure, of course, is Labour. The repeated image of illness creates a cognitive environment within which the Government's activities can be assessed. This repeated use of medically based metaphorical types indicates how cognitive metaphors of specific kinds may be developed. Single metaphors indicate a simple comparison between reality and the image of illness, but over time some individuals will come to accept the image in a cognitive and literal sense.

It must be admitted, however, that it is a chicken-and-egg situation attempting to decide whether the global environment is creating a specific cognitive frame against which specific ideological statements are then assessed, or whether the local ideological statements simply draw on existing frames and core metaphorical concepts to create a specific ideological picture of the political world.

The point of all this is that we can see how assumptions may already be pre-wired for the interpretation of various political metaphors. They may not simply be single instances created for a specific moment in time, but are, rather, frequently constrained by a core theme which has been ideologically constructed, and this may be revealed through both local and global structure.

This does not mean that all political metaphors are of this ideologically constrained type. Politicians also tend to employ metaphors for general purposes such as the exemplification of a specific point, or for light-hearted relief. Nevertheless, in terms of the general argument so far, we are now in a better position to consider the question we have been putting off until now, that is, the comparative question of choice between live and dead metaphors.

From what we have said, although *live* metaphors should generate more *weak* implicatures, the use of both local and global repetition suggests, however, that what seem to be individual instances of *live* metaphors may nevertheless have their interpretation constrained by habituated assumptions supported by internal and local sequential structures, or global information across texts. This makes some sense. Politicians are not in the business of taking risks, therefore it is unlikely that they would adopt a strategy of message presentation which left interpretation open ended. On the other hand, professional communication also requires that you maintain an audience's interest and attention, and the use of only simply bald facts or trite and dead metaphors would hardly be impressive. However, one can use as many live metaphors as one wants as long as the intended message, the 'landmark' assumption one wants accepted, is underscored by repetition. In this way one provides the hearer with directive evidence for sorting out the various strength of selected implicatures.

This is an empirical statement, in that one should be able to show that repetition of metaphors (as defined above; and not simply repetition of the same metaphor) confirm a conveyed message in a way that single or differentiated metaphors do not. In looking at how politicians employ metaphors it is quite clear that repeated metaphorical themes abound, and in one sense this is not surprising since the arguments which politicians present are not always necessarily new or different. Nevertheless, it would be possible to convey the same argument with different metaphorical themes, yet this choice does not seem to be a preferred option.

Conclusion

In this chapter the difficult area of metaphor was explored in relation to a number of political aspects of communication. The pragmatic basis of metaphor was explored in some detail because the concept is one where little agreement exists and controversy abounds. It was argued that metaphors are clearly pragmatic constructs, and that they are processed for their pragmatic relevance taking account of the relative strength of the assumptions they generate as input into any processing system. This was exemplified in the case of a single situated political metaphor, and further explored in a local and global sense by looking at text-internal sequential structures and metaphorical repetition across time.

6

A Political Question

Technically the best interview was with John Biffen. That was when I persuaded him last autumn to affirm that the Government could not further reduce its expenditure. It got in all the news bulletins, all the front pages, and in fact it was a very dramatic thing for him to say, contradicting Government policy. It worked perfectly because he never resisted *a question, we simply went through the whole thing . . . by the end I'd got the lot, everything I could conceivably want.*

Brian Walden: quoted in S. Harris,
'Interviewers' Questions in Broadcast Interviews'

Introduction

Questions play a central role in the political process. Politicians question each other within the system of parliamentary debate, and they field and respond to questions from journalists within the domain of the public eye, most specifically within the broadcast interview. There is a common-sense view of the political response to questions, and it is one which suggests that politicians are evasive, attempting to avoid answering questions in a direct manner: 'Journalists are renowned for asking questions and politicians are renowned for evading them' (Dillon, 1990; see also Bull and Mayer, 1988). What exactly does this mean, however? In what sense do politicians evade questions?

On the surface the issue seems straightforward enough, one is evading a question when one is refusing to answer it. However, it is not always the case that one has the information to supply a simple answer to a question. In (1) we would not want to say that *B* was in some way not answering the question. The option of either 'yes' or 'no', for example, need not always be available, and even where such options are available to give only one or the other response may be misleading in itself.

(1) *A*: Is Mary going to the party?
    B: I believe so.

The difficulties involved in deciding what is and what is not an answer to a question have been particularly highlighted in the field of artificial intelligence, where many of the problems faced in producing efficient, co-operative dialogue systems arise where the system slavishly follows simple, goal-based processes, as opposed to becoming involved in a more complex activity which attempts to map the user's possible intentions and beliefs (see Stenton, 1988 for a review of some of the major issues). A classic question and answer example will illustrate the point.

(2) *A*: How many people failed John Wilson's course on phonology last year?
    B: None.

In (2) let us imagine we have a user, let's say a Dean, who is attempting to access some information from a data base. Let us also note that, unknown to the Dean, there is no course on phonology, taught by John Wilson or anybody else. In this context the computer has behaved in a perfectly logical manner, in that since there is no such course known to the data base, the null response is the only acceptable one (for a system of limited capability). However, the result is that the simple answer, here, has given the impression to the Dean that everyone who took John Wilson's course on phonology passed.

More advanced systems can get around this problem by modelling the speaker's erroneous belief (i.e. that there is a course on phonology) and correcting this assumption. Nevertheless, the point is that actually answering questions under certain conditions of belief can be just as misleading as so called evasive answers.

In order to assess evasiveness we must clearly define in what sense the question can or cannot be answered by a simple response. Where a simple answer would be misleading, or imply support for propositions which the hearer may actually oppose, then it is unacceptable to expect the hearer to comply with some naive, preconceived notion of a certain answer type, when the real problem is the question itself (see below).

It is not that I want to suggest that politicians do not manipulate their answers for specific purposes, but rather that politicians are too easily made the scapegoat in the analysis of broadcast interviews because there is a simplistic assumption that all questions, of whatever complexity, or type, may be straightforwardly answered without confusion or misleading consequences.

Further, we should not forget that questions asked within specific types of speech events, such as broadcast interviews, carry meanings and expectations which are socially grounded in the activity itself. Consider the following question put to the Rev. Ian Paisley, leader of the Democratic Unionist party in Northern Ireland.

(3) *B. Cowan*: About two weeks ago I stood in Bedford Street and watched people cleaning up after that car bomb planted there by the provisional IRA and I went straight back to the mid-1970s. Nothing has changed has it?

(BBC Radio Ulster: Talkback 1988)

The first thing to note is that in purely structural terms (to be discussed in more detail below), Cowan is merely asking Paisley if he agrees/disagrees that little has changed within Ulster in the last 20 years. Consequently, in response, Paisley could simply have said either yes or no. If he were to do this, of course, it would be likely that he would be asked the reasons for his choice. The situation here is similar to that of the classroom. When the teacher asks 'Do you think this poem has a fast rhythm?' frequently what this really means is 'tell me why you do/do not think this poem has a fast rhythm?' Similarly, in the broadcast interview, basic yes/no questions are rarely interpreted as that, but rather as indirect embedded Wh-questions (these terms will be explained and discussed below).

This type of speech event-based indirectness makes for good interview programmes in that the interviewee is expected, and expects, to give fairly detailed responses to any question type. Of course this is not always guaranteed, and I am not suggesting that one-word responses are unacceptable. The point I am making is that there are available interpretations of questions, generated by the speech event type one is involved in, which may allow one to go beyond the propositional content of the question form.

Despite the above claims, politicians clearly do manipulate their answers, (as much as interviewers manipulate their questions!) and clearly it is important that we understand both how and why this is done. We should be careful, however, not to adopt pre-theoretical structural or social ideals about what it means to answer questions, but we should rather attempt, within whatever limits, to establish the ground rules which constrain the inter-relationship between questions and their answers within an accessible theory. Only then can we say what it means for someone to answer or fail to answer a question.

In this chapter we will explore the nature of political questions/answers looking specifically at how politicians deal with speech events such as broadcast interviews, press conferences and parliamentary interactions such as question and answer sessions in Parliament. First, however, in order to make clear what it is we are dealing with when we talk of questions and answers, some consideration of these forms and their pragmatic status is a necessary initial step.

Questions and Answers in Pragmatics and Politics

There is a vast and growing literature on questions and answers. There are at least three extensive bibliographies in the area (Egli and Schleichert, 1976; Ficht, 1978; Dillon et al., 1988), and most recently a journal devoted entirely to the study (multi-disciplinary) of questions has emerged (*Questioning Exchange*, published by Taylor and Francis).

While there are various disciplinary focuses on questions/answers, three broad approaches may be delimited. The first I will refer to as the *logico-formal*. This approach attempts to delimit in formal and structural terms what questions are (see the papers in Hiz, 1978; Kiefer, 1983; and for a general review see Lyons, 1977). The second is what I refer to as the *functional* approach; here the focus is on the role of questions within various interaction situations. The concept of a question is given a basic common-sense definition within this perspective (for example: 'a question can be defined as a request for information,' Hargie et al., 1987), and on the basis of this definition a series of functional question types are then delimited; for example: open versus closed questions; probing questions; leading questions; echo questions and so on. The distribution and functional efficacy of these question types are then assessed in relation to specific (mainly professional) contexts, such as, inter alia, teaching, interviewing and counselling (see Dillon, 1990; Hargie et al., 1987). The third approach is the *sequential*. This approach, like the first, is definitional. However, rather than attempting to offer an abstract account of questions through some formal definition, the sequential approach argues that what is and what is not a question cannot be decided in terms of the internal structure, formal or logical, of any specific form, but rather it is determined through the sequential placement of that form within ongoing interaction; 'the point is that no analysis, syntactic, pragmatic, etc, of these utterances taken singly and out of sequence, will yield their import in use' (Schegloff, 1972: 107; see also Schegloff, 1988).

I have not mentioned, or named, any approach which might be called pragmatic. This is not to say this is not possible. Indeed, questions represent the canonical case of a speech act type (see Austin, 1962; Searle, 1969; 1975). Within speech-act theory questions would be defined in terms of their basic constitutive conditions. For example, Searle has defined questions in terms of the following types of rule:

Rule Types	*Question*
Propositional content	Any proposition or propositional function
Preparatory	1. S does not know the answer, i.e., does not know if the proposition is true, or, in the case of a propositional function, does not know the information needed to complete the proposition truly.
	2. It is not obvious to both S and H that H will provide the information at that time without being asked.
Sincerity	S wants this information.
Essential	Counts as an attempt to elicit this information from H.

While this approach is useful (see also Verschueren, 1985), it does not articulate anything about the essential pragmatic relationship between questions and their answers in terms of appropriateness and acceptability, other than within a limited intentional frame of wants and belief states. I do not suggest that such information is not relevant in producing a theory of questions and answers, merely that it does not fully reflect the variation of question types structurally available to participants (Searle does note the problem case of test questions, but is less clear on rhetorical questions; tag questions; embedded questions; indirect questions, etc.). In most respects, however, the speech – act approach, as a definitional perspective, belongs within the tradition of the logico-formal perspective.

All three perspectives have been applied, in one way or another, to political phenomena (see Harris, 1988 (logico-formal); Dillon 1990 and Bull and Mayer, 1988 (functional); Greatbatch, 1986 (sequential); Jucker, 1986 (logico-formal/functional)). Harris (1986), for example, draws heavily on the logico-formal tradition in exploring questions and answers in political interviews. Making use of the classic logico-formal argument that questions presuppose an unknown variable requiring a value (see Lyons, 1977; Wilson, 1981), she distinguishes between the propositions expressed in any question, and the presuppositions of that question. Consider the following question, put to Neil Kinnock by Donald McCormack of the BBC:

> (4)   Whereas Arthur Scargill is blamed for helping you to lose the Brecon by-election – the Notts miners are staunch traditional Labour supporters – why don't you hold out a helping hand to them?

Harris argues that this question contains two basic assertions:

> (a)   Arthur Scargill is blamed for helping you (Labour) to lose the Brecon by-election [agent deletion]
> (b)   The Notts miners are staunch traditional Labour supporters.

and the following presupposition:

> (c)   You are not holding out a supporting hand to them (Notts miners) *for some reason* [missing value]

In this analysis we can see how a formal approach allows the analyst to break up the question into various units, each of which plays a contributing role in establishing a specific universe of discourse (or knowledge frame) within which the answer will be assessed. Any answer which attends only to the issue of supplying a valid reason, which may act as a value for the missing variable, accepts the propositions expressed by McCormack in constructing his questioning turn (and indeed the presupposition of the question itself); even though, as Harris (1986: 74) suggests, these propositions may be 'disputable'.

The formal approach immediately highlights one of the difficulties facing politicians in answering questions, in that questions are rarely straightforward, but are, rather, frequently prefaced by a variety of statements (often controversial). If politicians attend to the propositions contained in these pre/post statements they may be seen as trying to avoid the question. On the other hand, if politicians fail to attend to such propositions they may be seen as accepting certain controversial claims as matters of fact.

Dillon's (1990) functional analysis of an example provided by Harris (1989) illustrates this point particularly well (the question is being put to a cabinet minister):

(5) Well now – when Mr Heseltine protested at the cabinet meeting on December 12th – over the fact that Mrs Thatcher had cancelled this meeting on December 13th – he raised a protest – which as you know – in his resignation statement he said – he said wasn't recorded in the cabinet minutes – and now he's gone back and said that he wants that protest recorded – can you say – as – as a bit of an expert on the constitution – probably more than a bit of an expert – can you honestly say – as a member of the cabinet – that you were happy that Mrs Thatcher allowed proper discussion by all the cabinet in detail of this very important decision for defence?

Dillon (1990: 100–1) breaks this question down into a range of presuppositions, assertions, attributions, propositions under question, and possible answers.

Presuppositions (P) – for validity of question

1 A decision on defence was taken.
2 The decision was very important.
3 The cabinet did not properly discuss the decision.

Assertions (Q) – about others

1 Thatcher cancelled the cabinet discussion.
2 Heseltine protested the cancellation.
3 Somebody omitted the protest from the record.
4 Heseltine resigned over the cancellation.
5 Heseltine is demanding his protest be entered in the record.

Attributions (R) – about respondent

1 You know that assertions Q are true.
2 You are an expert on the constitution.
3 You are a member of the cabinet.

Propositions (X) – in question

1 Thatcher allowed discussion.
2 Thatcher allowed proper discussion.
3 Thatcher allowed discussion by all the cabinet.
4 Thatcher allowed discussion in detail.

Questions (Y) – for answer

1 Do you agree that X [Is proposition X true]?
2 Can you say: 'I agree that X'?
3 Can you say: 'I agree that X' and be honest? [Is your alternative
   answer 'Proposition X is true' true? – viz., given truly?]

Answers (Z) – for respondent's choice

1 Yes
2 No

This is quite an extensive list of material that the respondent has to
deal with, although I think the description may be somewhat exaggerated. And as we shall see below, the claim that the respondent has
only two choices available in answering the question, i.e. 'yes' or 'no',
is both overly simplistic and overly limiting.

Nevertheless, Dillon has highlighted the fact that responding to a
question put by a political interviewer involves factors above and
beyond the content of the interrogative form itself. Such forms are
frequently embedded within a complex textual set of propositions
which must also be considered in any response. We must be careful
in our analysis, however, not to overextend the textual limits of any
propositional set, and I think Dillon may have been over-zealous in
his interpretation. Let us consider what Dillon makes of all this:

If the respondent denies attribution (R1) (you know that assertions Q are
true), he accepts a discrepancy between his opinion and reality – and may
be taken as incompetent or lying. If he denies R2 and R3, he states that his

own face is demeaning. On the other hand, if he affirms R1 (and/or 2 and 3) he is affirming Q1–5 and therefore denying either his confirmation of Q1 and 3 or his rejection of Q2, 4, 5 – wherefore he is stating that either he was lying or that his action was demeaning or that his face was demeaning, and he is further stating that either his colleagues or his prime minister's face is demeaning. (Dillon 1990: 102)

At a stroke this analysis represents two important facts. First, the complexity of many of the questions asked of politicians in interviews, and second the difficulty in delimiting formal units in terms of fine gradations. I would argue, for example, that nowhere in the question is there any explicit claim about what the respondent knows (so-called R1), other than that he knows that Heseltine in his resignation statement claimed that he (Heseltine) had raised a protest, and that this was not recorded in the minutes of the meeting. This only commits the respondent to Q4. Everything else stated within the question is based on what Heseltine claims about what took place (in his resignation statement, and elsewhere). If Heseltine's interpretation of what took place at the cabinet meeting is challenged (as indeed it was by a number of his colleagues) then many of the claims of the question are also automatically challenged.

This important feature of reported fact has been dramatically highlighted by the testimony of John Dean at the Watergate hearings. Ulrich Neisser (1989) has studied what John Dean said took place in particular White House conversations, and compared this with what actually took place, that is by looking at the transcripts of the tapes. Neisser notes that while he accepts fully that John Dean was telling the truth in relating what took place in conversations, Dean's exact testimony does not match the facts of the transcript. Neisser reasons that this results from Dean's wish to interpret the facts in a particularly personalized way.

A further aspect of Dillon's claims is that they depend heavily upon an acceptance of his distributional analysis of the various units he proposes. However, he does not offer any definition of these untis, they are assumed to be self-evident. This is the hallmark of the functional approach, where the impression of a formal analysis is given, but on closer inspection what is found is a neat and insightful descriptive analysis of phenomena yet to be explained.

For example, since most of what the questioner says is based on the interpretation of events supplied by Mr Heseltine, it is, in the main, material for debate. The questioner is in many ways offering an account of what was reported to have taken place, and reported propositions (such as X said that . . .) are much more problematic than straightforward propositional claims. I am not suggesting that Dillon has not uncovered a significant problem facing the respondent in this example. Merely, that Dillon may be reading more into the propositional form than is actually there in the context of production, and in consequence may be offering us an over-interpretation of available respondent selections.

The main difficulty with the functional approach can be more simply highlighted in the description of so called 'implicational leading questions' offered by Hargie et al. Hargie et al. describe 'implicational leading questions' in relation to the implications they express; a question such as (6) implies that any negative answer 'places the respondent in a position of apparently being unpatriotic' (Hargie et al., 1987: 75).

> (6) Anyone who cared for his country would not want to see it destroyed in a nuclear attack or invaded by a foreign power, so don't you think any expenditure on an effective defensive deterrent is money well spent?

Exactly what the implication is here is not made explicit by Hargie et al., perhaps because they feel that it is obvious. The assumption seems to be that a negative answer denies the whole of the opening statement, that is, that the person cares about the country, etc. But how is this done? On this point Hargie et al. offer no clear explanation. In a similar sense to Dillon, certain claims are asssumed to be self-evident. Hargie et al. tell us that certain forms may create implications following specific responses, but since they do not tell us how this is done the phenomenon has merely been highlighted but not explained.

The explanation here hinges significantly on the pragmatic behaviour of the particle 'so', along with the use of the contracted negative. Blakemore (1987: 87; see also Schiffrin, 1987: ch. 7) points out that 'so' acts as 'an instruction to interpret the proposition it introduces as a logical consequence'. Consequently, the presupposition contained within the yes/no question in (6), that expenditure on nuclear deterrence is money well spent, is not merely presented, but rather produced as a logically necessary proposition which follows from the previous proposition. To deny the presupposition of the question is therefore to deny the proposition from which the question follows as a logical consequence.

This is further confirmed by the use of the contracted negative in the initial position of the yes/no question. Such contracted forms are used to suggest that the proposition under question is one which is taken to be true, or assumed to be true (taken for granted); compare (7a) and (7b):

(7a) Do you want to go to the cinema?
(b) Don't you want to go to the cinema?

With the use of both 'so' and the contracted negative, the questioner in (6) is indeed 'leading', and such 'leading' is accounted for by the use of particular linguistic structures. Although this explanation is essentially formal in nature, this is not to say that a functional analysis does not have a role to play in the study of political questions and answers, merely that more attention must be paid to the analytic description of units selected for analysis in terms of their contextual distribution.

We should not assume, however, that the logico-formal approach is without its flaws. The logico-formal approach is useful in so far as it attempts to provide a clear definitional starting point for exploring what questions are, but it has a number of weaknesses. For example, this approach is often insensitive to the interactive nature of questions in the real world. The result of this, for a number of theories, is that they predict answers which would never be acceptable in any real-time context. For example, Grewendorf (1981: 264) is highly critical of Åqvist's (1975) theory of direct answers, which states that 'an answer to a question Q should constitute a (just) sufficient epistemic condition for the truth of core Q'. Grewendorf notes that (9), as an answer to (8), would constitute a true answer within a logic of questions and answers, but that it would be pragmatically odd.

(8) Who murdered John?
(9) The murderer of John is the murderer of John.

Schegloff (1988), an advocate of the sequential approach, offers a more general criticism of any formal method. He argues that such formal accounts cannot possibly distinguish what is a question from what is not, since this distinction is only made within the ongoing construction of interactive texts. Schegloff is absolutely correct when he suggests that many forms with a surface interrogative structure, or even with a semantic structure indicating an unknown variable (or piece of information), may not be interpreted as questions because of their sequential location, or indeed in the case of a number of classic indirect speech acts, because of conventional expectations (Searle,

1975; Clark, 1979). However, the fact that a syntactically defined declarative form might act as a question, or that a syntactically defined interrogative might act as a statement, is simply a reaffirmation of something linguists have been aware of for some time, i.e. that form and function do not necessarily match on a one-to-one basis (see for example Sinclair and Coulthard, 1975). Nevertheless, this does not mean that chaos rules; there are highly predicted correlations between interrogative forms and question functions. Conversationalists must have access to a basic set of formal rules, otherwise they have nothing to manipulate in context. In a kind of Gricean way it is the existence of basic underlying principles which allows speakers to re-code utterances in terms of their sequential location.

Schegloff (1977: 83) points out that in (10) it would not be easy to tell what is and what is not a question, at least in purely formal or structural terms:

(10) *B1*:   Why don't you come and see me some//times?
     A1:   I would like to.
     B2:   I would like you to. Lemme//just –
     A2:   I don't know just where this address is.

Schegloff argues that the first turn here is an invitation and not a request, and this is partly justified by the next turn structure. This seems acceptable, but it does not guarantee that B1 is not also a question. What we seem to have here is a classic case of an indirect speech form, and such forms can perform more than one action. Like other indirect forms, B1 could be treated as a question (with an answer such as 'because I don't have the time'), as an invitation (as Schegloff suggests) or as both a question and an invitation (I would love to but I don't have the time).

It is well known that in the case of some indirect forms, they have become so conventionalized that one interpretation has taken preference over the other (consider the case of 'Can you pass the salt?': see Clark, 1979). But this is not a sequential fact, it is a formal and structural fact. The sequential information merely encodes how the hearer has selected from a range of option types, which are given different predictive weightings depending on the initial structure chosen.

Clark (1979), has shown, for example, that in the case of indirect requests one can make different predictions as to whether such forms will receive an answer only, an action only, or an answer with the action which fulfils the request. These predictions are based on the structure of the form chosen: for example, table 2 indicates the differential results for a series of different questions put to merchants about their closing time, such as 'What time do you close?' and 'Would you mind telling me what time you close?'

Although sequence plays a role in determining how an utterance has been interpreted, this does not guarantee that there are no other valid interpretations based on the formal structure itself. Indeed, the choice made by the hearer in the production of his/her sequential response takes into account and weighs the various options provided by the structure (i.e. in the case of an indirect request the differential weightings attached to question and request components).

This is really the point. In dealing with questions as real-time constructions it is best to take into account both formal and sequential facts in attempting not only to code the form, say for functional purposes, but also to take account of the way in which the question and answer relate to each other as typed turns; by this I mean that it is the formal structure of the question which initially determines how the answer will be interpreted and constructed.

The upshot of all this is that in exploring political questions and answers I do not want to restrict myself to only one argument position. In looking at the pragmatics of questions and answers in political contexts I want to draw upon relevant evidence from both the sequential and formal areas in making not only decisions about how specific meanings are being constructed and reacted to, but also in relation to

Table 2 Percentage of merchants giving answers and information to five requests

Statement	Answer Alone	Answer plus Information	Information Alone	Other
What time?	0	0	97	3
Could you?	0	0	97	3
Would you mind?	0	23	70	7
Do you close?	13	57	27	3
I was wondering?	3	60	37	0

Merchants asked each request N = 30 in each case
Source: adapted from Clark, 1979: 455

considering the functional distribution of question/answer pairs within specific speech event types.

Questions in the House

In this section we will look at the role of questions and answers within the House of Commons. Howarth (1956) notes that the first question in the House of Commons was asked in 1721, and it was only in 1950 that the first question was asked in the American House of Representatives. Both of these facts may seem surprising, but Howarth is not suggesting that these were the very first questions ever asked, merely that these dates represent the first time in which a question was used for purposes other than speaking to a motion. Within the British parliamentary system, when E. Cowper in 1721 put the first question to the Government, he initiated a process that was to become part of the parliamentary procedure itself.

The impact of this development meant that the holders of power could be questioned about their actions, a process which has made governments and their representatives uncomfortable ever since. Only 50 years after the first question, the Earl of Grafton was led to comment: 'If called upon in Parliament for information which every member in either House has a right to expect they either give no reply or evade the question' (*Parliamentary History*, vol. 19, c. 326, quoted in Howarth, 1956: 35).

From the viewpoint of the Government, Pitt noted in 1784 that he did not feel he should necessarily be required to answer questions, justifying his refusal in relation to the questions put: 'interrogatives which I do not think gentlemen entitled to put on me'. As this brief historical note reveals, evasion is nothing new, being as old as the first question itself.

The use of questions within the parliamentary process is now well established (for a historical review see Chester and Bowring, 1962), and they arise not only within parliamentary debate, but within specific sessions set aside for questioning (for example, Prime Minister's question time), in both oral and written forms (see Hansard). In this section I want to focus specifically on that part of Hansard set aside for 'oral answers to questions'. There are two reasons for this. First, the data, like that of the previous chapters, is organized for live production; second, this question and answer session bears a number of similarities to that of the cross-examination of the broadcast interview for which we have recent and detailed research information (see Jucker, 1986).

As we noted above, questions may be defined in a variety of ways. To begin with, however, we will accept a common-sense approach to the distribution of questions and answers within the specifically designated oral session of parliament we have selected to focus on, returning later to more thorny formal analytic issues, such as the relationship between form and function (see for example, Sinclair and Coulthard, 1975; Beaugrande, 1981; Stubbs, 1983).

Within the common-sense approach we will accept an idealaized grammatical position that questions may be recognized by their structural form, for example, through the use of interrogative forms, like who, what, where, when and how; through specific grammatical movement rules which re-order subject auxiliary positions to produce questions like, 'Is John X', 'Are the girls Y', 'do/does the boys/John like Z'; or through the use of modal verbs such as can, could, should, will and so on.

One might argue that what we have here is a list of yes/no interrogative forms, as opposed to yes/no questions, and Wh-interrogative forms as opposed to simply Wh-questions. Jucker (1986) argues this point by noting that both yes/no questions and Wh-questions may come in a variety of syntactic forms. Consequently, yes/no interrogative questions are merely a restricted sub-set of yes/no questions in general, being constrained to a limited set of syntactic forms. He applies a similar argument to Wh-interrogative questions, these being equally constrained, in this case in terms of a limited set of Wh-words. There is some plausibility in this argument, but in this chapter I will stay with the accepted formulation of yes/no question and Wh-question since my main concern is with function; the form is being used as a simple starting point for the discussion.

Distributing Questions in Parliament

In looking at the distribution of Wh- and yes/no question types within oral question and answer sessions, an analysis of a number of selected sessions in 1986 (N = 10) indicated that, on average, there were 42.7 questions asked per session. Three sessions were selected at random from this set and a more detailed count of the individual structures employed was made:

Has (4)	Can (7)	Will (47)	When (2)	Where (0)
How (0)	Why (8) May (5)	Does (28)	Is (19)	Neg (4)
Who (1)	Should (2)	What (8)	Did (1)	Which (1)
Would (1)				

various forms, but also why it occurs. Further, with such information, drawing up content analysis categories might prove less problematic.

In looking at this distribution it is interesting to note the significant proportion of what we are referring to as yes/no questions, as opposed to Wh-questions (nexus versus X-questions, in more classical terms; see Jespersen, 1933). Out of a total of 139 questions, 116 are yes/no with only 23 being a Wh-type. Within the yes/no – Wh-Q distinction, the Wh-question is normally seen as a more 'open' form; which simply means that the answer is not constrained in the way an answer to a yes/no question might be. Wh-questions presuppose an unknown variable which requires a value, where this value, unlike the limited set of answers to a yes/no question, is selected from any one of a number of complex sets. For example, a question such as (11) presupposes (12). Any answer must select a value from a set of places.

(11)   Where is Harry?
(12)   Harry is somewhere.

It is assumed that yes/no questions constrain the answer to either yes or no, 'or an equivalent affirmative or negative' (Hargie et al., 1987: 66), although this is a simplification (see Bolinger, 1978: 103, who wants us to reject the notion of yes/no questions altogether). As Stubbs (1981; see also 1983) points out, the choice of answer to a yes/no question may also include other systems of choice as well as the simple positive or the simple negative: for example, a system of choice which indicates degrees of certainty/uncertainty, as shown in figure 3.

An answer such as 'I'm not sure' would co-select both 'no' and − certainty (Stubbs, 1981: 26). As Stubbs is aware, however, although selectional choices are represented in a binary manner, selection is made in terms of a continuum. In responding to a yes/no question by saying 'I'm not sure,' one is not really selecting 'no' with + or − certainty, but rather a point on a scale which lies closer to 'no' than to 'yes'.

The point that Stubbs is making is that there is an expectation that whatever occurs in the slot following a yes/no question will provide

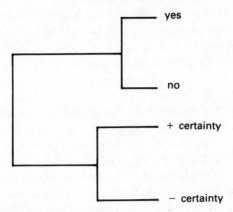

Figure 3 Selectional choices in answering yes/no questions

information to the questioner which assists him/her to locate the answer in terms of a yes/no continuum. This is most clearly reflected in the simple binary choice of either yes or no; but the speaker may use a variety of methods and ways of speaking to indicate points on a scale between these absolutes.

These arguments are, however, mainly concerned with the semantic import of what a proper answer to a yes/no question might be. And it is frequently this aspect of questions that analysts are concerned with when they claim that a question has not been answered (see below). But we must also consider a question's pragmatic import if we are to understand the role of questions and answers in real interaction.

Yes/no questions may rarely be answered with either a simple yes or no, or any of the variants on the positive/negative continuum. Consider the following question put to the Secretary of State for Northern Ireland.

(13) Can something be done to encourage those parties (Unionist and Democratic Unionist) back to the house? (Hansard, 1986: 1057)

In terms of the logic of questions and answers, it seems perfectly acceptable that this question could be answered with either 'yes' or 'no'. But implicit is the fact that this question is not simply asking

whether a certain thing is or is not possible, but also for the respondent
to provide some explanation for whichever choice he makes. A legitimate semantic response to this question would be either yes or no,
but this would not be pragmatically acceptable (acceptability, being
relative to the level of structure one is operating with, see Goodman
(1984) on *radical relativisim*). The question, of course, is why not?

A number of pragmatically based reasons can be given. From the
perspective of speech-act theory we might argue that (13) is an indirect
speech act, which could mean something like 'tell us what can or what
cannot be done.' In this sense we might ask is it a question at all? Is
it not the case that the utterance is performing a number of acts, only
one of which may be that of questioning? For example (13) may be
both a question and an act of requesting some explanation for an
answer selected. One problem with this direction of argument is that
attempts to adequately explain how indirect speech acts operate has
proved notoriously difficult. Several formal solutions have been
offered (Gordon and Lakoff, 1975; Searle, 1975; Searle and Vandereken, 1985) but these consist often of nothing more than translation
procedures.

Adopting a Gricean model we might try and argue that within the
context of a debate on the role of the Anglo-Irish agreement in
Northern Ireland (an agreement rejected by the Unionist parties; and
as part of their campaign of rejection these parties boycotted the
proceedings of Parliament), that a particularized implicature is generated in that the speaker may not have said as much as is required at
this point in the exchange. By this I simply mean why else would the
speaker ask the question in this context other than to find out *what*
can be done (if anything) to bring these parties back to the House?

This argument is similar to one which I put a number of years ago
(Wilson, 1980), where I argued that all questions, and indeed their
answers, are constrained by what I called a 'reason for contract'. By
this I meant that all questions are asked for a reason, and that this
reason must be marked in some way. For example, this may be within
the structure of the question as in (14); within the discourse itself
(15); in terms of the context of the talk (16); or in terms of mutual
knowledge (17):

(14)   What time is it? *I have a train to catch.*
(15)   And they took all my money.
       How *much* did you have?
(16)   Can I have a nail? (where the speaker has a hammer in
       hand and is nailing a box)

(17)   Do you know it is 9.10? (where it is mutual knowledge
       that the speaker/hearer has a train to catch at 9.00).

Put in Gricean terms this would mean that the principle 'say as
much as required', when applied specifically to questions, means
that the speaker, as well as making clear what information he/she is
requesting, should also provide a reason for the question, and the
respondent should also take account of this reason in providing an
answer. This would account for why it is that a simple yes/no is not
possible in some cases. It is not that the question has not been
answered (at least semantically) but rather that the pragmatic implicature (reason) has not been attended to.

The significance of this fact is revealed where one fails to adhere
to the rules. Try asking a close friend (without any contextualization)
the question 'What age is your mother?' Unless this question is marked
in some way in terms of the 'reason for contract', then the question
itself will be queried; either immediately, or following an answer.

(18)   What age is your mother?
(b)   Why do you want to know?
(b)   65, why do you want to know?

These facts indicate that providing a justification or reason for either
the question or the answer plays a significant role in deciding the
pragmatic well-formedness of questions and answers. Treating questions as simply yes/no types simplifies their potential pragmatic function. This may be seen in the functional description of such question
types as 'closed' questions. Yes/no questions, according to Hargie et
al. (1987) are a sub-type of closed questions, in that they may be
adequately answered by yes or no.

This looks very much like a semantic interpretation, since it is
within the limiting semantic frame, abstracted away from real interaction, that yes/no seems reasonably acceptable. More specifically, however, Hargie et al. (1987) note the following definition of closed
questions: 'the respondent does not have a choice in his response
other than those provided by the questioner' (King, 1972: 158).
Under one interpretation this would provide for a very restricted view
of normal interaction. The problem is really one of how 'closed' is to
be interpreted. Within the functional frame the interpretation seems
to be a quantitative one, that is closed questions provide for simple
responses, or restricted responses. This may indeed be true as a

general probabilistic claim, but clearly yes/no questions are not closed if one is free to provide a justification, or to comment on the likelihood or uncertainty of particular outcomes. I can imagine a quite lengthy response is possible to a question such as 'Are you Irish?' (an example of a closed question given by Hargie et al., 1987) given the right context. I can also imagine that such a form might just as easily receive a yes/no; so how are we to know what is a simple yes/no response and therefore 'closed', and what is a complex form and therefore 'open'?

From the sequential viewpoint one might argue that we cannot know a priori what the answer will be, since interpretation is an ongoing process, that is it is something which is locally managed by the participants themselves. Consequently, we can only recognize yes/no questions where they are defined as such by the participants. This would need to be done retrospectively, presumably. But if this were so, then the analyst would have to look both forwards and backwards within his/her data in order to determine how a particular form is interpreted. Such a procedure would not be available to the participants themselves, only analysts can look forward to the finished product. However, there is one sense in which the concept of closed versus open does indeed correlate with certain question types.

This may be understood from a formal perspective, which in one sense merely articulates in more structural detail what I believe is at the heart of the functional claim. The principle here is that if we treat all questions as presupposing an unknown variable requiring a value, this restricts any answer, or rather its interpretation, to being relative to the propositional constraints of the variable.

Yes/no questions determine their answers in relation to whether the answers can or cannot be located on a continuum or scale of yes/no possibilities. In this case the answers to (19) are both legitimate, but we would hardly call the second type a 'closed' response, at least in functional terms.

(19) Are you Irish?
(a)   Yes/no.
(b)   Well, assuming that by Irish you mean simply someone who was born in Ireland, raised in Ireland, educated etc. in Ireland then I am Irish. Although there are some who would argue that one must be of pure Irish stock whatever that might be, and under that interpretation there might be some doubt. But that seems such a pedantic way of looking at things.

The point is, however, that under King's interpretation (or rather my formal interpretation of his interpretation) of closed questions (noted above) both responses may be seen as equally limited; by this I mean that the second response is merely quantitatively longer: in propositional terms it will still be interpreted as locating the response at a point on the yes/no continuum.

Yes/no questions are therefore closed in a propositional sense, but not in relation to the quantitiative amount, or detail, which any answer may contain, nor indeed in terms of the contribution of this information to the ongoing interaction.

Given this propositional constraint we are in a better position to consider why it is that the vast majority of questions within the oral answers session of parliament are (in basic terms) of a yes/no type. Any answer, of whatever complexity, will, or can, be ultimately reduced to a point on a scale of positive and negative values. An MP who puts a question knows that he is unlikely to get a simple 'yes' or 'no', since such responses would indicate acceptance of many of the other propositions attached to the question. Nevertheless, by putting the question in a yes/no form, the MP, and the audience, are free to interpret any response as locating the minister at a specific point on a yes/no continuum. Where such an interpretation is not possible, then the minister has not answered the question. This claim may now, however, be structurally validated. What this means is that where any answer to a yes/no question cannot be located on a positive/ negative scale then we may have an example of evasion. In this case, however, we will have a structural account of what we mean by evasiveness.

Before we look somewhat more closely at this last point, I want to consider one other noticeable fact about the scores for the distribution of parliamentary questions outlined above, that is the fact that 'will', as a question form, is used twice as often as all Wh-forms put together, and nearly twice as frequently as its nearest yes/no rival 'does'.

'Will' is a modal form which can be used with the third person as addressee, and this is how it is most often employed in the parliamentary context (see chapter 4). Palmer (1979) suggests that where 'will' is used in the interrogative mood it carries an implication that the action under question *should* be carried out. In other words, there is a strong assumption that any question using 'will' indicates a request which is expected to be fulfilled. For example, 'Will you pass the salt?' is a much stronger indirect request form than 'Are you able to pass the salt?' If this is the case, then any rejection of the indirect request element of a 'will' question becomes that much more problematic.

Further, 'will' is also considered to be more polite than 'can' (see Bolinger, 1989 for a recent overview of some of the complexities involved in the analysis of 'can') although 'can' is said to function in the interrogative mood in a similar way to 'will'. Once again, with increased politeness as a variable, rejecting any indirect request made through the interrogative use of 'will' creates a problem situation for the respondent. Because of the increased politeness of 'will', any rejection of the indirect request is essentially a 'face threatening act' (Brown and Levinson, 1978). Rejecting any indirect request requires interactional sensitivity. As the general politeness of the indirect act increases the problem of sensitively constructing a rejection becomes more complex. If, as we have suggested, 'will' carries an increased politeness marking, while at the same time indicating a specific expectation that the response/request will be fulfilled, then it is a useful discourse marker (to use Schiffrin's (1987) phrase) for making any refusal or rejection that much more difficult for the respondent. Such a claim seems consonant with the context of parliament, where despite rivalries and antagonisms, members are expected to maintain a civilized and respectful form of confrontation. By constructing a parliamentary question using 'will', members can indicate their expectation of a response while at the same time laying claim to adherence to a specific polite form.

These facts suggest some reasons why 'will' may be the preferred form within the oral question and answer sessions. First, it commits (through implication) the hearer to the action; and second, it is a polite request, and, therefore, any simple rejection of the request reflects back on the individual who has refused to perform what has been implicated as a reasonable action.

The actions requested through the use of 'will' are rarely reasonable from the minister's viewpoint however:

(20) *Mr Mallon* : *Will* the Secretary of State confirm that a sizeable section of the population of Northern Ireland is in favour of the accord and wants to see it working? *Will* the Secretary of State consider directing some of his remarks to that section of the community at the earliest possible opportunity instead of expressing his own inherent Unionism at every opportunity?

(Hansard, 1986c: 1054, my italics)

(21) *Mr J. Enoch Powell*:   *Will* the right honourable Gentleman try
                              to come to an understanding that what-
                              ever happens over Easter and in the
                              weeks beyond, the ultimate responsibility
                              will lie, as ever, with the ambiguities and
                              insincerities of the policy of successive
                              British governments towards Northern
                              Ireland and its people?
                                  (Hansard, 1986c: 1061, my italics)

(22) *Mr Heffer*:   *Will* the Government inform their col-
                              leagues in America that they should con-
                              sider United States history? The United
                              States gained power after a struggle
                              against the British, and only later did it
                              have democratic elections. Nicaragua is
                              in precisely the same position. Nicaragua
                              has a democratically elected government.
                              The United States of America should not
                              support those who are trying to over-
                              throw a democratically elected govern-
                              ment who are carrying out policies on
                              behalf of the people.
                                              (Hansard, 1986d: 135)

Consider, where we treat 'will' as being used to both question and
perform an indirect request, the consequences of a positive response
to any of these questions. In the first one, if the Minister agrees, or
were to give a positive response, he would be admitting to a bias on
his part ('expressing unionism at every opportunity'). If he were to
say 'no' he would be suggesting that he will not direct his remarks to
a certain section of the Northern Irish community, in this case a
mainly nationalist section.

Clearly, the Minister cannot do either of these things, and in one
sense he cannot therefore answer the question, at least in purely
semantic terms. But implicit within the question is the reason for its
production; in this case, Mr mallon is expressing the view that the
Minister is spending too much of his time worrying about those who
disagree with the Anglo-Irish agreement (the Unionists), instead of
getting on and attending to those who support the agreement. It is
this fact which the Minister responds to, firstly, by accepting that a

large section of the nationalist population are in support of the agreement, but then noting that even they must recognize that for the
ultimate aims of the agreement to be achieved the Unionist community
must be drawn into the dialogue.

Mr King: . . . I recognise that one of the consequences of the agreement
was a recognition among the nationalist community of the opportunity of
progress by constitutional means rather than by having to support the men
of violence. I thought that I had made my views very clear on this point.
At the same time, it is not in the nationalist interest to have the degree of
misunderstanding and discontent that undoubtedly exists among the Unionist
community over the Anglo-Irish agreement. I am anxious that those fears
and misunderstandings should be relieved and that genuine concerns should
be met in discussions with the Unionists on a number of aspects such as
methods of consultation and involvement that are available to them as well.
(Hansard, 1986c: 1054)

With the second example the Minister once again faces a dilemma.
If he simply responds with 'yes' he indicates that he 'will try to come
to an understanding'. This would presuppose a previous failing and
denigrate the Minister's *face*. If he were to simply say 'no', however,
then he would seem unsympathetic and arrogant. The Minister
responds in the following way:

Mr King: We all have a responsibility at present to, not to anticipate trouble,
but to seek in every way we can to discourage trouble taking place. I hope
that I can look to the right hon. Gentleman in his position as a Member of
the House to join with all hon. Members in saying that the right way to
resolve the difficulties, ambiguities or uncertainties is by discussion and
consultation and that at no time can there be a case for violence and confrontation.
(Hansard, 1986c: 1062)

In this response, the Minister seems to have avoided the question
altogether. He merely makes a claim that all reasonable people, in
particular legally elected politicians, should not predict problems
ahead, but work to the resolution of those more general problems
recognizable at present. Only in the most convoluted sense can this
response be located at a point on a positive/negative continuum, and
for this reason I would say this is not an answer, but merely a response
(a response being any turn with locatable propositional relevance, but
which cannot however be said to have answered the question in terms

of its structural location on a positive/negative continuum: see above).
This is a structurally defined case of evasion.

The response to the third question is one which rejects the premise
on which the question is based, that is that the Nicaraguan Government cannot be defined as a democratic one.

Mr Eggar: The armed forces and nearly all the national institutions in
Nicaragua are under the control of the Sandinista political party. The draft
constitution under discussion in Nicaragua provides for the formalization of
these powers. Does the hon. Gentleman believe that this is a democratic
system?

(Hansard, 1986d: 136)

Taking Mr Eggar's last question as rhetorical we might argue that
since the claim is that Mr Heffer is mistaken, then it follows that the
action he has requested is based on this mistaken premise, and cannot
therefore be carried out. Indirectly, therefore, the question has been
answered, since it is obvious, in a trivial logical sense, that the answer
is no.

Where questions, or the premises on which they are based, are
rejected, it is not necessarily the case that the assumed response will
always be negative. One could reject the premise of a question but
still provide a positive response:

(23) *Q*:   When you fly to New York on Monday will you speak with
            the President?
     A: It is not Monday but Wednesday that I go to New York,
            however when I get there I will certainly speak to the
            President.

(adapted from Jucker, 1986)

This brief discussion reveals some of the complexity involved in
the analysis of both questions and answers within the parliamentary
context of the oral answers to questions sessions. One might argue
that the term question in this context is a misnomer, in that the
politicians who are involved in the questioning of ministers seem to
be doing much more than merely requesting information. This is
undoubtedly true, but I would argue that any of the other actions
they are attempting to perform (criticize; demean; insult) emerge
from the primary action of the question itself, as it is used against

the background of both stated propositions, and both general and shared knowledge.

Questioner and Respondent

As well as considering the propositional relationship between questions and their answers, one can also look at, again in basic quantitative terms, how the overall duration of questions effects the overall duration of response received. Quantificational studies have revealed a variety of interesting facts about the relationship between a question's duration and the duration of the response. Several studies by matarazzo (described in Jucker, 1986) indicate that the average length of a response is affected by the length of the question, although the relationship is not fully correlated. In one experiment it was shown that as questions increased in length (measured in seconds) so did the answers. However, while the length of the response doubled as the question length went from 5 seconds to 10 seconds, it did not increase threefold when the question length increased to 15 second (discussed in Jucker, 1986: 27).

In a study of news interviews on Radio 4, Jucker (1986) confirmed this general pattern, as shown in figure 4. As Jucker notes, although scores for 4 to 6, and 8 to 10 secs follow the expected pattern, the scores for 2, 12 and 14 secs do not. What this indicates is that the duration of question and duration of answer correlate most strongly around the average (7.5 seconds). It follows from this that since only 15 per cent of all interviews fall into the categories of values lower than 3 seconds, or higher than 11 seconds, the general claims of Matarazzo still hold.

Within a political context, Ray and Webb (1966) noted that for the Presidential press conferences of John F. Kennedy the case was as shown in figure 5.

Ray and Webb (1966: 900, quoted in Jucker, 1986–29) sum up the relationship between questions and answers and their duration in terms of what they call the 'Matarazzo effect':

the Matarazzo effect is a verbal conditioning phenomenon within an interview, rather than a tendency which manifests itself on each question answer pair. Thus while individuals interviewed do not give long answers just because questions are long, their answers should increase in length if the interviewer's comments are long.

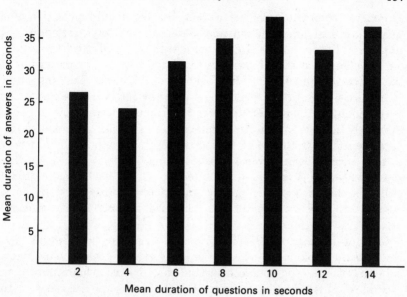

Figure 4 Answer lengths in relation to question lengths
(adapted from Jucker, 1986: 37)

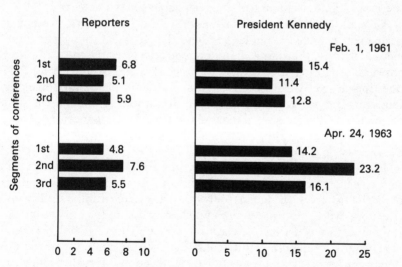

Figure 5 Mean duration of questions and answers in two exemplary Kennedy
news conferences
(adapted from Jucker, 1986: 29)

A general comment may be made here. We should note that this quantificational phenomenon may be accounted for in relation to a number of the comments already made within this chapter. In particular the claim that simple answers to complex questions may commit the respondent to a series of propositions which he/she does not accept (see Harris, 1986). Consequently, where the interviewer's comments become longer, the number of potential propositions a simple response implicitly accepts or rejects increases. Not surprisingly, most interviewees attend to this issue by increasing the length of their answer to take account of the various propositions. This is not to say that the interviewee attempts to counter or accept each one in turn, although this is possible, merely that their response must be more complex to take account of the increased number of propositions attached to the question.

Most of the research on correlations between question duration and response duration has, to a greater or lesser extent, dealt with interview contexts of one type or another; contexts, that is, where more than one question is asked by the interviewer of the same interviewee. In the oral session of parliament we have a a slightly different context, because it is generally the case that each question is asked by a different participant of the same minister. However, like the interview there is a limited amount of time set aside for the activity.

An analysis of 137 question–answer pairs for the oral session of parliament revealed a similar result to that found in broadcast interviews, that is that long questions positively correlate with long answers. Adapting the method used by Ray and Webb (1966), 137 question–answer pairs were located and a count of the total lines (as found in the Hansard transcription) for question and answer was calculated. A correlational analysis revealed a significantly strong correlation between the duration of the question and the duration of the answer (r of 0.92; p at 0.001).

The significance of this result may in part be accounted for by the very structure of the oral answer session of parliament. Since Members of Parliament (in the main) only have the opportunity to ask one question, with only rarely the opportunity for follow-up questions, supplementary questions, or clarificatory comments, as available in the interview, they must carefully construct their question for maximum impact in terms of its propositional ramifications. Equally, since the minister responding is not necessarily going to have time to come back at a later stage and refer to points he/she made have missed in attending to the answer, he/she will pay particular attention to the propositions (and presuppositions) of the question and attend to these accordingly.

This is not to say that each and every question is dealt with in this way. Complex implicational questions, for example, may not be easily dealth with in this manner (see above). In such cases we may predict evasion or simple rejection of the premises of the question. This general principle should apply whether we are dealing with broadcast interviews, press interviews or parliamentary sessions (see below).

The Function of Parliamentary Questions

In looking at the function of questions one might adopt a variety of strategies. Hargie et al (1987: 61) identify 12 interactional functions for questions:

1 To obtain information
2 To maintain control of the interaction
3 To arouse interest and curiosity concerning a topic
4 To diagnose specific difficulties a respondent may have
5 To express an interest in the respondent
6 To ascertain the attitudes, feelings and opinions of the respondent
7 To encourage maximum participation of the respondent
8 To assess the extent of the respondent's knowledge
9 To encourage critical thought and evaluation
10 To communicate, in group discussion, that involvement and overt participation by all group members is expected and valued
11 To encourage group members to comment on the progress of other members of the group
12 To maintain the attention of group members, by asking questions periodically without advance warning

Most of these functions seem relevant to an actively positive view of interaction. It is not clear how many of them would apply within the oral session of parliament (obviously 10 to 12 seem less relevant). The problem is that a while a question such as 'Does the minister not understand?' might be said to select (4), it is difficult to think of any circumstances where the minister would admit to any lack of understanding (a possible misinterpretation of a question perhaps), since to make such an admission would be particularly problematic for the minister. The reality is that the oral session of parliament uses questions for frequently negative purposes.

This is picked up in Jucker's (1986: 77–94) work which indicates that for news interviews, questions can perform 13 different face threatening acts (adapted from Dillon, 1990: 97–8):

1 Commit yourself to do something:
   Q: Is it in your mind to invite Mr Tchernenko to come to Britain?
   A: Well no no don't jump too quickly, one of the things, if you're doing diplomacy is you must go stage by stage.

2 State your opinion:
   Q: Well do you think we might get better value for money out of the coal industry, if it were in private hands or partly in private hands?
   A: Well I'm not talking well I'm not talking about denationalizing the coal industry.

3 Confirm your [demeaning] opinion:
   Q: You're surely not suggesting as you seemed to in the course of that answer, that strikes and unions are responsible for three million plus unemployment in this country?
   A: No. Mr C. I'm not suggesting . . .

4 Accept discrepancy between your opinion and your actions:
   Q: Is there not a certain irony though in the fact that you'll be talking to Mr Botha on the very day when the England rugby team will be playing in South Africa contrary to the agreement and very much against the wishes of this Government?
   A: I see no irony about it at all.

5 Accept discrepancy between your opinion and reality:
   Q: If we were to tie a polygraph on to you you wouldn't, it wouldn't go ping when you are saying things like that?
   A: No I'm happy to be able to refute that proposition, there is absolutely nothing that I am hiding.

6 Accept that the reason for doing the action is demeaning:
   Q: . . . the point that Mr Q made, that this is all politically motivated, that the idea is merely to save money . . .
   A: No I can't accept that because . . .

7 State that the action is demeaning:

   Q: But you say you wished you destroyed the document, that is virtually thwarting the law, is it not? which is almost as bad.

   A: No it's, that's that's something that happens before the legal process begins and that's what, that's what I'm talking about.

8 Confirm the demeaning action:

   Q: Now, first of all that criticism I quoted from Mr. Q that these patients had actually had to be re-admitted to hospital because they weren't being treated properly, what do you say to that?

   A: These patients are being discharged as part of an overall national and regional policy, which says . . .

9 Take responsibility for the demeaning action:

   Q: But don't you accept, Mr J, that it's the duty of your prison school to make sure that pupils don't stray and commit robberies or thefts?

   A: . . . admit it totally and we have this as our duty number one.

10 Justify the demeaning action:

   Q: Well then why did you go about it in this, some people have said 1984 way, suddenly people find that they are being denied what they thought until now was freedom – on their desk a piece of paper saying, from now on you can't join a trade union, full stop.

   A: I think then you actually make a decision of this kind . . .

11 Take action against something [demeaning]:

   Q: That you are going to do about the canker of long term youth unemployment that is the unemployment is the thing that bothers most people in this country.

   A: But Mr C, that's exactly what I have been saying.

12 State that the other's face is demeaning:

   Q: But the Government hired Mr M at a considerable salary in order to put the industry right. If they are now rejecting his advice is that not foolish?

   A: I think they've taken a lot of his advice.

13 State that your face is demeaning:

   Q: Prime Minister you say that Britain is historically and by inclination pro-American but do you accept there is a majority of people in this country which is opposed to this deployment of cruise missiles here?

A: I see a number of polls, but I do not think, when it comes to the majority of people, that the issues have ever been fully explained.

As Jucker points out this list is not exhaustive, and further points out that not all face-threatening acts are cases of one category or the other.

Locating such examples within parliamentary question and answer sessions is not difficult however:

Mr Willie Hamilton: Is he [the minister] prepared to have a look at the senseless housing policies inflicted on the people of Glenrothes and elsewhere by the Government?

(Hansard, 1986f: 986)

A positive response here would demean the face of the Government, i.e. by accepting that their housing policy is 'senseless'. Implicitly, as well, in this case, one might argue that any positive response by the Minister would also demean his own face as he is not only a member of the Government but explicitly responsible for housing within the areas Mr Hamilton is concerned with.

Because there is a potential overlap of a number of Jucker's categories (depending on the linguistic context), and because his categories have been adequately explored within the news interview context, they will not be re-applied here, although the idea that questions function to attack *face* seems a more reasonable assessment of what may be happening in the oral session of parliament than attempting to apply Hargie et al.'s more positive (and more general) model.

We need not be as specific as this however, since questions, as speech acts, may have a variety of functions (only one of which may be *face threatening*; such FTAs may also function to obtain information for example). What I want to do instead is to argue for a basic category function for the majority of questions within the parliamentary session. This basic category function will also allow for the utterance to be interpreted in other ways (face threatening, inquiring, etc.). The basic category function will however, I hope, capture the basic aim of parliamentary questions, that is, reflect their unique function within this specific speech event.

The basic category function will be described in an informal manner, in relation to a set of basic steps:

Step 1: Present some time set of circumstances/facts.
Step 2: Establish these as either (a) propositions or (b) presuppso-
        tions of the question.
Step 3: Question the minister's knowledge/awareness/acceptance of
        the stated propositions (resuppositions).
Step 4: Link (implicitly or explicitly) through an invited inference,
        the propositions/presuppositions to a conclusion.

Steps 1 and 2 are inter-related. What happens here is that a series of
assertions (or a single assertion) are put under question, for example:

(24) *Mr Alton*: Given the concern registered by Dr Garret
                  FitzGerald during his recent visit to the United
                  Kingdom about the continued discharges of radioac-
                  tive waste from Sellafield, was the issue discussed
                  at the last meeting of the inter-governmental body?
                  If not will it be on the agenda of the next meeting?
                  Does the right hon. Gentleman agree that the report
                  of the Select Committee on the Environment on the
                  discharge of radioactive waste should be considered,
                  and the continuation of discharges, which is making
                  the Irish sea the most radioactive body of water in
                  the world, is undermining good Anglo-Irish
                  relations?
                                        (Hansard, 1986c: 1057)

In this example there are three questions, the first two are attached
to the following assertions:

(a) Dr Garret FitzGerald visited the United Kingdom
    recently.
(b) Dr Garret FitzGerald expressed his concern about radioac-
    tive discharges from Sellafield.

The second question is attached to the following assertions:

(a) The report of the select committee on the Environment
    on the discharge of radioactive waste should be discussed
    by the inter-governmental body.
(b) Discharges of radioactive waste are continuing.
(c) The Irish sea is the most radioactive body of water in the
    world.

(d)   Discharges from Sellafield are undermining Anglo-Irish relations.

There are also a number of presuppositions in this question, most significantly that associated with the use of 'continued', which presupposes that these discharges have happened before.

The last question asked by David Alton begins 'Does the right hon. Gentleman agree'. This takes up step 3, and this kind of gambit is frequently used in questioning:

(a)   Is the Minister aware that?
(b)   Does the Minister accept that?
(c)   Does the Minister believe that?

With each of the three steps, Mr Alton has established a series of assertions/presuppositions to which he seeks agreement. The Minister cannot simply disagree by responding to this yes/no question with a 'no', because a number of the propositions put are true; on the other hand a number of others are disputable (i.e. that the Irish Sea is the most radioactive body of water in the world). We have discussed the general situation faced by a respondent in this kind of context above (see also Harris, 1986; 1989). Important as well, however, is step 4, in which an invited inference may be constructed in terms of what has been presented, as shown in example (1).

Example (i)
   The Irish Sea is the most radioactive body of water in the world.
   The radioactivity in this water is caused by discharges from Sellafield.
   The condition of the Irish Sea is undermining Anglo-Irish relations.
   Assume that radioacitivity is bad.
   Assume that the British want good relations with the Irish.

Discharges from Sellafield should be stopped (reconsidered / discussed).

This is, of course, not a purely logical construction, but it is a reasonably rational one, similar to the type of pragmatically based rational arguments noted by Leech (1983). The concept of an invited inference adds a further level of pragmatic structure to a variety of complex questions. Indeed, the main aim of many politicians in putting questions is to establish the invited inference as opposed to really querying whether the minister does or does not know X.

In many ways all four steps act as means to an end, specifically the construction of an inductive conditional. I use the term inductive here because the deductive logical form of P→Q would not seem to be appropriate, in that this rule states that if P is true then Q must be true. The situation with real-world examples cannot be so easily resolved. An instance is shown in example (ii).

Example (ii)
All dumping of nuclear waste should be stopped.
Sellafield dumps nuclear waste.

Sellafield should stop dumping nuclear waste.

In the real world (unlike the world of logic, where form may be more significant than context, and where truth is generally bivalent) even if a politician accepted the first two premises (and accepting these is not quite the same thing for politicians as saying they are true, in any formal sense of truth) it would not guarantee that he/she would accept the conclusion. Politicians would argue that further conditions must be taken into account such as, accept premise 1 but only as an ideal for the future; premise 2 is true, but the waste is treated and not as dangerous as some have believed, etc.

Consequently, these kinds of syllogisms are best treated in the sense of induction argued for by Rescher (1980), where the output, the conclusion, is the best answer available. The problem in politics is that the best answer available depends on the evidence you provide for the input, and this is where politicians disagree. Nevertheless, one of the main aims of the questioner seems to be to establish certain premises from which certain actions would follow (rationally) if the premises where true, and it is these actions which are expected of the Government.

We might think of the four steps I have outlined as being used to construct a kind of inductive syllogism of the form KNOW X → ACT Y?, which states that if X is known to be the case then action Y should be taken. The syllogism is inductive in that the evidence for what is known cannot be stated irrefutably, hence ministers can reject the claims of the question by claiming alternative evidence while at the same time accepting the premise, or they can question the probability of any premise which acts as an input into the first part of the syllogism. Consider the following question which I have broken up into antecedent and consequent:

(25) *Mr Lambie*: Is the Minister aware that for the first time in the history of the Scottish new towns we are experiencing a housing shortage as second generation families start to apply for new rented houses?

(If there is a housing shortage then ....)

    Mr Lambie: ... Will he give the development corporation the permission and the resources to start building immediately new houses for these second generation families?

(Hansard, 1986f: 985)

Whether we think of the process of questioning in the House of Commons as a simple inductive action, or a series of informal steps creating propositions, presuppositions, and invited inferences, there is a further level at which the questions operate. Questions in the House often operate along party lines, so one frequently finds (although not always) that the information to be established in steps 1 and 2 is grounded within a party-political context. By this I mean simply that the responsibility for the state of affairs outlined in any question through steps 1 and 2 is attached to a specific party. We saw this above with Mr Hamilton's question, but here is an even more explicit case:

(26) *Mr Maxton*: Is the Minister aware that the thousands of people in Glasgow who are waiting for housing improvement grants would be astonished to hear that he is blaming local authorities for failure to provide them? The Government's failure to provide sufficient funds to remove the backlog is the problem.

(Hansard, 1986f: 990)

In this example, the Government are squarely to blame for the state of affairs presented within the question. Questions of this type are frequently put by the parties who are in opposition to the party of government. Equally, however, the members of the ruling party can construct their questions to opposite effect. In this situation the questioner takes the opportunity to establish a case which has arisen directly out of Government action, and establishes an invited inference that the Government should continue with its present actions:

(27) *Mr Hirst*: Does my right hon. Friend agree that there has been a broad welcome from the business community, which sees the reforms as helping redress the appalling imbalance in business rates north and south of the border? Is he aware that the business community also warmly welcomes the protection which will be given to it during the transitional period of rating reform? Will he contrast the worth of the Government's proposals with the fact the Labour Party will do nothing to reform the rates, and with the rather loopy idea which is circulating in alliance circles that rates should somehow be linked to the profits of a business?

(Hansard, 1986f: 986)

As well as what we might call *negatively established* (questions of blame and negative responsibility), and *positively established* (questions of praise and positive responsibility) questions, there are also what could be called *neutrally established* questions, where the responsibility for any particular state of affairs is not clearly levelled at any one party. Although considering the nature of the parliamentary oral session we are dealing with, such questions are difficult to find; (25) above may, however, be seen as an example of this type.

Evading Questions

At the beginning of this chapter we noted that it is commonplace to claim that politicians do not answer questions within interviews. I questioned what exactly was meant by the concept of evasion, and throughout the analysis of this chapter it has been made clear that drawing hard and fast lines around what is and is not an answer to a question is not a straightforward issue. This fact was noted by Jucker (1986) in one of the few detailed analyses of questions and answers within political interviews. Jucker (1986: 141) notes a further and more specific difficulty with moodless questions (lacking a finite verb) as found, for example, in the third move in (28):

(28) *AAA*: But what about imports from within the EEC into this country?

    BBB: I think imports from within the EEC we can't do all that much about and it's the rules are very complicated and some people er try to get round those rules by various devices.

    AAA: Fiddles of various kinds?

    BBB: I think that might be extending it a bit but that could well be said to be true.

The problem here, argues Jucker, is that is not clear what kind of answer the interviewer is trying to elicit in the third turn, since it is not clear what kind of question (propositionally) has been asked. Consequently, where one cannot easily see what the aim of the question is, it becomes difficult to see what an acceptable answer might be.

Such a problem does not, however, seem to have been encountered by Bull and Mayer (1988), who have managed to develop a typology of question evasions:

1 Ignores the question
2 Acknowledges the question without answering it
3 Questions the question
4 Attacks the question
5 Attacks the interviewer
6 Declines to answer
7 Makes political point
8 Gives incomplete answer
9 Repeats answer to previous question
10 States that the question has already been answered
11 Apologizes

                         (adapted from Bull and Mayer, 1988: 10)

Bull and Mayer's approach is essentially functionalist, as the term has been defined above, and it pays no attention to any of the work on the formal analysis of questions and answers; nor to Jucker's work. Indeed, Bull and Mayer (1988: 4) comment: 'there has been little if any systematic study of question evasion in political interviews . . . we have no idea of the extent to which this occurs, nor of how they manage to be evasive.' This is to some extent true, but as we have already noted, Jucker (1986) has offered a variety of insights into how politicians organize and structure their responses, taking account of the detailed history of difficulties involved in defining questions, and as a consequence, what explicit and acceptable answers to such questions might be.

Bull and Mayer, unfortunately, supply no arguments of any kind to indicate how they reached their decisions of what is and what is not evasion in general, nor indeed how they managed to develop the various levels of refinement noted above (other than to tell us that they developed the protocol jointly, resolving disagreements through discussion).

They suggest, as a starting point, a distinction between answers, evasions and answers by implication. An example of an answer by implication is given as (29) where the interviewer (Sir Robin Day) asks Mrs Thatcher whether the chiefs of staff should resign in the context of a Labour Government which decommissioned Polaris:

(29) I know what I would do I just could not be responsible for the men under me in those circumstances it wouldn't be fair to put them in the field if other people had nuclear weapons . . . but they are free to make their decision that's a fundamental part of the way of life in which I believe.

Bull and Mayer (1988: 6) comment: 'Thus, in giving this answer she makes her own view quite clear without ever explicitly stating that she believes it would be the duty of the chiefs of staff to resign.'

In essence this seems correct, but as with the example of an implicational leading question noted above, there is no explanation of how this interpretation operates. Any implication here, however, emerges only from the fact that one is seeking to make sense of the answer (in a Gricean way) in terms of the propositional constraints of the question, which suggests, of course, that implicitly (or explicitly) Bull and Mayer must have drawn upon such facts to reach their conclusion. This is the whole point; any protocol analysis of answers is only as successful as the theory of questions on which it depends. It is important that this theory be made explicit in order that one may assess the efficacy of the programme. This seems much more reasonable than relying only on the authors' own negotiated agreement.

As an example of just one of the problems which may arise because Bull and Mayer have failed to do this, consider the import of accepting that answers can be implicative. If, as Bull and Mayer accept, answers can attend to questions indirectly, by some form of implication, then it seems equally logical that where a politician is making a political point (see 7 in the protocol) then that very point may be implicative, that is, it might actually serve as an answer to the question.

Alternatively, take the case of the so called 'negative answer', defined as answers which state what 'will not happen instead of what will happen' (Bull and Mayer, 1988: 16). The example provided by Bull and Mayer is that of the response by Neil Kinnock to a question about 'whether the Labour party will have an incomes policy'.

> (30) Now all governments because they are governments have had incomes policy taxation itself is a policy for incomes what I'm setting aside is the idea either the the guiding lights of Selwyn Lloyd or the legislated incomes policy of Mr Jenkins and Mr Wilson in the sixties or the incomes policy of fixed norms or Ted Heath's counter inflation incomes policy.

Once again it is certainly true that Kinnock is teeling us what he will not have as opposed to (explicitly) what he will have, but since the question asked simply if he would have an incomes policy (it is unfortunate that Bull and Mayer do not provide a complete transcript of the question), Kinnock has in fact answered the question. In this case one might argue that he has answered it by implication, a logical implication in this example, since Kinnock states that being a government necessarily entails having an incomes policy.

Could we also argue, perhaps, that what Kinnock has said functions to attack the question (number 4 in the typology) since the answer is, at one level, a logical given. It is difficult to debate this point, since Bull and Mayer have not given us any structural or formal clue as to where their typological categories come from, nor, indeed how these categories overcome and take account of the issues of form and function; sequencing; moodless questions; and so on.

Taking up one point made by Bull and Mayer, there is indeed little work on how evasion operates, but in order that we might take some steps forward in developing a view on this issue we should at least pay some attention to the problematic relationship between questions and their answers (definitional and relational); only then can we understand not only what evasion is and how it manifests itself in various forms, but also why it occurs. Further, with such information, drawing up content analysis categories might prove less problematic.

In this section I want to take a tentative step forward in considering evasion, in this case evasion as defined in relation to a specific theory of questions and answers. The aim is not so much to resolve all the problems and issues of defining what evasion is and how it operates, but rather to look at the possibilities opened up by approaching evasion from the perspective of formally established rule expectations as opposed to negotiated intuitions.

In looking at evasion I want to explore a number of question–answer pairs from the presidential press conferences of Richard Nixon. There are a number of reasons for this. First, I will be interested in those questions and answers which attend specifically to the Watergate issue of Nixon's Presidency. One might expect, particularly in the early days of the unfolding story of the Watergate scandal, evasion to operate. Second, as Helen Thomas notes, 'the most remarkable news conferences in White House history were held in the Nixon era' (Thomas, 1978: i). Third, Nixon's relationship with the press, through his refusal for long periods to hold press conferences, was almost confrontational, and therefore one in which one might predict tough questions requiring careful handling. This allows us to look at those who question as well as those who answer (rejecting Bull and Mayer's uncritical comment that 'reporters are only doing their job'). Fourth, the press conference is an interesting mid point between the oral session of the House of Commons, and the processes involved in the broadcast interview.

Within the press conference there is a formal control similar to that in parliament; further, more than one questioner is involved, but like the news interview the questioners are journalists and not themselves political representatives constrained by party loyalties. And fifth, unlike Kennedy (as noted by Ray and Webb, 1966), Nixon does not balance the relative length of his answer to the relative length of the question. Using the technique established by Ray and Webb, an analysis of a sample of 33 question–answer pairs within the Nixon presidential press conferences revealed no significant directional correlation between length of question and length of answer (r 0.058 n.s).

Nixon's mean length of response was 17.5 (S.D. 12.0) compared with the results of a similar analysis of Kennedy ($N = 30$) who had a mean length of response at 11.3 (S.D. 7.6) ($z = 2.5$ $p < 0.001$). This indicates that Nixon tends to give lengthy responses to questions in general.

Nixon on Evasion

As I noted above, in considering evasion it is important to clarify the theory of questions which is being used. Earlier, I defined yes/no questions as forms which predict, or expect, a response which locates the answer on a positive/negative continuum. Responses which one can not locate on such a continuum are not therefore answers. Admittedly, there will be cases where it is difficult to specifically pinpoint whether the response is or is not locatable on a positive/negative continuum. Nevertheless, this formal starting point serves as an important heuristic guide in examining so-called evasion.

In the case of what we have been called Wh-questions, a similar tactic is possible. In this case, such questions are defined in terms of the propositional set, indicated by the unknown variable presupposed by the question. For example, a *where* question presupposes an unknown variable constrained to the set of *places*. A *when* question presupooses an unknown variable constrained to the set of *time* (see Huddleston, 1976; 1984; Lyons, 1977; Wilson 1981). Consequently, responses to Wh-questions can be assessed in relation to whether or not they can be delimited in terms of the set of options determined by the propositional organization of the question.

As with yes/no questions this is not a perfect solution. We noted above Jucker's worry about moodless questions, where the surface form does not explicitly tell us what the constrained set will be. However, with such problematic cases (among others) we do have one analytic step which we can take. We may draw upon a sequential argument to at least supply us with information about how the respondent interprets the question, and how in turn the questioner reacts to the answer given, that is, whether they make the question explicit in a return move; call for clarification; or reject the answer explicitly.

Even this process cannot guarantee categorical success; nevertheless the reader will at least be able to see how the analyst has reached a particular conclusion, and concur or reject accordingly.

Let us begin with what is a clear example (at least according to the theory of questions I have accepted) of a response which is not an explicit answer to the question (see Johnson, 1978a: 308):

(31) Q: There seems to be an expansion of what executive privilege was in the past, and you

	were quite critical of executive privilege in 1948 when you were in Congress . . .
The President:	I certainly was.
Q:	You seem to have expanded it from conversation with the President himself to conversation with anyone in the executive branch of the Government and I wonder, can you cite any law or decision of the courts that suppports that view?
The President:	Well, Mr Mollenhoff, I don't want to leave the impression that I am expanding it beyond that. I have perhaps not been as precise as I should have been. And I think yours is a very legitimate question because you have been one who has not had a double standard on this. You have always felt that executive privilege, whether I was complaining about its use when I was an investigator or whether I am now defending its use when others are doing the investigating – I understand that position.

Let me suggest that I would like to have a precise statement prepared which I will personally approve so that you will know exactly what it is. I discussed this with the leaders and we have talked, for example – the Republicans like Senator Javits and Senator Percy, are very interested in it, not just the Democrats, and I understand that. But I would rather, at this point, not like to have just my-off-the-top-of-my-head press conference statement delineate what executive privilege will be.

I will simply say the general attitude I have is to be as liberal as possible in terms of making people available to testify before Congress, and we are not going to use executive privilege as a shield for conversations that might be embarrassing to us, but that really don't deserve executive privilege.

In this example Nixon indicates his willingness to clarify the way in which he will define the parameters of executive privilege, and that such parameters, whatever they turn out to be, will not be used as a simple protective device for avoiding Government embarrassment. But the question asked whether Nixon could cite any law or previous legal decision for any form of extension of executive privilege beyond conversations with the President, and by extension of the 'reason for contract' (see above) to provide just such an example. Nixon does neither of these things. This is clearly not an answer to the question.

Considering the question at a more detailed level, as suggested by Bull and Mayer (1988), it will be clear that this answer is not behaving in a unitary way, but reflects several supporting and interacting moves. Bull and Mayer's typology of question evasions gives the impression that each answer is of a particular type. They say, for example, that 46 per cent of evasions for both Thatcher and Kinnock were of the *making a political point type*. Nixon's answer might also be seen in that way, since he gives reassurance, and certainly some self-justification for his behaviour. But he also implies that he can't answer the question at this point in time, preferring to leave a detailed response until he has prepared a precise statement (more than a 'just my-off-the-top-of-my-head press conference statement'). Is this then also part of the 'declines to answer category' (see above)? Further, Nixon attempts to ingratiate himself with the questioner, down-grading his (Nixon) own face ('I perhaps have not been as precise as I should have been'), while up-grading the questioner's face ('you have been one who has not had a double standard on this'). This process of partial ingratiation does not seem to be covered in Bull and Mayer's typology, unless this perhaps falls under the broad category of 'acknowledge the question without answering it'.

This is not to suggest that typological analyses are not possible, nor, indeed, that Bull and Mayer's suggestion is not a useful start; rather what we need is much more data from a wider range of sources, as well as some clearly articulated account of how the units within the typology are not only recognized but also how they may interact with each other in evasion strategies.

There should also be much greater attention paid to the linguistic and pragmatic cues involved in strategic evasion. For example, Nixon begins his response with the use of 'well' as a qualifier. As R. Lakoff (1973: 473) tells us: *'well* is used in case the speaker senses some sort of insufficiency in his answer'. Further, within conversational analysis, 'well' has been treated as indicating a dispreferred move, or a 'pre-disagreement preface' (see Pomerantz, cited in Jucker, 1986: 150); and Owen (1983) has suggested that 'well' may be used to provide for face threat minimization in the response (see also Schiffrin, 1987: 102–27).

We can see in the Nixon example that potential evasion was already pragmatically pre-marked (but not guaranteed) by Nixon's very first move. Schiffrin (1987) has noted that, in general, 'well' does not tend to precede answers which give the information required by the question.

Ultimately, Nixon is suggesting that the most reasonable way to respond to the question is to provide all the necessary detail for the delineation of executive privilege. It would be unreasonable for the questioner to expect a half-baked answer at this point. What is unstated here, however, is whether this more detailed information would include any citation from the law or decisions of the court. There is no explicit attempt by Nixon to claim that any more detailed information would not include such citations, on the other hand there is no explicit claim that it would.

Nevertheless, in the context of the question one must infer that any further information supplied would include such citations, otherwise the reasoning behind the answer, as an answer, fails. What I mean here is that Nixon's arguments rests on a claim that the information necessary to respond to the question is not readily available at this point in time, but that he will prepare this information for a later date, when, presumably, at that later date the question will be answered. Now since the presupposition of the question is that Nixon has or does not have any legal precedents for his present actions, then any future information supplied must attend to the resolution of the alternative values within the presupposition: you can/can not cite, etc.

So much for intuitive logic. However, in this example Nixon can also decide to attend to the propositions within the overall questioning move as opposed to the presupposition, in this case those propositions concerned with Nixon's attitude to executive privilege over a period of time. And indeed the answer Nixon gives is more suggestive of a response at this level. With a response at this level, which could simply be a detailed description of how Nixon views executive privilege at the time of the question, Nixon could claim to have answered the question. Of course all he would have done would be to have merely attended to a number of propositions associated with the question. Since we would not, however, know anything about the legality of Nixon's position on executive privilege, he would not have answered the question.

Interestingly, this is an example of how the answer can utilize the propositions associated with the questioning move to the respondent's advantage. Earlier we saw how the propositions attached to questions place the respondent in a difficult or awkward position (vis-à-vis a specific positive or negative response: see above, also Harris, 1988: Dillon, 1990), where a simple affirmative or negative response might commit the respondent to propositional claims which he/she did not accept. In Nixon's response, he has taken the propositions, rather than the direct legal issue associated with the presupposition of the question, and suggested that he would supply future information which would clarify his position relative to these propositions. Since these propositions are attached to the legal issue (presupposition), it also looks like this information might also be supplied in the future, but this is not guaranteed, and Nixon could not really be seen as being inconsistent if such information were not supplied.

Let us look now at what, on the surface, seems the complete opposite of evasion:

(32) *Q*:　　　　　Mr President, isn't there an essential difference between your investigation of the Hiss case and the request of this subcommittee to Mr Dean to appear? In the former, foreign affairs was involved and possibly security matters, where here they only wish to question Mr Dean about the breaking into Watergate.

The President:　Yes I would say the difference is very significant. As a matter of fact, when a committee of Congress was investigating espionage against the Government of this country, that committee should have had complete co-operation from at least the executive branch of the Government in the form that we asked. All that we asked was to get the report that we knew they had already made of their investigation.

　　　　　　　　　Now, this investigation does not involve espionage against the United States. It is as we know espionage by one political organisation against another. And I would say that as far as your question is concerned, that the argument would be that the congress would have a far greater right and would be on much stronger ground to ask the Government to co-operate in a matter involving espionage against the

> Government than in a matter like this involving
> Government.
>
> (Johnson, 1978a: 329)

One of this first things to take into account in analysing this response is the question itself. As we noted earlier in discussing questions and answers within the British Parliament, it is the case that questions carry (as well as set propositions and presuppositions) certain invited inferences. For instance, in (31) one might argue that there were a number of invited inferences in the question: since Nixon had once been against an extension of executive privilege, and now he seemed to be extending it, then he was involved in a contradiction; i.e. executive privilege should be extended and executive privilege should not be extended. Further, where it is extended and there are no legal precedents for doing so then the invited inference is that Nixon is behaving, potentially, in an unconstitutional way.

Now in the case of (32), one must bear in mind that there had been some debate as to whether White House aides should be allowed to testify before the Ervin Committee. With this in mind the question invites the inference that if the case about which the aides were being asked involved espionage then there might be a good reason for them not to testify: if the case, however, concerned an internal criminal matter, then there would not seem to be any problem. Consider, in this instance, the phrase 'they only wish to question Mr Dean about breaking into Watergate.' The use of 'only' here minimizes the action, and suggests that the action, in comparison with other possibilities, is (in the view of the speaker) non-threatening.

Nixon's answer seems, at first blush, to be in agreement with this assessment, in that it seems to be a positive response to the question, agreeing that there is indeed a great difference between cases involving espionage and those involving internal matters. The result of accepting what the questioner has put leads to a different conclusion for Nixon however. The questioner argues that there is no good reason not to testify in relation to matters of internal concern, but there may be good reasons where national security is concerned. Nixon turns the logic of this around. His answer suggests that because espionage against a government is such a serious thing, the Congress are on 'stronger ground', have greater rights, to expect co-operation from the Government. The invited inference here, is that with internal politics they (the Congress) should be less involved and less concerned, because in terms of the contrast set up they would be on weaker ground.

There is a subtle distinction here, which is difficult to grasp at first. But basically it is like saying that the law should have special privileges where, for example, terrorist cases are involved. In Northern Ireland, for example, civil human rights are, the Government would argue, necessarily reduced in the fight against terrorism (for example, individuals can be held in custody without charge for up to seven days). This is necessary under the extreme case of terrorism, but not necessary under civil law. Nixon is making a similar case for giving evidence to certain committees; it is necessary in the case of espionage, but much less acceptable in internal political cases. In this example Nixon has managed to directly answer the question, but, at the same time, to deny its underlying inference.

Is this evasion then, or an answer to the question? In terms of the basic structural theory we are operating with, it is an answer to the question. On the other hand, Nixon has evaded any commitment to accepting that aides should testify in internal political cases, even if he agrees that such cases are less serious than those involving espionage. Once again we see the complexity involved in dealing with questions and their answers, and much more work is required at this level before we can truly begin to focus on the distribution of a typological range of avoidance or evasive types.

My aim in briefly looking at these examples from Nixon was twofold. First, I wanted to indicate how the view of evasion developed in this chapter might operate. Second, building on this, to indicate how several of the pragmatic issues raised throughout the chapter might be brought to bear in a specific case.

Conclusion

In this chapter we have extensively considered the function and formal nature of questions and answers, and explored various aspects of the questioning process within differing political contexts. It was argued that questions are pragmatic phenomenon, and throughout the chapter an effort has been made to indicate the pragmatic parameters of questions and question types, as well as indicating in broader terms how pragmatic aspects of questions may be utilized in the analysis of what politicians say. The major issue of evasion was raised and considered in relation to what it would mean to fail to answer a question. A structural definition of evasion was offered, which, although broad-ranging, offered a basis for debate, and a starting point for considering what it is that we think politicians are doing when we believe they are not answering questions.

7

Conclusion

Introduction

The stated aim of this text was to apply selected pragmatic concepts to the analysis of political talk, where the term 'political talk' was restricted to the real-world linguistic activities of practising politicians. The term 'pragmatic concept' proved somewhat more difficult to pin down, the elusive nature of the general pragmatic enterprise being aptly documented by Levinson (1983).

There are two ways in which one might describe the notion of a *pragmatic concept* as it is applied in this work: the first, as outlined in the introduction, refers to the interaction of delimited L-, P- and O-pragmatic concerns; the second is in terms of the analytic objects/ descriptions themselves, the pragmatics is what pragmatic analysts do answer (a possibility also noted by Levinson, 1983). Within this frame, my emphasis was on meaning implicated (Lycan's (1986) implicated relations) beyond the surface or literal form of the language itself, the basic meaning in context view.

Meaning is a particularly slippery term, as is indeed the term context, and the construction of meaning within contexts, or specifically political contexts, involves more, of course, than a purely linguistic dimension. My aim was not, however, through any holistic analysis of the social, socio-historical, ideological, intersubjective, textual and other levels or layers or meaning, to reveal any underlying truth, or reality, subverted by political talk. Which is not to say this is not possible (although any truth will of course be relative), or that on one level of interpretative relativism that I have not, to some extent, done this. Rather, my aim was to bring to bear on the analysis of political talk a pragmatic perspective in order to see what this might reveal about the linguistic organization of politicians' linguistic production.

Studies of political language which focus, or which claim to focus, only on the language of the political enterprise are criticized from two main directions. The first suggests that the linguistic description of political language represents only one level of analysis, even where one wants to focus only on political language (see for example Richardson, 1989). This seems reasonable to me – all forms of analysis are idealizations to some extent – but it is equally reasonable if one *only*, or mainly, wants to focus on the structure of the language itself, as opposed to the many other levels or directions in which an analysis of language might lead. This is where the second type of criticism comes in. Here there is an assumption that one cannot explore the discourse of language independently of concepts such as power, ideologies, ethics and social representation (see, for example, Chilton 1987 and Klein, 1988).

There is a certain truth in this claim, and I have no doubt that several of the analytic statements I have made in this text reflect, or are relevant to, concepts of power and control, or indeed may be effected or manipulated for specific ideological purposes (consciously or unconsciously). This point was made early on when I noted the comparison between Nixon's behaviour in producing the statement 'no one presently employed in the White House' (see pp. 22–3), and a child's negative response to the question 'Did you eat some of the cookies?' where the child has in fact eaten all of the cookies. There is certainly something interesting going on in both cases beyond the language itself; nevertheless, the aims, goals and objectives of the manipulation in both cases is determined, initially, from an understanding of what has been manipulated, in both cases a pragmatic feature of the linguistic system.

This very type of manipulation may serve as the lead into more specific political issues, where one wishes to take this direction. Chilton (1987) attempts to show, for example, that Grice's co-operative principle is affected within an international- relations frame because there are clearly political contexts where the aim would be not to co-operate. The first thing to note is that Chilton's very conception of contextual and political manipulation of co-operation only emerges from a consideration of Grice's model within certain selected and specific contexts; in other words, as a minimum, this pragmatic model has acted as a heuristic catalyst for the consideration of issues beyond language. On one level, then, language can be a starting point for further analysis, but such further analysis can only proceed once the linguistic concepts are delimited, agreed, and recognized.

This is what I have been concerned with in this book. Not the search for any base structures which are then ideologically transformed in some textual sense to create a specific political view of the world (as Hodge, 1989 would advocate), but much more simply a pragmatic description of the choices politicians have made, a real (political) world consideration of pragmatic concepts in action.

Findings and Implications

There are two basic levels on which the analytic endeavours of the previous chapters may be considered. The first relates to what we can learn from the application of pragmatic concepts to political language, and the second is what can we learn about pragmatics itself from applying pragmatic concepts to political language.

Both questions are necessarily inter-related. Applying pragmatics to political language, as a specifically selected form of language in use, we may gain confirmation of our pragmatic theories: real-world proof that pragmatic concepts are in operation in real talk, as opposed to the contextually sterile examples frequently employed by both linguists and philosophers. Further, and related to the second question, we gain the opportunity to reconsider and further develop our theories where their application is not fully vindicated in the light of specific data.

Take, for example, the important theory of 'relevance' developed by Sperber and Wilson (1986). This theory has had a significant impact on pragmatic theorizing in the past few years, being used to solve a variety of core linguistic issues (see for example, Kempson, 1987). Nevertheless, in chapters 4 and 5 we have had opportunity to pause and consider exactly what are the ramifications of the relevance theory in specific contextual cases. Like Chilton's (1987) arguments about Grice's co-operative principle, we could argue that 'relevance' is effected by the contextual needs of the participants. Individuals are not slaves to either of these theories, but rather make use of the basic principles outlined by them relative to their own contextual and individual needs. Importantly, however, the very conception of the relevance theory proved essential for us as a way into an understanding of the data; this is developmental, data analysis and theory (potential) development working hand in hand.

Further, less controversial linguistic elements, for example the selection of pronouns, turned out to be socio-pragmatically discrete in the hands of politicians. The analysis provided in chapter 3 not only highlighted this fact, but provided a potentially new, ideologically sensitive linguistic tool. One's ideological orientation, it was suggested, could in part be mapped onto the quantitative selection of particular pronominal types.

On a more individual basis the pronominal claims of chapter 3 undoubtedly reflect issues of power, status and social identity. The simple fact that certain pronouns are avoided altogether by socialist politicians, for example, 'one', suggests that this pronoun carries negative connotations for these politicians. You don't need to be a political or cultural analyst to figure this much out. It is legitimately available from the gross distribution of elements within the political talk itself.

As I noted above, and stated in chapter 1, we must also not forget that language, as a basic tool, is available to everyone. This is not to say that every person uses it in the same way; the arguments of this text clearly indicate otherwise. However, the arguments also seem to indicate that political manipulation has much in common, on a variety of levels, with manipulation as applied by other social groups. In chapter 4, the suggested protective manipulation of personal identifications, as indicated by the selection of restricted or open (referential/ attributive) referring expressions, can be found not only among politicians, but among parents, Deans, schoolteachers, policemen and anyone else who has the opportunity to self refer via either personal or role identification.

I state once again, this is not an argument in defence of politicians, but a cautionary note for those who believe the function of the analysis of political language is to provide a critique of specific political issues, for example 'militarism'. It is not enough to simply marshal arguments about the way particular individuals use language to represent certain facts; the critique itself is involved in the very same process.

This may sound very much like a 'cop-out' for linguistic analysts (the intellectual paper-tiger argument of Van Dijk). We should remember, however, that the sociolinguistic description of language championed by scholars like Labov and Trudgill in the 1960s and 1970s had a significant impact on educational attitudes to accents and dialects. The argument here has always been based, firstly, on difference not deficiency, that is, that accents and dialects differ from each other, but that this fact in itself is not linguistic evidence for any one accent or dialect being superior to any other. This is not to say that the social injustice caused by a biased view of language is acceptable, but the defeat of such linguistic prejudice must begin by making clear the illogicality of the linguistic foundations of that very prejudice, by showing, that is, that any one dialect or accent is as acceptable as another in linguistic terms.

Linguistic arguments of superiority were often justified in terms of such things as logic, or historical accuracy. Interestingly, arguments against the language of politicians (specifically in the area of 'nuke-speak'; see Chilton, 1985) are based on very similar premises. Richardson (1989) notes that analysts criticize politicians' use of language in relation to its logic, its unfairness, its lack of truth. As she has shown, however, the very same arguments can be questioned and turned back on their proponents.

The way forward in the analysis of political language is for analysts to make their own agenda clear, or as clear as it can be within a postmodernist world. My aim was to apply pragmatic concepts in the description of political talk, and to that end I believe I have, to some extent, been successsful. I accept that political neutrality is a myth, as much as I accept the historical and social location of the construction of my text; nevertheless, like John Searle (1984), once I have said this much, 'I want to go to work;' this book is the result of my work on the application of pragmatics to political talk.

Appendix

Table A.1 Speeches used in this study

Pre-scripted			Unscripted
Thatcher	Foot	Kinnock	Foot
Speech A	Speech D	Speech G	Speech J
Central Council 27 March 1982	Press Conference 19 April 1982	Party Conference 6 October 1983	Party Conference October 1982
Speech B	Speech E	Speech H	Speech K
Central Council 26 March 1983	Party Conference 16 November 1982	Party Conference 3 February 1984	Party Conference October 1983
Speech C	Speech F	Speech I	
Small Business Bureau Conference 8 February 1984	Party Political Broadcast 8 December 1982	Party Conference Summer 1984	

Table A.2 Numbers of pronouns found in speeches A to I

	Thatcher			Foot			Kinnock		
	A	B	C	D	E	F	G	H	I
Approx. total no. words	5540	6230	3300	560	790	790	1440	2160	6400
Total no. of pronouns	310	346	117	6	32	28	92	113	258
Pronouns % of total words	5.6[a]	5.5	3.5	1.1	4.0	3.5	6.4	5.2	4.0
No. of I/Me in speech	38	37	10	1	2	1	16	3	39
% of pronouns	12.3	10.7	8.5	16.7	6.2	3.6	17.4	2.6	15.1
We/Us	150	141	40	1	12	13	25	30	89
% of pronouns	48.4	40.7	34.2	16.7	37.5	46.4	27.2	26.5	34.5
Our/Ours	58	62	15	–	7	5	8	15	33
% of pronouns	18.7	17.9	12.8	–	21.9	17.8	8.7	13.3	12.8

You	12	13	15	1	–	2	12	8	5
% of pronouns	3.9	3.8	12.8	16.7	–	7.1	13.0	7.1	1.9
One^2 + You^2	4	2	1	–	–	–	–	–	–
% of pronouns	1.3	0.6	0.8	–	–	–	–	–	–
One^3 + You^3	1	23	9	–	–	–	–	5	5
% of pronouns	0.3	6.6	7.7	–	–	–	–	4.4	0.8
He/She	11	16	3	–	3	–	10	11	14
% of pronouns	3.5	4.6	2.6	–	9.4	–	10.9	9.7	5.4
It	–	–	1	1	1	2	2	3	5
% of pronouns	–	–	0.8	16.7	3.1	7.1	2.2	2.6	1.9
They/Them	28	51	20	2	6	3	19	35	67
% of pronouns	9.0	14.7	17.1	33.2	18.8	10.7	20.5	31.0	26.0
Those	8	1	3	–	1	2	–	3	4
% of pronouns	2.6	0.3	2.6	–	3.1	7.1	–	2.6	1.5

[a] Individual % figures rounded to one decimal place.

Table A.3   Numbers of pronouns found in unscripted speeches J and K

	Foot	
Speeches	J	K
Approx. total no. words	6510	6820
Total no. of pronouns	451	564
Pronoun % of total words	6.9[a]	8.3
No. of I/Me in speech	110	191
% of pronouns	24.4	33.9
We/Us	164	87
% of pronouns	36.4	15.4
Our/Ours	40	48
% of pronouns	8.9	8.5
You$_1$	18	33
% of pronouns	4.0	5.9
One^2 + You^2	–	–
% of pronouns	–	–
One^3 + You^3	10	11
% of pronouns	2.2	2.0
He/She	27	109
% of pronouns	5.0	19.3
It	–	8
% of pronouns	–	1.4
They/Them	77	69
% of pronouns	17.1	12.2
Those	5	8
% of pronouns	1.1	1.4

[a] Individual % figures rounded to one decimal place.

References

Åqvist, L. (1975) *A New Approach to the Logical Theory of Interrogatives*. Tubingen: Niemeyer.

Ariel, M. (1985) *Givenness Marking*. Unpublished PhD: Tel-Aviv University.

Ariel, M. (1988) Referring and Accessibility. *Journal of Linguistics*, 24, 65–87.

Atkinson, J. M. (1984) *Our Masters' Voices*. London: Methuen.

Atkinson, J. M. and J. Heritage, (1984) *Structures of Social Action*. Cambridge: Cambridge University Press.

Atlas, J. D. and S. Levinson (1980) A note on a Confusion of Pragmatic and Semantic Aspects of Negation. *Linguistics and Philosophy*, 3, 411–14.

Austin, J. L. (1962) *How To Do Things With Words*. Oxford: Clarendon Press.

Bates, E. (1976) *Language and Context: The acquisition of pragmatics*. New York: Academic Press.

Beaugrande, R. De (1981) *Text, Discourse and Process*. London: Longman.

Bell, A. (1984a) Language Style as Audience Design. *Language in Society*, 13, 145–204.

Bell, A (1984b) Good News–Bad Copy: The syntax and semantics of news editing. In P. Trudgill (ed.) *Applied Sociolinguistics*. London: Academic Press.

Bitzer, L., and T. Rueter (1980) *Carter vs Ford: the counterfeit debates of 1976*. Wisconsin: University of Wisconsin Press.

Blakemore, D. (1987) *Semantic Constraints on Relevance*. Oxford: Basil Blackwell.

Boër, S. E. and W. G. Lycan (1980) Who Me? *Philosophical Review*, 89, 427–66.

Boër, S. E. and W. G. Lycan (1986) *Knowing Who*. Cambridge, Mass: MIT Press.

Bok, S., (1978) *Lying: moral choice in public and private life*. New York: Vantage Books.

Bolinger, D. (1973) Truth is a Linguistic Question. *Language*, 49, 3, 539–50.

Bolinger, D. (1978) Yes/No Questions are not Alternative Questions. In Hiz, 1978.

Bolinger, D. (1989) Extrinsic Possibility and Intrinsic Potentiality: 7 on May + 1. *Journal of Pragmatics*, 13, 1–23.

Boorstin, D. (1962) *The Image, or What happened to the American Dream*. New York: Athenum.

Botha, R. P. (1987) *The Generative Garden Game*. Stellenbosch Papers in Linguistics (16): University of Stellenbosch. Published as *Challenging Chomsky* (1989) Oxford: Basil Blackwell.

Boyd-White, J. (1984) *When Words Lose Their Meaning*. Chicago: University of Chicago Press.

Bratman, M. (1984) Two Faces of Intention. *The Philosophical Review*, 93, 3, 375–405.

Brown, P. and S. Levinson (1978) Universals in Language Usage: politeness phenomena. In E. N. Goody (ed.) *Questions and Politeness: strategies in social interaction*. Cambridge: Cambridge University Press.

Brown, R. and A. Gilman (1960) The Pronouns of Power and Solidarity. In T. A. Sebeok (ed.) *Style and Language*. Cambridge, Mass: MIT Press.

Bull, P. and K. Mayer (1988) How Margaret Thatcher and Neil Kinnock Avoid Answering Questions in Political Interviews. Paper presented to British Psychological Association, London.

Butler, C. (1984) *Interpretation, Deconstruction and Ideology*. Oxford: Clarendon Press.

Cameron, D. (1985) *Feminisim and Linguistic Theory*. London: Macmillan.

Carnap, R. (1950) *Logical Foundations of Probability*. London: Routledge and Kegan Paul.

Carston, R. (1987a) A Re-analysis of some Quantity Implicatures. In Horn and Levinson, 1987.

Carston, R. (1987b) Saying and Implicating. In Horn and Levinson, 1987.

Castãneda, H. N. (1968) On the Logic of Self Attribution of Self Knowledge. *Journal of Philosophy*, 65, 439–56.

Castãneda, H. N. (1975) Individuation and Non Identity. *Philosophical Quarterly*, 12, 131–40.

Chafe, W. (1982) Integration and Interaction in Speaking, Writing and Oral Literature. In D. Tannen (ed.) *Spoken and Written*

Language. Norwood, New Jersey: Ablex

Chester, D. N. and N. Bowring (1962) *Questions in Parliament*. Oxford: Clarendon Press.

Chilton, P. (ed.) (1985) *Language and the Nuclear Arms Debate: nukespeake today*. London: Francis Pinter.

Chilton, P. (1987) Co-operation and Non Co-operation: ethical and political aspects of pragmatics. *Language and Communication*, 7, 3 221–39.

Chilton, P. (1988) *Orwellian Language and the Media*. London: Pluto Press.

Chomsky, N. (1965) *Aspects of the Theory of Syntax*. Cambridge, Mass: MIT Press.

Chomsky, N. (1986) *Knowledge of Language: its nature, origin and use*. New York: Prager.

Christie, C. (1987) Activity Types and Psychotherapy. Paper presented at the International Pragmatics Conference, Antwerp, Belgium.

Clark, H. H. (1979) Responding to Indirect Speech Acts. *Cognitive Psychology*, 11, 430–77.

Clark, H. H. and E. Clark (1977) *The Psychology of Language*. New York: Harcourt, Brace Jovanovich.

Cohen, P. R. (1985) *Heuristic Reasoning about Uncertainty: an artificial intelligence approach*. Boston: Pitman Advanced Publishing program.

Cole, P. (ed.) (1981) *Radical Pragmatics*. New York: Academic Press.

Cole, P. and J. L. Morgan (eds) (1975) *Syntax and Semantics, vol. 3: Speech Acts*. New York: Academic Press.

Coleman, L. and P. Kay (1981) Prototype semantics: the English word lie. *Language*, 57, 1, 26–44.

Cooper, D. (1986) *Metaphor*. Oxford: Basil Blackwell.

Cowan, B. (1988) *Talkback*. BBC Radio Ulster.

Crystal, D. (1988) *The English Language*. Harmondsworth: Penguin.

Davidson, D. (1984) *Inquiries into Truth and Interpretation*. Oxford: Clarendon Press.

Derrida, J. (1978) *Writing and Difference*. (Trans. A. Bloss) Chicago: University of Chicago Press.

Devitt, M. and K. Sterelny (1987) *Language and Reality*. Oxford: Basil Blackwell.

Dillon, J. T. (1990) *The Practice of Questioning*. London: Routledge.

Dillon, J. T., J. Golding, and A. Graesser (1988) Annotated Bibliography of Question Asking. *Questioning Exchange*, 2, 81–5.

Donnellan, K. S. (1966) Reference and Definite Descriptions. *Philosophical Review*, 75, 281–304.

Downs, W. (1984) *Language and Society*. London: Fontana.

Durkin, K. (1983) Review of Kress and Hodge. *Journal of Pragmatics*, 7, 1, 101–4.

Edleman, M. (1971) *Politics as Symbolic Action*. New York: Academic Press.

Edleman, M. (1978) *Political Language*. New York: Academic Press.

Edleman, M. (1988) *Constructing the Political Spectacle*. Chicago: University of Chicago Press.

Egli, V. and H. Schleichert (1976) A bibliography on the Theory of Questions and Answers. *Linguistische Berichte*, 41, 105–28.

Epstein, J. P. (1982) The Grammar of a Lie: its legal implications. In R. J. De Pietro (ed.) *Linguistics and The Professions*. Norwood, New Jersey: Ablex.

Erickson, P. (1985) *Reagan Speaks: the making of an American myth*. New York: New York University Press.

Facts About (1982) The Facts About 'Us People'. *Washington Post*, 26 April, Sect. A. 16.

Fasold, R. (1984) *The Sociolinguistics of Society*. Oxford: Basil Blackwell.

Ficht, H. (1978) Supplement to a Bibliography on the Theory of Questions and Answers. *Linguistische Berichte*, 55, 92–114.

Foucault, M. (1972) *The Archaeology of Knowledge*. London: Tavistock.

Fowler, R., B. Hodge, G. Kress and T. Trew (1979) *Language and Control*. London: Routledge.

Frederiksen, J. R. (1981) Understanding Anaphora: rules used by readers in assigning pronominal referents. (Tech. Report› no. 3–4462) Cambridge, Mass: Bolt Beranek and Newman Inc. (ERIC Document Reproduction Service No Ed 205 930).

Garfinkel, H. and H. Sacks (1970) On Formal Structures of Practical Action. In J. McKinney and E. Tiryakian (eds) *Theoretical Sociology*. New York: Appleton-Century Crofts.

Gazdar, G. (1979) *Pragmatics: implicature, presupposition and logical form*. New York: Academic Press.

Gazdar, G. and D. Good (1982) On the Notion of Relevance. In N. Smith (ed.) *Mutual Knowledge*. London: Academic Press.

Geis, M. (1987) *The Language of Politics*. New York: Springer Verlag.

Gibbs, R. W. (1987) Mutual Knowledge and the Psychology of Conversational Inference. *Journal of Pragmatics*, 11, 561–88.

Givon, T. (1979a) *On Understanding Grammar.* London and New York: Academic Press.

Givon, T. (ed.) (1979b) *Syntax and Semantics*, vol 12: *Discourse and Syntax.* New York: Academic Press.

Givon, T. (ed.). (1983) *Topic Continuity in Discourse: a quantitative cross language study.* Amsterdam: John Benjamins.

Goffman, E. (1967) *Interaction Ritual: essays on face to face behaviour.* Harmondsworth: Penguin.

Goffman, E. (1981) *Forms of Talk.* Oxford: Basil Blackwell.

Goldman, A. (1978) Epistemology and the Psychology of Belief. *Monist*, 61, 525–35.

Goodman, N. (1984) *Of Mind and Other Matters.* Cambridge, Mass: MIT Press.

Gordon, D. and G. Lakoff (1975) Conversational Postulates. In Cole and Morgan, 1975.

Grace, G. W. (1987) *The Linguistic Construction of Reality.* London: Croom Helm.

Graesser, A. C. and J. B. Black (1985) *The Psychology of Questions.* Hove: Lawrence Erlbaum Associates.

Greatbatch, D. (1986) Some Standard Uses of Supplementary Questions in News Interviews. *Belfast Working Papers in Language and Linguistics*, 8, 86–123.

Green, D. (1987) *Shaping Political Consciousness.* Cornell: Cornell University Press.

Green, G. M. (1989) *Pragmatics and Natural Language Understanding.* Hove: Lawrence Erlbaum Associates.

Green, M. (1982) There He Goes Again. *Nation*, 6, 273–4.

Grewendorf, G. (1981) Answering as Decision Making: a new way of doing pragmatics. In H. Parret, M. Sbisa, and J. Verschueren (eds) *Possibilities and Limitations of Pragmatics.* Amsterdam: John Benjamins.

Grice, H. P. (1961) The Causal Theory of Perception. *Proceedings of the Aristotelian Society*, supplementary vol. 35, 121–52.

Grice, H. P. (1975) Logic and Conversation. In Cole and Morgan, 1975.

Gruber, H. (1987) Political Language and Textual Vagueness. Paper delivered at the International Pragmatics Association, Antwerp.

Gurwitsch, A. (1978) Galilean Physics in the Light of Husserl's Phenomenology. In T. Luckman (ed.) *Phenomenology and Sociology.* Harmondsworth: Penguin.

Halliday, M. A. K. and R. Q. Hasan (1986) *Cohesion in English.* London: Longman.

Hansard (1986a) *Parliamentary Debates (Oral Answers) House of Commons Official Report.* 20 March, 94, 82, 396–516.

Hansard (1986b) *Parliamentary Debates (Oral Answers) House of Commons Official Report.* 21 March, 94, 83, 517–90.

Hansard (1986c) *Parliamentary Debates (Oral Answers) House of Commons Official Report.* 27 March, 94, 87, 1054–150.

Hansard (1986d) *Parliamentary Debates (Oral Answers) House of Commons Official Report.* 7 May, 97, 108, 124–236.

Hansard (1986e) *Parliamentary Debates (Oral Answers) House of Commons Official Report.* 12 May, 97, 111, 430–538.

Hansard (1986f) *Parliamentary Debates (Oral Answers) House of Commons Official Report.* 2 July, 100, 141, 928–1097.

Hargie, O., C. Saunders and D. Dickson (1987) *Social Skills in Interpersonal Interaction.* London: Croom helm.

Harland, R. (1988) *Superstructuralism.* London: Methuen.

Harman, G. (1986) *A Change in View.* Cambridge, Mass: MIT Press.

Harre, R. (1988) Accountability within Social Order: the role of pronouns. In C. Artaki (ed.) *Analysing Everyday Explanation.* Beverley Hills: Sage.

Harris, R. (1984) *The Making of Neil Kinnock.* London: Faber.

Harris, R. J. (1974) Memory for Presuppositions and Implications: a case study of verbs of motion and inception-termination. *Journal of Experimental Psychology* 103, 594–7.

Harris, S. (1986) Interviewers' Questions in Broadcast Interviews. *Belfast Working Papers in Language and Linguistics*, 8, 50–86.

Harris, S. (1989) Questions in Political Broadcast Interviews. *Questioning Exchange*, 3, 10–25.

Hayes-Roth, B. and F. Hayes-Roth (1979) A Cognitive Model of Planning. *Cognitive Science*, 3, 275–310.

Heritage, J. (1985) Analysing News Interviews: aspects of the production of talk for an overhearing audience. In T. Van Dijk (ed.) *Handbook of Discourse Analysis*, vol. 3. New York: Academic Press.

Heritage, J. and D. Greatbatch (1986) Generating Applause: a study of rhetoric and response at party political broadcasts. *British Journal of Sociology*, 91, 110–57.

Hintikka, J. (1974) Questions about Questions. In M. K. Munitz and P. K. Unger (eds) *Semantics and Philosophy* New York: New York Unversity Press.

Hiz, H. (ed.) (1978) *Questions.* Dordrecht: Reidel.

Hodge, B. (1989) Discourse in Time: some notes on method. In B. Torode (ed.) *Text and Talk as Social Practice.* Dordrecht: Foris.

Horn, L. (1987) Negation and Quantity. In Horn and Levinson, 1987.

Horn, L. (1988) Pragmatic Theory. In F. Newmeyer (ed.) *Cambridge Survey of Linguistics*, Vol 1. Cambridge: Cambridge University Press.

Horn, L. and S. Levinson (eds) (1987) *Course Material for the Pragmatics Seminar 11 274*. Standford: Linguistics Institute.

Howarth, P. (1956) *Questions in the House: the history of a unique British institution*. Oxford: Bodley Head.

Huddleston, R. (1976) *An Introduction to English Transformational Syntax*. London: Longman.

Huddleston, R. (1984) *An Introduction to English Grammar*. Cambridge: Cambridge University Press.

Hudson, K. (1978) *The Language of Modern Politics*. London: Macmillan.

Husserl, E. (1962) *Ideas: general introduction to pure phenomenology*. New York: Collier.

Hymes, D. (1977) *Foundations of Sociolinguistics*. London: Tavistock.

Jasinski, J. (1988) The Privatization of Rhetorical Language. Paper delivered at the Speech Communication Association of America, New Orleans.

Jespersen, O. (1933) *Essentials of English Grammar*. London: Allen Unwin.

Johannesen, R. L. (1985) An Ethical Assessment of the Reagan Rhetoric. In K. R. Sanders, L. Lee Kaid and D. Nimmo (eds) *Political Communication Yearbook (1984)*. Carbondale: Southern Illinois University Press.

Johnson, G. W. (1978a) *The Nixon Presidential Press Conferences*. London: Heyden.

Johnson, G. W. (1978b) *The Kennedy Presidential Press Conferences*. New York: E. M. Coleman.

Johnson-Laird, P. N. (1983) *Mental Models*. Cambridge: Cambridge University Press.

Johnson-Laird, P. N. and A. Garnham (1980) Descriptions and Discourse Models. *Linguistics and Philosophy*, 12, 371–93.

Jucker, A. H. (1986) *News Interviews—a pragmalinguistic perspective*. Amsterdam: John Benjamins.

Kahneman, D., P. Slovic and A. Tversky (eds) (1982) *Judgement Under Uncertainty: heuristics and biases*. Cambridge: Cambridge University Press.

Karttunen, L. (1973) Presuppositions of Compound Sentences.

Linguistic Inquiry, 4, 169–93.

Karttunen, L. (1974) Presupposition and Linguistic Context. *Theoretical Linguistics*, 1, 3–44.

Karttunen, L. and S. Peters (1979) Conventional Implicature. In Oh and Dineen, 1979.

Katz, J. J. (1987) Common Sense in Semantics. In E. LePore (ed.) *New Directions in Semantics*. London: Academic Press.

Kempson, R. M. (1979) *Presupposition and the Delimitation of Semantics*. Cambridge: Cambridge University Press.

Kempson, R. M. (1987) Grammar and Conversational Principles. In Horn and Levinson, 1987.

Kiefer, F. (ed.) (1983) *Questions*. Dordrecht: Reidel.

King, G. (1972) Open and Closed Questions: the reference interviews; *RQ. Reference and Adult Science Division*, 12, 157–66.

Kirkpatrick, J. J. (1981) *The Reagan Phenomenon*. Washington: Public Policy Research Institute.

Klein, B. (1988) After Strategy: the search for a post-modern politics of peace. *Alternatives*, 3.

Kovecses, J. (1986) *Metaphors of Anger, Pride and Love: a lexical approach to the structure of concepts*. Amsterdam: John Benjamins.

Kress, G. and B. Hodge (1979) *Language as Ideology*: London: Routledge.

Kuipers, B., A. J. Moskowitz and J. P. Kassirer (1988) Critical Decisions under Uncertainty: representation and structure. *Cognitive Science*, 12, 177–210.

Laberge, S. and G. Sankoff (1980) Anything You Can Do. In G. Sankoff (ed.) *The Social Life of Language*. Philadelphia: University of Philadelphia Press.

Labov, W. and D. Fanchel (1977) *Theraputic Discourse: psychotherapy as conversation*. New York: Academic Press.

Lakoff, G. (1972) Hedges: a study in the meaning criteria and the logic of fuzzy concepts. *Papers from the 11th Regional Meeting of the Chicago Linguistic Society*, 183–228. Chicago: University of Chicago Press.

Lakoff, G. and M. Johnson (1980) *Metaphors We Live By*. Chicago: University of Chicago Press.

Lakoff, R. (1973) Questionable Answers and Answerable Questions. In B. Kachru *et al.* (eds) *Papers in Honour of Henry and Renee Kahane*. Urbana: University of Illinois Press.

Lavandera, B. (1988) The Study of Language in its Socio-cultural Context. In Newmeyer, 1988, vol. 4.

Leech, G. (1983) *Principles of Pragmatics*. London: Longman.

Levinson, S. (1979) Activity Types and Language. *Linguistics*, 17.5/6, 356–99.

Levinson, S. (1983) *Pragmatics*. Cambridge: Cambridge University Press.

Levinson, S. (1987) What's Special about Conversational Inference. In Horn & Levinson, 1987.

Lewis, D. (1969) *Convention*. Cambridge, Mass: Harvard University Press.

Lewis, D. (1972) General Semantics. In D. Davidson and G. Harman (eds) *Semantics of Natural Language*. Dordrecht: Reidel.

Lwaitama, A. F. (1988) Variations in the Use of Personal Pronouns in the Political Oratory of J. K. Nyerere and A. H. Mwinyi. MS. To appear in *Belfast Working Papers in Language and Linguistics*, 10.

Lycan, W. (1986) *Logical Form in Natural Language*. Cambridge, Mass: MIT Press.

Lyons, J. (1977) *Semantics*. (2 vols) Cambridge: Cambridge University Press.

McTear, M. F. (1986) *Children's Conversation*. Oxford: Basil Blackwell.

Maitland, K. (1988) Why Choose Me: The pragmatics of English pronouns. Unpublished DPhil: University of Ulster.

Maitland, K. and J. Wilson (1987) Ideological Conflict and Pronominal Resolution. *Journal of Pragmatics*, 11, 495–512.

Milroy, J. and L. Milroy (1986) *Authority in Language*. London: Routledge and Kegan Paul.

Montgomery, M. (1985) *Introduction to Language and Society*. London: Methuen.

Murray, S. O. (1981) Review of *Language and Ideology*. *American Journal of Sociology*, 87, 743.

Neisser, U. (1989) *Interview: what is truth?* London: Channel Four Productions, Independent Television.

Newmeyer, F. J. (1980) *Linguistic Theory in America*. New York: Academic Press.

Newmeyer, F. J. (ed.) (1988) *Cambridge Survey of Linguistics*. (4 vols) Cambridge: Cambridge University PRess.

Norris, C. and I. Whitehouse (1988) The Rhetoric of Deterrence. In N. Coupland (ed.) *Styles of Discourse*. London: Croom Helm.

Nunberg, G. D. (1978) The Pragmatics of Reference. Indiana University Linguistics Club.

Ochs, E. and B. B. Schieffelin (1979) *Developmental Pragmatics*. New York: Academic Press.

Oh, C. K. and D. A. Dineen (eds) (1979) *Syntax and Semantics, vol 11: Presupposition.* New York: Academic Press.

Ortony, A. (ed.) (1979) *Metaphor and Thought.* Cambridge: Cambridge University Press.

Orwell, G. (1969) Politics and the English Language. In W. F. Bolton and D. Crystal (eds) *The English Language, vol 2.* Cambridge: Cambridge University Press.

Owen, M. (1983) *Apologies and Remedial Interchanges.* Berlin and New York: Mouton.

Paivio, A. (1979) Psychological Processes in the Comprehension of Metaphor. In Ortony, 1979.

Palmer, F. R. (1979) *Modality and The English Modals.* London: Longman.

Pêcheux, M. (1978) Are the Masses an Inanimate Object? In D. Sankoff (ed.) *Linguistic Variation: Models and Methods.* New York: Academic Press.

Popper, K. (1963) *Conjectures and Refutations: the growth of scientific knowledge.* London: Routledge.

Popper, K. (1978) *Unended Quest.* London: Paladin.

Prince, E. (1981) Towards a Taxonomy of Given-New Information. In Cole, 1981.

Putnam, H. (1971) In Discussion with B. Magee. In B. Magee, *Men of Ideas.* London: BBC Publications.

Quine, W. V. O. (1969) *Word and Object.* Cambridge, Mass: MIT Press.

Quirk, R., S. Greenbaum and J. Svartvik (1985) *A Comprehensive Grammar of The English Language.* London: Longman.

Reagan, R. (1987) *R. Reagan Talks to America.* Greenwich: Devin Adair.

Rees, A. (1983) Pronouns of Person and Power: a study of personal pronouns in public discourse. Unpublished M. A. dissertation: University of Sheffield.

Rescher, N. (1980) *Induction.* Oxford: Basil Blackwell.

Richardson, K. (1989) Criticising the Critics: Arguments in the analysis of nuclear arms discourse. Paper presented to Conference on Conversation, Discourse and Conflict, Trinity College, Dublin.

Ricoeur, P. (1978) *The Rule of Metaphor.* (Trans. R. Czerny) London: Routledge and Kegan Paul.

Ross, L. and A. Anderson (1982) Shortcomings in the Attribution Process: on the origins and maintenance of erroneous social assessments. In. Kahneman *et al.*, 1982.

Sacks, H. and E. Schegloff (1977) Two Preferences for the Organisation of Reference to Persons in Conversation and their Interaction. In U. Quasthof (ed.) *Sprachstrucker Socialstrucker*. Berlin: Scriptor Verlag.

Sadock, J. M. (1978) On Testing for Conversational Implicature. In P. Cole (ed.) *Syntax and Semantics, vol 9: Pragmatics*. New York: Academic Press.

Sanford, A. J. and S. C. Garrod (1985) On the Real Time Character of Interpretation during Reading. *Language and Cognitive Processes*, 1, 43–59.

Sapir, E. (1964) Conceptual Categories in Primitive Languages. In D. Hymes (ed.) *Language, Culture and Society*. New York: Harper Row.

Schegloff, E. (1972) Notes on Conversational Practice: formulating place. In D. Sudnow (ed.) *Studies in Social Interaction*. New York: Free Press.

Schegloff, E. (1977) On some Questions and Ambiguities in Conversation. In W. U. Dressler (ed.) *Current Trends in Text Linguistics*. Berlin: De Gruyter.

Schegloff, E. (1988) Presequences and Indirection: applying speech act theory to ordinary conversation. *Journal of Pragmatics*, 12, 55–62.

Schenkein, J. (ed.) (1978) *Studies in the Organisation of Conversational Interaction*. New York: Academic Press.

Schiffrin, D. (1987) *Discourse Markers*. Cambridge: Cambridge University Press.

Schon, D. (1979) Generative Metaphor: a perspective on problem setting in social policy. In Ortony, 1979.

Searle, J. (1984) *Voices (Post-Modernism)*. London: Channel Four Productions, Independent Television.

Searle, J. R. (1969) *Speech Acts*. Cambridge: Cambridge University Press.

Searle, J. R. (1975) Indirect Speech Acts. In Cole and Morgan, 1975.

Searle, J. R. (1979a) Metaphor. In Ortony, 1979.

Searle, J. R. (1979b) *Meaning and Expression*. Cambridge: Cambridge University Press.

Searle, J. R. (1983) *Intention*. Cambridge: Cambridge University Press.

Searle, J. R. and D. Vandereken (1985) *Foundations of Illoctionary Logic*. Cambridge: Cambridge University Press.

Seidel, G. (1985) Political Discourse Analysis. In Van Dijk, 1985: vol 2.

Sharrock, W. and D. C. Anderson (1981) Language, Thought and

Reality Again. *Sociology*, 15, 287–93.

Silk, P. (1987) *How Parliament Works*. London: Longman.

Silverman, D. (1973) Some Neglected Questions about Social Reality. In P. Filmer, M. Phillipson, D. Silverman and D. Walsh, *New Directions in Sociological Theory*. London: Collier-Macmillan.

Sinclair, J. and M. Coulthard (1975) *Towards an Analysis of Discourse*. Oxford: Oxford University Press.

Smith, N. V. and D. Wilson (1979) *Modern Linguistics: the results of Chomsky's revolution*. Harmondsworth: Penguin.

Sperber, D. and D. Wilson (1986) *Relevance*. Oxford: Basil Blackwell.

Stenton, S. P. (1988) Dialogue Management for Co-operative Knowledge Based Systems. *Knowledge Engineering Review*, 3, 99–121.

Strawson, P. F. (1950) On Referring. *Mind*, 59, 320–44.

Strong, T. B. (1984) Language and Nihilism: Nietzsche's critique of epistemology. In M. Shapiro (ed.) *Language and Politics*. Oxford: Basil Blackwell.

Stubbs, M. W. (1981) Discourse, Semantics and Syntax: some notes on their relationship. *Belfast Working Papers in Language and Linguistics*, 5, 1–71.

Stubbs, M. W. (1983) *Discourse Analysis*. Oxford: Basil Blackwell.

Tannen, D. (1979) What's in a Frame? Surface evidence for underlying expectations. In R. Freedle (ed.) *New Directions in Discourse Processing*. Norwood, New Jersey: Ablex.

Thomas, H. (1978) Introduction. In Johnson, 1978a.

Urban, G. (1986) Rhetoric of a War Chief. *Working Papers and Proceedings of the Centre for Psychosocial Studies*, Chicago, 5, 1–27.

Van Dijk, T. (1985) *Handbook of Discourse Analysis*. (4 vols) New York and London: Academic Press.

Verschueren, J. (1985) *What People Say They Do with Words*. Norwood, New Jersey: Ablex.

Verschueren, J. (1987) *Pragmatics as a Theory of Linguistic Adaptation*. Antwerp: IPRA Working Document 1, Belgian National Foundation.

Wardhaugh, P. (1986) *An Introduction to Sociolinguistics*. Oxford: Basil Blackwell.

Weinberger, C. W. (1986) U. S. Defense Strategy. *Foreign Affairs*. 64, 4, 675–97.

The White House Transcripts (1974) Edited by the staff of the *New York Times*. The New York Times Co.

Whorf, B. L. (1956) *Language, Thought and Reality*. (ed. J. B.

Carrol) Cambridge, Mass: MIT Press.

Wilks, Y. (1982) Comment on Sperber and Wilson. In N. Smith (ed.) *Mutual Knowledge*. London: Academic Press.

Wilks, Y. (1986) Relevance and Beliefs. In T. Myers, K. Brown and B. McGonigle (eds) *Reasoning and Discourse Processes*. London: Academic Press.

Wilks, Y. and J. Bien (1981) Beliefs, Points of View and Multiple Environments. Cognitive Studies Centre, University of Essex.

Wilson, D. (1975) *Presuppositions and Non Truth Conditional Semantics*. London: Academic Press;

Wilson, D. and D. Sperber (1986) Inference and Utterance Interpretation. In T. Myers, K. Brown and B. McGonigle (eds) *Reasoning and Discourse Processes*. London: Academic Press.

Wilson, J. (1980) Why Answers to Questions are Not Enough in Social Discourse. *Belfast Working Papers in Language and Linguistics*, 4, 60–85.

Wilson, J. (1981) Come On Now Answer the Question: an analysis of constraints on answers. *Belfast Working Papers in Language and Linguistics*, 5, 70–101.

Wilson, J. (1989) *On The Boundaries of Conversation*. Oxford: Pergamon.

Yule, G. (1981) New, Current and Displaced Entity Reference. *Lingua*, 55, 41–52.

Index